THE NOVELS OF LOUISE ERDRICH

American Indian Studies

Elizabeth Hoffman Nelson and Malcolm A. Nelson
General Editors

Vol. 11

PETER LANG
New York • Washington, D.C./Baltimore • Bern
Frankfurt am Main • Berlin • Brussels • Vienna • Oxford

CONNIE A. JACOBS

THE NOVELS OF LOUISE ERDRICH

Stories of Her People

PETER LANG
New York • Washington, D.C./Baltimore • Bern
Frankfurt am Main • Berlin • Brussels • Vienna • Oxford

Library of Congress Cataloging-in-Publication Data
Jacobs, Connie A.
The novels of Louise Erdrich: stories of her people / Connie A. Jacobs.
p. cm. — (American Indian studies; vol. 11)
Includes bibliographical references and index.
1. Erdrich, Louise—Criticism and interpretation. 2. Women
and literature—United States—History—20th century. 3. Indians
in literature. I. Title. II. American Indian studies; v. 11.
PS3555.R42 Z73   813'.54—dc21   00-056402
ISBN 0-8204-4027-2
ISSN 1058-563X

Die Deutsche Bibliothek-CIP-Einheitsaufnahme
Jacobs, Connie A.:
The novels of Louise Erdrich: stories of her people / Connie A. Jacobs.
−New York; Washington, D.C./Baltimore; Bern;
Frankfurt am Main; Berlin; Brussels; Vienna; Oxford: Lang.
(American Indian studies; Vol. 11)
ISBN 0-8204-4027-2

Cover art by Barbara Tobin Klema
Cover design by Dutton & Sherman Design

© 2001 Peter Lang Publishing, Inc., New York

All rights reserved.
Reprint or reproduction, even partially, in all forms such as microfilm,
xerography, microfiche, microcard, and offset strictly prohibited.

Printed in the United States of America

THIS BOOK IS DEDICATED to the memory of my father,
Albert Augustine, and my mentor, Sophie Cooney S.J.,
who inspired this work but did not live to see it completed.

ACKNOWLEDGMENTS

THE CREATION OF A BOOK is an act of love and courage by the author and an acknowledgment of faith by those who support her—colleagues, friends, and family. In this spirit, I would like to pay tribute to those who so willingly helped me bring this project to completion. James Giles, David Barrow, Mary Sue Schriber, and Winifred Creamer read early drafts and helped this fledgling project in its formative stages. My editor, Heidi Burns, has been ever vigilant and ever supportive. Greg Sarris's comments helped me reshape portions of chapter three, and Robert Nelson's insightful and thorough reading of the manuscript in its final stages made all the difference.

Elaine Walstedter at the Fort Lewis Library came to my rescue innumerable times by helping me gain access to some of the more obscure pieces of information I needed. Lisa Atchison helped me shape the maps, Barbara Klema designed a wonderful cover, and Olive Holmes provided the much needed technical support, for which I am most grateful.

I have been blessed with a large cheering section who always believed this book would be published. To the incredible ladies of the TWRAHS book group, thank you for encouragement and good cheer. To Barbara and Peter, your friendship was always an unwavering base of support. To officemates Lisa and Chris, thanks for always believing in me and urging me to look beyond the daily work to bigger goals. To colleagues Vicki and Molly, now it's your turn. To Judy, Mary Jo, Lynnda, Jane, Wendy, Marilynn, John, and Alice who were always there in all stages of the book to urge me on, my deepest gratitude. My mother Louise, brother Ed, and sister Kathy were always willing to listen, to encourage, and to applaud. Most of all, my children Amy, Beth, and Greg and husband Steve gave me the privacy, help, and ultimate love that guided this project to completion.

Portions of this book have been read at various conferences:

The Graduate Conference at Northern Illinois University, The National Association of Ethnic Studies Conference, Popular Culture and American Culture Conference, and the ALA Symposium, Native American Literary Strategies for the New Millennium.

Contents

Preface xi
Maps xvii
List of Abbreviations xxi

1 Continuing the Tradition: Louise Erdrich and the
   Native American Literary Renaissance 1
   Native American Authors Write Back 1
   The Native American Literary Renaissance 3
   Defining Native American Literature 6
   Critical Work in Native American Literature 10
   Five Characteristics of Native American Fiction 12
   Writing as an Act of Recovery 17

2 Traditional Storytellers 19
   How Storytelling Functions in the
   Native American Literary Tradition 19
   How Folklorists Have Studied the Function of Stories 28
   How Orality Theory Provides a Fuller Context
   for Erdrich's Work 32
   Transitional Texts between Oral and Written Narratives 38
   Erdrich's Novels as Storytelling Sessions 45

3 Louise Erdrich, A Contemporary Traditional Storyteller 51
   Erdrich's Life and Work 53
   Erdrich's Use of the Autobiographical Voice in Her Novels 60
   Erdrich's Use of Story Cycles to Frame Her Novels 69
   The Historical Ojibwa 70
   Traditional Ojibwa Beliefs 71
   The Formation of the Turtle Mountain Band 77
   Erdrich's Non-Reservation Novels 82
   Erdrich's Incorporation of Tribal and Anglo History 85

4 The Power of Love as Medicine: Louise Erdrich's Family Stories ... 105
   Defining "Family" 106
   Erdrich's Use of Families in the Novels 108

    The Circular Narrative Structure of Erdrich's Family Stories ...108
    Touchstone Family Stories 117
    Family Characteristics 134
    Love Medicines..145

5 "POWER TRAVELS IN THE BLOODLINES, HANDED OUT BEFORE
    BIRTH": LOUISE ERDRICH'S FEMALE MYTHIC CHARACTERS 147
    Secondary Heroes...148
    Fleur's Bear Power...151
    Animal Helpers and Totems..152
    The Historical Pillagers 153
    Fleur's Immortality..154
    The Bear in Ojibwa Culture..155
    Fleur's Bear Medicine..158
    Fleur's Wolf and Marten Characteristics.................................160
    Fleur's Guardian, Misshepeshu..161
    Fleur, an Anishinaabe Medicine Woman................................165
    The Antelope People...169
    Mythic Dogs..172
    The Mythic World of *The Antelope Wife* 173
    Erdrich, the Maker of Myths 173

6 LOUISE ERDRICH, AN AMERICAN STORYTELLER..............................175
    The American Literary Canon and Multiculturalism.............175
    Writing out of the Dominant Culture 179
    Erdrich and the American Literary Tradition 181
    From Myth to Rhetorics 184
    Continuance of the Mythic for Native Americans.................186
    The Importance of Stories and of Storytelling........................187

NOTES..191
APPENDIX: IMPORTANT DATES IN THE HISTORY OF THE
    TURTLE MOUNTAIN BAND OF CHIPPEWA INDIANS...................219
WORKS CITED 223
INDEX..249

Preface

IF YOU ARE READING THIS PREFACE, then I can assume that you, my audience, are among the small but passionate group of scholars who believe that Native American literature represents some of the most powerful, most artfully expressed, and most culturally relevant writing today. There is no need to have to convince you of the merits of the work of the foremost Native American writers: Sherman Alexie, Louise Erdrich, Joy Harjo, Linda Hogan, N. Scott Momaday, Simon Ortiz, Greg Sarris, Leslie Marmon Silko, Luci Tapahonso, Gerald Vizenor, and James Welch. There is no need to argue the significance of the people who first occupied America being able to tell their stories to an audience that now extends beyond their particular tribe to readers across the Americas and across the oceans.

When I first discovered Louise Erdrich, I was in a traditional graduate school program in the 1980s at a midwestern university where Native American literature was a scant part of the curriculum, a situation happily remedied in many colleges and universities by the beginning of the twenty-first century. What I originally found so compelling about the work by Native American authors in general and Erdrich specifically was its powerful voice, its artful use of the oral tradition, and the subtle yet cogent ways in which its literature is subversive. This subversive quality, not unlike that found in the writings of African-American authors, fascinated me in the same way that Richard Wright in the Memphis library found in the writing of H. L. Mencken a voice whose critique of the dominant society echoed Wright's deeply held yet unarticulated thoughts. Erdrich and other Native writers compel us to look more closely at the prevailing American myths, about the morality of removing people from their land and justifying the subsequent killings with western European ideas of Manifest Destiny born out of racist notions of cultural superiority. Works of Native American authors challenge the hegemony of

Anglo culture and argue for the inclusion of native voices in the American story. These works nudge Anglo Americans out of our complacency to accept the mythic tale of America's ascendancy and destiny, our deeply held beliefs in the primacy of western culture, and our stereotypes of native people so pervasively and devastatingly presented in the seventeenth and eighteenth centuries by the Puritans, in the nineteenth century by the government and western military forces, all picked up and packaged for posterity by Hollywood in the twentieth century.

These remain the foremost reasons why Native American literature continues to exert such a pertinacious influence on me. I am not a Native American, but in the literature of native authors, I see a cultural relevancy nowhere expressed so urgently and with such sensuous language. Native authors are literally and literarily writing for their lives and the lives of their tribal people as they tell the story of people whose voices have been appropriated ever since Europeans arrived on American shores. Through the power of the written word, indigenous people have found the avenue to tell their story in their own words.

Erdrich infuses western language with Chippewa epistemologies, and in her novels, she assumes the mantle of the tribal storyteller who connects one story to the next, encodes history in her stories, and uses stories to instruct, to teach; rather than sitting around a campfire throughout the winter months listening to these tribal stories, we as readers can pick up her novels and read them at any time, not heeding tribal taboos of storytelling outside of the traditional storytelling season. We can read the story of a tribe through linked novels, can watch tribal members grow up, marry, have children, and can view the spectrum of tribal life in the twentieth century through the stories Erdrich tells of her people.

There are many compelling voices in the Native American literary pantheon, but Erdrich remains to date the only author whose novels collectively form the story of her people in the twentieth century. Through her humor, compassion, sense of the mythic presence still pervasive in tribal life, poetic language, and encompassing of so much cultural history, Erdrich invites readers into her tribal world. It is a place I want to experience and linger in, and once entering her fictional tribal world, I am loathe to reemerge.

With Momaday, Vizenor, Silko, and Welch serving as literary

forebears, Erdrich joined the Native American Literary Renaissance with *Love Medicine* and established herself as one of the gifted and original Native voices. Her quartet, *Love Medicine* (1984), *The Beet Queen* (1986), *Tracks* (1988), and *The Bingo Palace* (1994) becomes a chorus of mingling voices from the Plains of North Dakota. *Tales of Burning Love* (1996) continues the stories of several characters from the quartet, and *The Antelope Wife* (1998) with its new cast of characters and new locale is a novel of love, betrayal, alcoholism, and the ultimate power of community and tradition to heal, themes found in all her novels. The artistic manner in which she poetically renders her narrative, uses elements from traditional Chippewa[1] storytelling to impart her story, and vividly and compassionately recounts in a fictional format the lives of her people during the last century immediately situated her as one of the leading contemporary novelists for both Indian and non-Indian audiences alike.

Erdrich's works now predictably land on the *New York Times* best-selling books list as well as on a variety of college syllabi. Another indicator of her status as a leading contemporary author is the amount of critical material scholars generate on her work. Literary critics analyze her use of the oral tradition and the storytelling foundation of her work, especially *Tracks*, her use of Chippewa history and culture, her narrative style, the function of humor in her work, feminist approaches to the novels, and her collaboration with Dorris on the novels.[2]

While scholars have examined diverse areas of Erdrich's work, this book broadens the discussion by filling in critical gaps. Chapter one traces the rise of written Native literature into its flowering as the Native American Literary Renaissance and situates Erdrich's work within this rich cultural literary heritage. A discussion of recognizable characteristics of Native American stories as well as my take on using the all-encompassing and polemical term Native American literature is this chapter's focus. In chapter two, I review orality studies and how this field informs what is happening in Native American literature today and, more specifically, how the theories from this field help enrich an understanding of how Erdrich reworks traditional materials. Erdrich and Silko, although critics like to pit them against one another because of Silko's harsh review of *Beet Queen*, practice traditional Indian storytelling in similar ways, which orality studies help explain.

After I place Erdrich in a framework of Native American literature and orality theory, I analyze the ways in which she utilizes the tradition from her specific tribal background, the Turtle Mountain Band of Chippewas. This becomes a comprehensive study of the novels and how her characters represent different aspects of traditional Anishinaabe life and how a traditional story cycle structures her books.

Erdrich's novels are family stories, and chapter four describes in detail the various families and how they connect and interrelate in her novels. The family units comprise the heart of the novels, and a unifying theme in the books is the binding and healing nature of the community and families.

The still efficacious mythic presence in Chippewa life is the focus of chapter five. Erdrich's novels are the stories of families on the North Dakota Plains and in the nearby cities who struggle for survival in an unpredictable and harsh physical environment within a changing world of government policies. Their stories are those of individuals, those of families, those of communities, and those of a tribe. What connects all the stories is the presence of characters of mythic dimension, including Fleur, who appears throughout the quartet. This chapter illustrates how Fleur connects the novels, and how she functions as a contemporary embodiment of an age-old Chippewa mythic and cultural element. Sweetheart Calico, the Antelope Wife, serves a similar function in *The Antelope Wife*.

The concluding chapter addresses Erdrich's place as a storyteller in contemporary American fiction. Her work echoes other American authors who write series novels and short-story cycles, and in this chapter I examine how the category of Native American writer (and all categories, for that matter) serves to compromise her writing accomplishments. Since Erdrich identifies herself as a Native American writer, this chapter assesses her novels as a Native American writer working within the framework of the American literary tradition.

This book seeks to provide readers with a more comprehensive framework for reading Erdrich's novels. Its intended purpose is to advance a more complete picture of her work within the spectrum of literary studies and most specifically within the context of Native American literature. Its unstated goal is to emerge readers more fully and richly in Erdrich's novels, a repository of cultural history, an ever dynamic and lively region, and a place where families, love, community, culture, tribal tradition, and myth are inscribed as cultural markers that sustain the Chippewa people. Erdrich as a contemporary Chippewa storyteller invites Native and non-Native listeners into her world of stories, and this study is meant to serve an academic accompaniment for readers who desire to more fully and completely emerge themselves in Erdrich's fictional world.

MAPS

Ojibwa Boundaries, Late 1800s

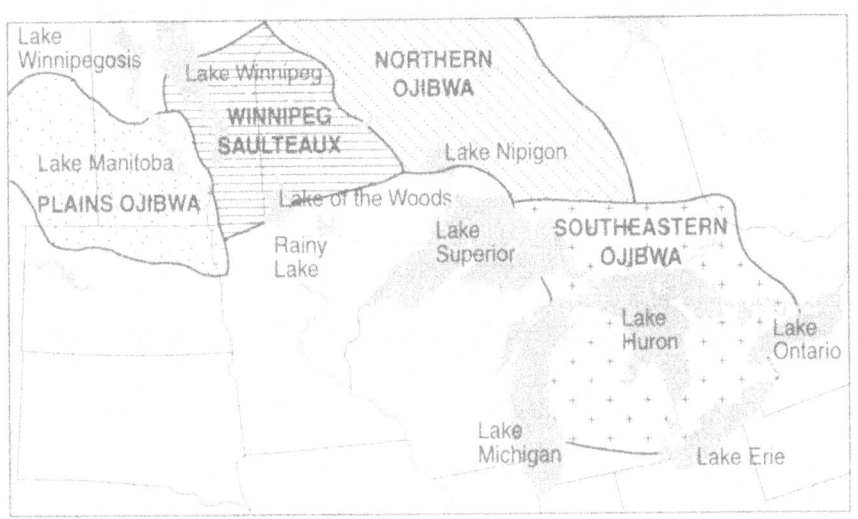

Map by Lisa Snider Atchison

Twentieth Century U.S. Plains-Ojibwa Reservations and Reserves

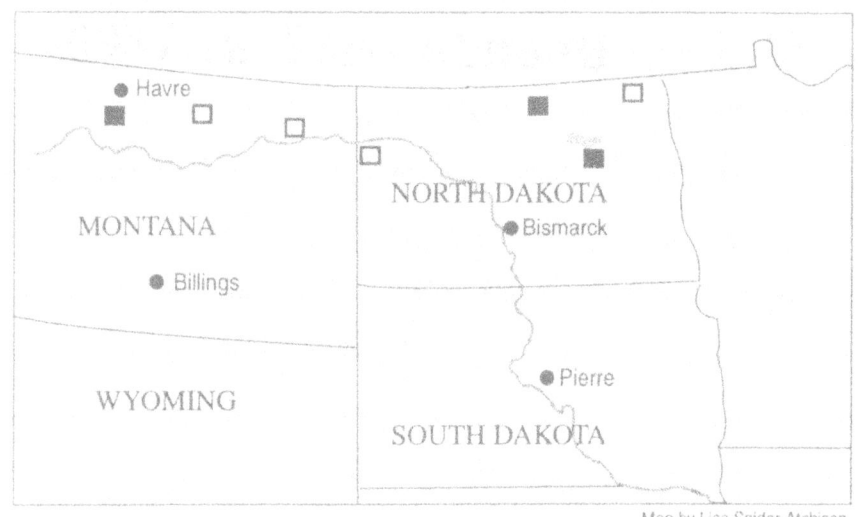

Map by Lisa Snider Atchison

KEY:
- ■ Full-blood reservation
- ☐ Métis communities
- ● Major cities

MAPS

The Historical and Current Turtle Mountain Homeland

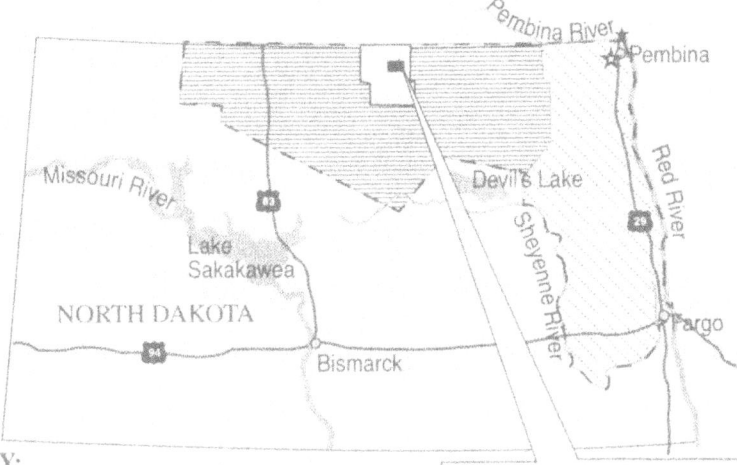

KEY:

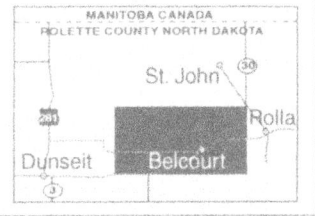

Map by Lisa Snider Atchison

- / The original lands claimed by the Turtle Mountain Chippewa comprised about 1/5 of state of North Dakota.

- ★ 1797 – Northwest Company of Montreal establishes a trading post.

- ☆ 1843 – Norman Kittson establishes Pembina trading post.

- 1863 – Little Shell, leader of the Turtle Mountain Band of Chippewa Indians, cedes 11 million acres of the Red River Valley.
  Also in 1863: Red Lake and White Earth reservations are created in Minnesota for the Chippewa. Increase in white farmers, decrease in buffalo herds.

- 1882, October – Without the consent of the Turtle Mountain Chippewa or any payment made as compensation, the General Land Office opens up between 9–10 million acres of land claimed by the tribe for Anglo settlement.

- 1882, December – President Chester Arthur signs an executive order creating a 24 x 32 mile reservation in Rolette County.
  Reservation contains excellent farmland.
  Reservation intended for 300–400 full-bloods — does not account for the 1,000 Métis.

- 1884 – The reservation is again reduced in size. The Government opens up to Anglos 20 of 22 townships of the best farmland set aside for the Turtle Mountain Chippewa in 1882. The Government claims they were acting in deference to the full-bloods who did not want their lands in severalty. The Government tells the Métis to take their allotment on public lands.

- 1904 – The McCumber Agreement originally made in 1892 is finally ratified. The Tribe officially cedes the 9–10 million acres they still claimed. The Tribe is compensated 10 cents/acre, which is now known as the "ten cent treaty."
  The Government allots 160 acre tracts to 326 families. 700 male tribal members are forced to take off-reservation land in Rollette County near Devil's Lake, on public lands, and in Montana, thus effectively dispersing the tribe.

ABBREVIATIONS

ABBREVIATIONS FOR THE NOVELS OF LOUISE ERDRICH APPEAR AS FOLLOWS:

- AW: *The Antelope Wife*
- BP: *The Bingo Palace*
- BQ: *The Beet Queen*
- LM: *Love Medicine*
  Note: All references are to the revised edition of *Love Medicine*.
- T: *Tracks*
- TBL: *Tales of Burning Love*

Chapter 1

Continuing the Tradition: Louise Erdrich and the Native American Literary Renaissance

Louise Erdrich prevails as the most popular contemporary Native American author. With a lyrical and innovative narrative style that has captivated general readers as well as academics, she tells stories of Turtle Mountain Chippewa Indians and the descendants of European immigrants who inhabit the uncompromising yet fiercely beautiful North Dakota Plains and nearby cities. Her best-selling books perennially appear on the *New York Times Book Review List;* her novels and poetry are taught in a myriad of academic classrooms including Native American Literature, Women's Literature, Minority Writers, American Literature, Comparative Mythology, Political Fictions, and Contemporary Literature; her work is widely anthologized; she has garnered an impressive array of literary awards; and scholars have written extensively about her work. Her popularity and the widespread recognition of the quality of her writing acknowledges that she has won her place among the ranks of the foremost Native American authors and found her way into an American literary canon that only within decades has opened its doors to minority writers. Her place in the Native American Literary Renaissance and American Literary Canon as well as a study of how her North Dakota novels plus *The Antelope Wife* reflect Erdrich as a contemporary tribal storyteller is the primary focus of this book.

Native American Authors Write Back

Other Native American writers laid the groundwork for Erdrich that allowed her to appear on the literary scene and capture the attention of readers who now, with enthusiasm, supported novels about Indian peoples written by Indian authors.

In 1984, with the publication of her award winning first novel *Love Medicine*, Erdrich became a rising star in the newly emerging Native American Literary Renaissance. This movement was born out of the need of Native peoples to represent themselves and to tell their stories with their voice and from their perspective because from the beginnings of the American literary tradition, the Anglo voice represented Native Americans. Consequently, Anglo authors played a pivotal role in forming America's perception of Native peoples. In both fiction and non-fiction, non-Native writers romanticized, vilified, and marginalized Native Americans. Mary Rowlandson's "infidels," "bloody/merciless heathens, "murderous wretches," Longfellow's peacemaker Ojibwa/Iroquois Hiawatha, James F. Cooper's noble Chingachgook, Herman Melville's daring harpooner Tashtego, Mark Twain's murderous Injun Joe, Helen Hunt Jackson's heroic Ramona, the brave/bloodthirsty Lakota and Cheyenne warriors who defeated General George Armstrong Custer, Walt Whitman's "half-breeds" and "squaws,"[1] Oliver Le Farge's pure and innocent Navajo Laughing Boy, Ernest Hemingway's promiscuous "squaw" Prudence Mitchell, and William Faulkner's "incorruptible" Sam Fathers[2] comprise a composite picture that, along with Hollywood's depictions of Native Americans as the foe of settlers and cowboys, still forms for some contemporary Anglos their portrait of an Indian.[3]

To be sure, there were a handful of Native Americans picked for their acculturation skills who through missionary conversion and early boarding schools gained literary skills and wrote about their people. Up until just into the twentieth century, there were the voices of Samson Occom (Mohegan) 1723–1792, William Apes (Pequot) 1798–1839, Elias Boudinot (Cherokee) 1802–1839, George Copway or Kah-ge-ga-gah-bowh (Ojibwa) 1818–1869, John Rollin Ridge (Cherokee) 1827–1867, Simon Pokagon (Potawatomi) 1830–1899, Sarah Winnemucca Hopkins (Paiute) 1844–1891, Charles Eastman or Ohiyesa (Lakota) 1858–1939, Alexander Lawrence Posey (Creek) 1873–1908, John Milton Oskison (Cherokee) 1874–1947, and Gertrude Simmons Bonnin or Zitkala-Ša (Lakota) 1876–1938.[4] However, these Indian writers barely made a dent in the perceptions of Native Americans that more established Anglo writers had formed.

Therefore, in the twentieth century with most Native peoples settled on reservations, the old ways were irrevocably gone. The pressure from missionaries, the boarding schools, and the BIA to adopt a more "civilized" lifestyle left Native people stranded between two worlds. To return to their traditional homelands and lifestyles was not an option, but completely assimilating into the Anglo world would necessitate negotiating their Indian heritage. The struggles with identity and injustices found a new arena in which to be fought in the twentieth century. With tribal members having access to schooling, widespread advanced literacy became the opportunity for Indians to use writing as the most powerful of political tools. They could now read the treaties, write their histories, and present their stories to the reading world. Literacy brought the opportunity for Native Americans to tell their stories and to become a potent voice in the American political system. For the first time, large numbers of American Indians were able to use the English language with an Anglo audience.

As Native Americans became more acculturated, intermarried with other Americans, and moved into the cities, their opportunities for advanced education increased. With the advent in the last half of the twentieth century of Native Americans in larger numbers attending college and becoming more fluent in English than in their Indian language, the conditions for a new group of Native American storytellers arose. These storytellers are not tribal elders but rather well educated Indians of various tribal origins and with mixed amounts of Indian ancestry who seized upon literacy as a persuasive tool for revising and transforming Anglo America's portrait of Indians. These college educated, acculturated writers used the pen to lead the way in creating a literary/political tradition that became the vehicle by which Indian voices entered the American mainstream.

The Native American Literary Renaissance

N. Scott Momaday's 1969 Pulitzer Prize-winning novel *House Made of Dawn* was the harbinger of this literary tradition that within a few short decades became an integrated part of the American canon.[5] Arnold Krupat's *The Voice in the Margin: Native American Literature and the Canon* provides a comprehensive review of the literary, historical, and cultural processes that coalesced in the late 1960s to create a more inclusive mood where new groups of writers could try out their voices. He notes how in the 1970s people traditionally excluded from representation in society and literature asserted their right to assume a place alongside members of the dominant culture, and the voices of minorities generally and Native Americans specifically aroused popular interest in their culture and literature (118). The political and cultural energies of the 1960s and 1970s provided an atmosphere in which the voices of people of color, women's voices, and the voices of ethnic populations could begin to rip open the tightly woven fabric known as the American literary canon. Within a decade, the canon had been radically altered by scholars who heard and included these emerging voices; and within a relatively short period of time, the secure foundations on which most university syllabi were based began eroding.

Philip Fisher defines this paradigmatic transformation by describing what took place in American studies as a shift from myth to rhetorics. His interpretation of the literary revolution that changed the body of the American literary canon twenty-five years ago is worth noting: "One way to characterize this newness would be to say that, in this generation of American studies, interest has passed from myth to rhetorics. Myth in this perhaps too simple formula is always singular, rhetorics always plural. *Myth* is a fixed, satisfying, and stable story that is used again and again to normalize our account of social life. . . . *Rhetoric*, in contrast is a tactic within the open questions of culture "(232). He further characterizes the shift to rhetorics as a new manifestation of regionalism now defined by race and gender (242). He points out, "This new regionalism demanded and made claims for a wider membership within the university on behalf of women, blacks, and others while supplying the new members with an automatic subject matter: themselves, their own history and rights within the national array of culture" (242). Fisher describes a new mood in the academy, one which has become less exclusionary and more open; and his remarks thus provide a context in which a reader can more fully appreciate the literary renaissance of Indian writers, who now claim the written word as their own and produce fiction and poetry that tells the stories of their people. They reclaim the territory long held by anthropologists, missionized Indians, canonical writers who precede the Native American Literary Renaissance, and contemporary Anglo writers such as Frank Waters, Oliver La Farge, Hal Borland, and Forrest Carter[6] who appropriate the authority to speak for the Indian way of life.[7]

The literary voices of Native Americans were clearly emerging and being heard by a wider and more receptive audience when *House Made of Dawn* became the first contemporary Indian work that asserted its otherness, its voice from a people who had not been a part of the literary mainstream. Momaday (Kiowa), who earned his Ph.D. at Stanford, forges a mythic tale of a shattered World War II Pueblo Indian veteran who struggles to find a place in a world that no longer makes sense. Momaday's singularly acclaimed voice soon was joined by a chorus of talented Native American writers, who, within ten years, carve out a literary domain now peopled by hosts of talented writers.

Finding an exact definition of this newly recognized literary field, Native American Literature, is fraught with difficulties. To be sure, Kenneth Lincoln's 1983 pronouncement that "To date, Indian poets and novelists are generally unknown outside tribal circles" (207) is no longer valid. However, Indian and Anglo critics differ as to what all is encompassed under the rubric Native American Literature. The late anthropologist and writer Michael Dorris, Erdrich's husband, emphatically declared in a 1979 article that there is no such thing as an Indian literature. He reasons that any group of people comprising 300 cultural groups and speaking 200 different languages from seven different language families cannot intelligently be considered one single ethnic group. His training in anthropology influences his strident insistence that a group of people designated as one could not logically be made up of hundreds of racially and culturally diverse people named Indians. He reasons, "If there had ever been a North American language called 'Indian,' the mode of communication within a society called 'Indian,' then there would undoubtedly be something appropriately labeled 'Indian literature.' But there was not, and is not" (147).

Dorris's point is well taken in light of Native Americans' history. His remarks are a jarring reminder of Indian struggles to identify themselves, and one arena in which this skirmish continues is over the application of the name Indian, used until the "politically correct" environment of the 1980s insisted that Native Americans was the more culturally sensitive term. The name Indian was misapplied wholesale to an entire population of 5 million people by a Spanish adventurer who misidentified the continent upon which he found himself.[8] Dorris acerbically sums up the issue: "Thus was born in the myopic minds of a few culturally traumatized and geographically disoriented individuals a new ethnic group" ("Native" 148).

Defining Native American Literature

The single term *Indian* used to designate multiple groups of people to this day is one striking representation of the power of the word that Momaday discusses in several of his works. He forces us to think profoundly about language and its potential political power when he writes, "A word has power in and of itself. It comes from nothing into sound and meaning; it gives origin to all things" ("A Word" 39).[9] Additionally, Paula Gunn Allen (Laguna-Sioux) argues, "Whoever controls your definition controls your sense of self" (Coltelli, *Winged Words* 18). The encompassing reduction of hundreds of culturally and racially different tribes of people into one misapplied nomenclature strikingly demonstrates the power of a dominant culture that, through language, reduced the identities of a marginalized people to one systematic category.

Louis Owens (Choctaw-Cherokee) accepts the encompassing term *Indian*, as do most scholars today, but he reflects on the question of who really should be classified as an Indian in the context of Native American literature. He considers:

> To begin to write about something called "the American Indian novel" is to enter a slippery and uncertain terrain. Take one step into this region and we are confronted with difficult questions of authority and ethnicity: What is an Indian? Must one be one-sixteenth Osage, one-eighth Cherokee, one-quarter Blackfoot, or full blood Sioux to be Indian? Must one be raised in a traditional "Indian" culture or speak a native language or be on a tribal roll? (3)

Frances Svensson reports that the United States Government set the standard of minimally one-fourth Indian blood in order to qualify for membership on a particular tribal roll (3). That the

Anglo government should take it upon itself to define their tribal membership is particularly galling to Native Americans. This concept of race is an imported European qualifier; since before the arrival of Anglos, race was not the important determiner of "what" or "who" one was. Instead, Indians identified themselves by their kinship and tribal groups.

As Owens points out, different tribes have different requirements for registration on their tribal rolls.[10] Since fewer than one-fourth of the people registered as Indians are full-bloods (Svensson 2), then "blood quantum" does not solely determine one's Indian affiliation. Rather, you need to move from the physical to the psychological in order to formulate a definition of "Indianness." Momaday seems to express best how Indian people form a sense of their identity when he states, "An Indian is an idea which a given man has of himself" (Chapman, *Literature* 97). This strong masculine voice found throughout Momaday's work excludes half of the Native American population; yet Indian scholars repeatedly refer to this definition, as it captures the essence of what it is to be an Indian in contemporary America. The fact is that more than half of the Indians today do not live on reservations or in other traditional tribal communities but rather flock to large urban centers like Chicago, Minneapolis, Denver, Omaha, Phoenix, Albuquerque, Los Angeles, and San Francisco to find work (Witt and Steiner 89). Also, a sizable percentage of Indians are mixed-bloods, or as Gerald Vizenor names them, "crossbloods [who] are a postmodern tribal bloodline" (*Crossbloods* vii). Owens notes that Vizenor's writing reflects a preoccupation with this theme, "At the heart of Vizenor's work lies a fascination with what it means to be of mixed Indian and European heritage in the contemporary world...." (225), and this very subject is explored by most contemporary novelists, who are, by and large, mixed-bloods themselves.[11]

Therefore, people who acknowledge their Indian ancestry, even if it is based on a small percentage of their blood, have chosen to adopt a certain stance, to wear a certain persona for the world, and to identify themselves with a group of people with whom they feel an emotional bond. To be Indian is to be "other," and the major mixed-blood contemporary novelists choose to be Indian.

Therefore, Momaday's definition rings true again and again as

Erdrich, Allen, Vizenor, Leslie Marmon Silko, Greg Sarris, Wendy Rose, and Linda Hogan write from an Indian frame of reference when they could have also chosen to identify themselves as Anglos. If you don't "look Indian," "talk Indian," or live in a traditional Indian community, then your Indianness must represent your identification with a particular worldview; and this is what is found in the writing of most the major mixed-blood contemporary writers who write out of their Indian heritage.

Those people identifying themselves as Indian have fought with words in their battle to establish themselves as legitimate members of the American literary canon. A proliferation of works appeared, written by Indians who emerged full of literary talent and energy after Momaday broke new ground with *House Made of Dawn*. In 1970, the first Convocation of Indian Scholars was held at Princeton where Dr. Alfonso Ortiz (Tewa) delivered the Convocation Call which sought the goal of having the Indian voice heard in the academy. By the time Dorris wrote his article in 1979, a field of highly acclaimed literature written by Indians was gathering momentum: James Welch (Blackfeet/Gros Ventre), *Winter in the Blood* (1974); Duane Niatum (Klallam) ed. *Carriers of the Dream Wheel*, a collection of contemporary Indian poetry (1975); Leslie Marmon Silko (Laguna), *Ceremony* (1977); and Gerald Vizenor (Ojibwa), *Darkness in Saint Louis Bearheart* (1978), as well as several books of poetry and essays. These works and others were individually impressive and groundbreaking, but they did not as yet constitute a new genre of literature.[12] The 1970s was the decade that decidedly shaped the field for the succeeding years, and it remained for other Indian voices to build the field into a distinctive literary arena.

In 1979, neither Dorris nor Erdrich, had individually or collectively gained recognition as Native authors; but Erdrich would earn several important literary prizes for her first novel, *Love Medicine*, published in 1984, and Dorris would garner an impressive array of awards for his own work.[13] But one only need glance at A. LaVonne Brown Ruoff's *American Indian Literatures* (1990), an important selected bibliography of American Indian Literatures, to see how the field expanded beginning in the 1980s.

The advent of the contemporary Indian novel may very well be what Dorris seeks as the embodiment of the "pan-tribal tradition of true 'Native American literature'" (Dorris, "Native" 156), since contemporary Indian novels reflect an identity that Indians give to themselves; and Dorris concedes in his article that the works of Welch and Silko constitute traditional tribal views depicting a shared Indian consciousness to the non-Indian world. Owens, writing eight years after Dorris's article, acknowledges the concern that encompassing all works written by Indians under the title Native American literature is problematic, but Owens argues that resolution to this thorny issue was fashioning itself in the 1980s, the most momentous decade yet for the Native American novel. In light of *Love Medicine*, *The Beet Queen*, and *Tracks* (Erdrich), *A Yellow Raft in Blue Water* (Dorris), *Fools Crow* (Welch), and *Griever: An American Monkey King in China* (Vizenor), Owens insists there is reason to believe that an Indian identity has emerged in literature. Writing in response to Dorris's 1979 article he concludes, "Perhaps better than any other form of writing by contemporary Indian authors, the novel has begun to fulfill Dorris's requirements" ("Acts" 56). Owens posits the contemporary Indian novel as an important factor in Indian cultural recovery, for Indian authors were now beginning to control the voice telling the lives of their people, wresting the authority to speak for tribes from non-Indians. This cultural recovery could only have begun once Momaday's groundbreaking, award winning work helped create an audience that was more receptive to hearing and understanding the Indian voice.

The concept "Native American novel" now designates literature written by Indians, about Indians, and with a decidedly Indian articulation of life. These works contrast with early writings by Native Americans which for the most part were little more than an occasion for converted Christian Indians to proselytize. Elias Boudinot and George Copway are good examples of "converted" Indian voices. Charles Larson was one of the first scholars to examine the degree to which Indian authors were originally assimilated writers, and it wasn't until later when more Native Americans were educated that the themes changed from Christianity to traditional Indian themes. Is this early writing then to be considered "Indian" literature? Indian scholars would say, "No," for what the early writers reflect is an Anglo viewpoint rather than a tribal one, and thus these early Christian Indian writers represent Natives who have assimilated into the Anglo culture while eschewing ancestral beliefs. While they are certainly still Indian writers, they do not reflect a traditional Indian way of viewing and operating in the world, and their writings become somewhat problematic to categorize. "Proselytizing Indian authors" perhaps comes the closest to clarifying how these authors do or do not fit into the mainstream of Native American literature. In the final analysis, it is one's worldview that Indian scholars argue determines if you are an Indian writer or a writer, born an Indian, who sees the world through the eyes of the Anglo culture.[14]

The contemporary Indian novel has become a medium through which talented Native writers can reshape and infuse a traditional western literary genre with their distinctive voice and worldview. Allen has come to believe that Indians can use the novel's format to define themselves in a culturally accepted western expression. She sees the novel as "a mapping of the possibilities, an exploration of our options as native people as we enter the twenty-first century surrounded by non-Indians (*Sacred* 100–01). Allen stresses the important role that contemporary Indian novels have taken on in the culture wars, "The novels respond to the question of whether we can remain Indians and still participate in and influence western culture or whether we will be junked or enshrined in museums of culture, victims of what Gerald Vizenor has named the 'word wars' and 'terminal creeds'" (*Sacred* 101).

Allen insists that the most important theme in Indian novels is not the conflict with the dominant Anglo culture but rather how Native Americans as a people will adapt and survive. Contemporary Indian novels are not pleas for understanding and acceptance; instead, they are poetic expressions of how and why Indians survive as a people. The poet Simon Ortiz (Acoma) sums up the importance of contemporary Indian novels when he asserts that Indian writers are "nowhere more articulate than in the novels" (Allen, *Sacred* 101), and this new contender in the American literary canon is now legitimized and supported by a field of scholars, critics, and publications.

Critical Work in Native American Literature

The Modern Language Association sanctioned the field with its *Three American Literatures*, edited by Houston Baker, Jr.,[15] and in the last 20 years, scholars such as A. Lavonne Brown Ruoff, Louis Owens, Charles Larson, and Andrew Wiget have specialized in the history of Native American literature.[16] Among the Native American scholars, Allen has been one of the most prominent Indian critics and authors, and her scholarship, especially regarding the feminine tradition in Native life, is particularly valuable.[17]

As editor of a course guide, *Studies in American Indian Literature: Critical Essays and Course Designs*, Allen considers important subfields into which Native American literature has diverged. Scholars tend to concentrate their work in one of these specialized subsets of the field: autobiography, translating and interpreting traditional oral texts, and analyzing how the oral tradition is reflected in contemporary Indian works.[18]

A related field to translating and interpreting traditional Indian narratives that has received an extensive amount of critical attention is the work folklorists and anthropologists have done with traditional materials. The reason this work is noteworthy to contemporary American Indian literature is to make the point that, until recently, the voice of the Indians was appropriated by the original anthropologists, highly respected professionals, who translated and interpreted Native texts according to their worldview and cultural orientation.[19]

Dell Hymes and Jerome Rothenberg have carved out a particular niche in the field of translation of Native texts with their specialization in ethnopoetics, the analysis of the various ways in which speakers use words. William Bright offers a definition of this new field that originated in the early 1970s as "an effort by scholars to capture the performance values and the poetic structure of oral literature" (341).[20] In addition to the work being done with translations of oral narratives, most prominent Native American scholars and critics, in both articles and books, explore the relationship between the oral traditions and written texts. The overviews of Native American literature by Ruoff, Wiget, Lincoln, and Allen all offer chapters that provide valuable insights on the importance of the oral tradition. Whereas the bulk of criticism on Native American texts concentrates on the oral tradition or the translations of oral texts, there exist as well several other specialties in the field that constitute interesting approaches to the literature. The areas of the trickster in Indian fiction, of the application of critical theories to the texts, and of feminist approaches offer insightful commentary to various works in the field.[21]

This overview of the critical work on Native American writing describes the many different areas in which scholarship is being conducted and suggests the breadth and depth of this relatively new genre in American literature. What all these various areas of scholarship within the field confirm is that Native American fiction has gained its place in the literary mainstream. However, even though it is now a part of the American literary tradition, it does not follow that readers can approach the texts relying on common Euro-American contexts and structures that underlie most canonical pre-1970s literature. Indian texts operate out of different frames of reference from those of most Anglo literature. This has become a central arena for recent scholarship, and what emerges from this critical work are five major characteristics of Native American literature. These features help define the perimeters of the Native American Literary Renaissance and the ways in which this literature differs from other American fiction.

Five Characteristics of Native American Fiction

First and foremost for Indian fiction is the oral tradition out of which it arises. The storytelling tradition is at the heart of most contemporary Indian fiction, which means that a writer/storyteller operates out of a shared knowledge base of myths and events in which communal understandings of events and implications are assumed because of a set of shared beliefs. This is a topic I further explore in chapter two; and it is the foundational underpinning of contemporary Indian fiction as it becomes a transformed and refigured version of the traditional art of storytelling.

Because stories arise out of a communal experience, the concept of a single author is an anomaly. To be sure, there is a single teller of the tales, but they speak as a communal voice. Ortiz explains, "Your voice is their voice ... a collective communal spirit" (Coltelli 110). Therefore, contemporary Native American authors convert the collective traditional tales and myths of their people into European literary forms that demand an author; their name appears as the sole creator of a work, but it is, instead, their rendering of a tribal story rather than their own original story. Welch's reconfiguration of the Gros Ventre warrior's journey into manhood in *Winter in the Blood,* Silko's *Ceremony* as retold Yellow Woman and Spider-Woman stories, Momaday's *Way to Rainy Mountain* as his personal journey woven into the mythic journey of the Kiowa people, and Erdrich's novels that tell the story of the Turtle Mountain Chippewa in the twentieth century are but a few examples of contemporary Indian authors retelling tribal stories.

Another important concept deriving from the storytelling tradition is the way in which stories now function in a written context. Most Indian authors seek to retain the flavor of the storytelling situation, positioning themselves as teller of the tale with the audience (reader) as receiver of the story as well as a participant in making meaning from it. Traditional storytellers adjust their performance to fit the nature of their audience, and the contemporary Indian novelist in this respect does not differ from traditional storytellers. Today, Native American authors write for an Indian and non-Indian audience alike thereby adjusting their storytelling now performed in print for a diverse audience. What remains a constant is the way in which Native American authors write out of traditional ways of passing along important tribal information through stories, which obligates readers to contextualize the story in a way not often demanded by non-Indian fiction.

The last major point to stress is that because traditional orality informs today's work, words are of paramount importance. The Indian culture transmitted traditions and values through spoken words, important words, words that needed to be remembered and passed on to future generations. There was no pan-Indian or even a single Indian alphabet when Sequoyah developed one in 1821 for his Cherokee nation. Other tribes formulated written systems in the twentieth century, but the oral component of communication remained of prime importance when history became reposited not in books but rather in stories told to each generation. With no fixed record of tribal history that chirographic cultures use to enshrine their past, the importance of what is said takes on even more significance in an oral culture that depends on spoken words to transmit and embody their culture. Thus, an oral culture values words for their ability to instruct, describe, and inform, for tribal realities were imparted solely through spoken words. These spoken words must be chosen with precision in order to transport the proper message not to the listener alone, but to all who thereafter listen to those words. If the spoken words were not remembered by tribal members, then history, culture, and tradition became lost to time; for in an oral culture, there was no repository of tribal life other than what was passed down orally from generation to generation (hide drawings being the only exception). It is, therefore, no coincidence that most of the major Indian fiction writers, Momaday, Vizenor, Silko, Welch, and Erdrich are also poets, wordsmiths, carriers of language, whose practice of conveying images and ideas in the compressed language of a poem permeates their fiction.

There are several other features of Native American literature which are distinctive characteristics derived from roots in an oral tradition. Alan Velie makes the point that stories were a part of everyday life, where every member of a tribe listened to the tales (*American* 7). It functioned to serve all tribal members in the various aspects of their life, and its teaching component made it an integral part of life. This differs from the function of most American literature, which champions the entertainment, technical, or creative value of a written work above its ability to instruct. Also, because stories inherently serve all tribal members, they additionally affirm one's identity in a group that shares its values. Stories affirm a communal identity and one's place within that community.

A second major characteristic of contemporary Indian literature is that in it time is cyclical, not linear. In *The Sacred Hoop*, Allen explains this concept:

> Another difference between these two ways of perceiving reality lies in the tendency of the American Indian to view space as spherical and time as cyclical, whereas the non-Indian tends to view space as linear and time as sequential. The circular concept requires all "points" that make up the sphere of being to have a significant identity and function, while the linear model assumes that some "points" are more significant than others. (59)

Stories do not end with their telling, but rather continue, transformed, in a circular manner, to link to other stories, to continue a new life in a new, never-ending life. The image of the circle is abundant in tribal life, from the sacred medicine wheels, to the round warrior shields, to the cyclical nature of the seasons, nature, and animal and human life. This element in contemporary Native

American fiction marks its "otherness" in a manner similar to that in which the elements of the oral tradition shape Indian literature today. This circular concept most often informs the organization of contemporary Indian novels, setting it in contrast to the more linear organization traditionally found in Euro-American literature. Allen's *Sacred Hoop* and Erdrich's *Love Medicine*, which begins and ends with June's story, are but two examples of this operating principle in Native American Literature.

Connected to the circular image is the Indian concept of the relatedness of all things, a third distinctive feature of Native American literature. People, animals, nature co-exist and are an integral part of the whole. In the same way, stories connect, people connect, events connect so that everything that happens is related to the story of life that never ends but continues and encompasses all aspects of being. Wholeness is connectedness, which is valued, while separateness, alienation, apartness are not desired, and this stands in contrast to the journey of the individual to find himself/herself, a theme predominant in American literature of the past two centuries. This idea of interconnectedness is applied to human behavior as well as to the stories, in which nothing is irrelevant, everything matters, and what has happened in the past is connected to the present and future in the same way that the present and future affect the past. Nothing is lost, events and people connect together in patterns often indiscernible to the participant. This is a pervasive feature of Indian fiction today, one that is often confusing to readers unaware of the tradition from which the story is told. Erdrich's novels are interlocking stories of people and the land they occupy—the Chippewa and immigrant people who populate a specific region in North Dakota and Minnesota.

The fourth distinctive feature of Native American literature is the prevalence of Trickster. While trickster characters appear in literature worldwide, they are not major components of Anglo American literature. They are, however, a pervasive presence in African-American literature (Brer Rabbit being the best known character) and in Indian tales, because both traditions emerge from an oral tradition and mythic past. In Indian literature, trickster figures assume various forms in different tribes and play particular cultural roles: coyote in the southwest, raven in the northwest, rabbit or hare in the Great Lakes, and "Old Man" for Blackfeet and

Crow.[22] Trickster plays tricks on unsuspecting humans, exhibits a voracious sexual appetite, lies, steals, and is guilty of outrageous acts of grossness. At the same time, though, the trickster figure is connected to the legendary aspects of tribal life. Vizenor calls trickster, "a liberator and healer in a narrative, a comic sign, communal signification and a discourse with imagination" (*Narrative* 187), and tricksters permeate his work (*Darkness in Saint Louis Bearheart, Griever: An American Monkey King in China,* and *The Trickster of Liberty*). However, trying to pin a definition on this elusive character is fraught with contradictions as Jarold Ramsey suggests, "Defining such a various creature is a little like trying to juggle hummingbirds, or arm wrestle Proteus" (*Coyote* 26). Trickster mediates in a world where events are often inexplicable and where human experiences defy meaningfulness. Ramsey views trickster as a crucial tribal figure who serves as a repository for unanswerable questions about the nature of human experiences, "The Indians and other tribal peoples seem to have relied on an age-old collective figure, unselfconscious and distinctly unheroic, to hold together indifferently well the various polarities of their experience, lest things seem to pull apart for the lack of a mediating center"(29). Paul Radin points out that this enigmatic figure is never static, for as each generation struggles to understand the complexity of its world, they must assign to the trickster traits and characteristics that seem to make no sense to a cohesive vision of life. He concludes, "And so he became and remained everything to every man—god, animal, human being, hero, buffoon, he who was before good and evil, denier, affirmer, destroyer and creator. If we laugh at him, he grins at us. What happens to him happens to us" (169).

Tricksters always enliven and enrich Indian fiction with their comic antics and mythic significance, and Erdrich's Nanapush and Gerry Nanapush are discernible Chippewa tricksters.

The fifth and perhaps most crucial distinction of Native American literature, one previously touched on, is the function it serves to Indians and non-Indians alike. The novels, stories, and poetry serve to represent a people defining themselves. No longer is the dominant culture speaking for them, interpreting their feelings, religion, and way of life. No longer are Indians represented by Anglos in a way that is pleasing or sensational, a commodity to be enjoyed and dismissed. Allen explains in an interview with Laura

Coltelli that, in Native American literature, Indian authors are finally able to take back the images of them given by Hollywood and the anthropologists and "claim themselves" (18). No longer are Native people subjected to the stereotypes forced on them, as Niatum points out in his thoughtful article "On Stereotypes." The fictionalized and romanticized Chingachgook, Hiawatha, and Ramona are finally replaced with portraits of "real" Indian people written by Indians.

Writing as an Act of Recovery

James Clifford believes that the phenomenon of Indians writing about themselves amounts to nothing less than "cultural continuity and recovery" (15). It *is* an act of recovery for a people to whom Congress awarded citizenship in 1924 (Indian Citizenship Act), whose tribal self-government was restored and devastating allotment system ended in 1934 (The Indian Reorganization Act), who were accorded Civil Rights in 1968 (Indian Civil Rights Act) and religious freedom in 1978 (American Indian Religious Freedom Act), and whose right to bury their ancestors and their grave goods came in 1990 (Native American Graves Protection and Repatriation Act). Women and slaves "recovered" their voices earlier than Native Americans. Frederick Douglass, Paul Dunbar, Sojourner Truth, Harriet Jacobs, W. E. B. DuBois, and the voices of the Harlem Renaissance represented the black voice without mediation from whites. Women began representing their way of life and their distinctiveness in the nineteenth century, first with the domestic novels by Louisa May Alcott and Harriet Beecher Stowe and then as regionalist writers like Sarah Orne Jewett, Mary Wilkins Freeman, Kate Chopin, Edith Wharton, and Willa Cather. From the domestic novelists to the regionalist writers to the modern voices, women began to tell the reality of their lives in their own voice.

Black and female voices merged in their effort to unlock the shackles placed on them by white males, but prior to the Native American literary renaissance, the Indians had no Seneca Falls Convention or Emancipation Proclamation to assert their new status and cultural and/or sexual voice. That representation remained muffled, except for a few lone pre-twentieth century authors who spoke from an Indian point of view in the first half of this century:

Mourning Dove, John Joseph Mathews, and D'Arcy McNickle.[23] Contemporary Native American fiction has accelerated this process of cultural identity begun in the late 1960s alongside the political activism of A.I.M , the occupation of Alcatraz, and the confrontation and occupation of Wounded Knee. To speak with their own cultural voice is indeed one of the greatest battles that Indians have fought and won, and Erdrich's novels of her Chippewa people evidence a literary as well as a cultural triumph.

Chapter 2

Traditional Storytellers

Louise Erdrich, like most Native American authors, writes out of an oral tradition, a topic scholars comprehensively address. Students of Indian literatures need only avail themselves of the wealth of information from Paula Gunn Allen, Kenneth Lincoln, Laura Coltelli, Andrew Wiget, A. LaVonne Brown Ruoff, Elaine Jahner, Karl Kroeber, Louis Owens, and Arnold Krupat in order to fully appreciate the oral context out of which contemporary Native American literatures arise. However, there are several additional notable aspects of storytelling that bear extended study for what they can tell us about traditional storytelling elements in Native American literature: how storytelling functions in the Native American literary tradition, how folklorists have studied the function of stories, and how orality theory provides a fuller contextual base in which to place Erdrich's work. Orality theory from the western tradition offers some intriguing, and yet unexplored, theoretical foundations from which to analyze contemporary Native American literature and to consider the possibility of a transitional text between the oral and written work. Erdrich in her North Dakota novels and *The Antelope Wife* and Leslie Marmon Silko in *Storyteller* represent contemporary Indian authors whose work approximates a traditional tribal storytelling session.

How Storytelling Functions in the Native American Literary Tradition

Traditional Indian communities cultivated a body of stories that enabled them to understand the world in which the people lived and to encode for future generations crucial tribal ways of understanding how they as a people perceive and operate in the world around them. N. Scott Momaday puts it this way, "Man tells stories in order to understand his experience, whatever it may be. The possibilities of storytelling are precisely those of understanding the human experience" ("Man" 104). From this longing to substantiate their importance and place in the natural world arise a body of different types of stories that explain, reinforce, and perpetuate tribal realities. Mythological or creation stories deal with a time before the people when the world was populated by the gods who decided to create and populate the earth with living beings. Accounts of creation differ from Ojibwa tales of Kitche Manitou creating all life and Sky-Woman giving birth to man and woman on her island home on earth, to Hopi tales of Spider Woman and Huruing Wuhti (a goddess of rocks, clay, minerals, and other hard substances), to the Modoc tales of Kumush, Old man of the Ancients, going to the underground world with his daughter and bringing back bones that he created into the Indian people.[1] These stories establish a tribal identity and become the basis for rituals that ensure through time a collective sense of self that by its distinctiveness marks the people as special beings in the order of creation.

Another body of stories concerns humankind's continual struggle to survive in a frightening and challenging world. In these stories, humans constantly seek and are provided with intermediaries, often in the form of the hero or the trickster, who come to their aid (bringing fire, domesticating animals, and slaying monsters) and teach them how to survive. Without such help, humans are hapless creatures in a mysterious world that overwhelms and entangles them. The importance of an intercessor for humankind is firmly established by tradition and will play an important part in contemporary literature, where characters are recovered from a hostile Anglo world through the intercession of a tribal mythic figure.

The last type of stories are those told by storytellers relating the history of the people. These include migration stories, historical accounts, and especially the stories encased within the living memories of tribal peoples. Arthur Amiotte (Lakota) emphasizes the importance of these stories, "They come close to an approximate living history of human events, and include specific references to actual landmarks and approximate dates.... Most crucially, these are personal accounts of life events, passed down through successive tellings from generation to generation, and they account for much of the content of Native ethno-history" (34).

Amiotte stresses that the mythical components of the first two types of stories are never fully absent from this category where they often manifest themselves in the form of dreams or supernatural healings directly linked to intercession from higher beings. Although various critics break down the corpus of narratives into different categories, the aforementioned three groups most succinctly characterize the stories within the oral tradition that reside at the heart of contemporary Native American literature.

Who are the storytellers? In most tribal communities, the role of the storyteller is borne by elders, valued as a repository of traditions, history, and tribal identity who have the wisdom of years to understand events and the respect of others to serve as bearers of the culture. Privileging the tribal elders as the storytellers is a pan-Indian custom, and their role is vital to ensure cultural survival. Silko writes, "The old people say, 'If you can remember the stories, you will be all right. Just remember the stories ("Language" 68)." Their responsibility is to pass on a living tradition to their grandchildren so that the continuity of tribal life is unending.

They tell stories for behavioral instruction, for historical perspective, for cultural nourishment, and for communal bonding. They tell stories on formal occasions, as well as informally when an occasion demands an example or moral teaching for the children. Through the elders' sharing tribal experiences and ways of knowing throughout their growing up years, the children reach maturity marked with the tribal identity. They may not understand the meaning of the stories in their early years, but their repeated recitation ensures that over time the children will come to understand and experience how the stories define them as a people and how they too are carriers of the tradition. Momaday experienced this when he recollected how he grew up with his father telling him the Kiowa story of arrowmaker. To this day, reflects Momaday, he continues to interpret and to ponder its importance in his writings ("Native" 11–4). Through these stories the young ones are imbued with a sense of tradition, a tribal imprint shaped by the elders' recitations of a corpus of stories that construct the identity of the people. It is for this very reason that so many children of the twentieth century sent off to boarding school lost a sense of identity

identity with their Indian community.

Winter nights are the most common time for storytelling, and there are specific natural events which mark the beginning and end of storytelling season, such as first frost to first flower, first snowfall to first thunder, or from the cessation of thunder and lightning to its resumption in the spring. In many tribes, there are taboos against storytelling in seasons other than winter, for only in winter when the animals are in hibernation is it safe to tell stories about them. Otherwise, you risk offending them and their spirits. With winter weather prohibiting cultivation and limiting outdoor activities, winter becomes the natural time set aside for storytelling, and thus it becomes an event greatly anticipated and enjoyed during this special time of the year.

For the Ojibwa, Erdrich's ancestors, winter marked the time when rice, berry, and maple syrup gathering, tanning, and fishing are suspended. In the summer, families gathered in small villages (five to fifteen families) located near fresh water and worked and socialized until the fall when ricing ended and families started moving to their winter lodges. This hunting lodge, located near game, provided the winter home where nights are long and there is ample time for stories that range in length from those heard in a single sitting to those which continued for weeks. Sister Bernard Coleman et al., who gathered stories from the Minnesota Ojibwa in the 1950s, tells of an elder on the White Earth Reservation remembering storytelling activities around 1900:

> In the winter evenings we would gather at the home of a woman story teller. When we arrived, we handed our contributions for the potluck to the old woman, and settled down to talk about personal happenings and current tribal problems. A special concern was the education of our children outside the home, for this means the breaking of family ties. Gradually, the atmosphere changed from the serious to the jovial when our old friend began to relate incident after incident about the tricks of Nanabozho. The evening closed with the potluck, lunch of boiled porcupine, rabbit or deer meat. (7)

Distinctive features of stories from the oral tradition manifest themselves in various ways in the works of Indian authors. A crucial element that Kroeber points out throughout his book *Retelling/Reading: The Fate of Storytelling in Modern Times* is the importance of continuous retelling of the stories in order to ensure cultural continuity. He emphasizes that a story is never in a "final" version, as it is once it passes from oral to written expression. A story is meant to be used and interpreted by successive generations, who apply lessons and explanations relevant to current situations from a shared tribal repertory. Therefore, a story is always a work in process that yields its meanings to the various interpreters across generations.

Traditional stories have no author, only tellers of the tales, interpreters of myths and legends that shape the consciousness of the tribe. The narratives in the oral tradition are for corporate use: for families who instruct their children, for holy people who ritualize sacred events, for the community at large for whom the stories define the collective life of a people, and for storytellers, gifted orators who creatively "perform" the stories for a tribal people who share the same mythic memory. Michel Foucault's concept of the author's absence in texts takes on interesting relevance in the context of Native American storytelling. Foucault's work refers to written texts he critiques "for their intrinsic and internal relationship" (140) while discounting the importance of the context of a work as the product of a single author. He cites as evidence that an author is not a fundamental component of a text the example of stories from oral traditions. He argues, "There was a time when those texts which we now call "literary" (stories, folk tales, epics, and tragedies) were accepted, circulated, and valorized without any question about the identity of their author. *Their anonymity was ignored because their real or supposed age was a sufficient guarantee of their authenticity*" (emphasis mine 143). Foucault's work concerns itself with written texts produced out of discourse communities, but at the same time, his premise that a literary work does not require an author's name to guarantee authenticity is a point well taken in relation to "authorless" texts from Native American oral tradition. His theories elucidate the essence of a tradition that assumes a work (story, legend, myth) to be a composite rendering of a people, and a storyteller (or author) as one designated to perform the "author-function." The teller of the tales is, therefore, nothing more than "a particular source of expression" (144).

Owens discusses this same issue when he considers the ethical issue contemporary Indian authors face when they put their name on to a work that is the product of the memories, rituals, and stories of a tribal community. He observes, "Try as he or she may, the Native American novelist can never step back into the collective anonymity of the tribal storyteller... through the inscription of an authorial signature, the Indian writer places him—or herself in immediate tension with this communal, authorless, and identity-conferring source..." (*Other* 11).

The modern concept of a single author for a text is, as Owens points out for Indian texts and Foucault points out for texts in general, a contradiction for an Indian society where stories have a communal base, are not tied to a single version of the "truth," and are the property of all who share them as a common reference for their identity. As Owens emphasizes, the concept of a single author just isn't Indian, and contemporary Indian writers who inscribe their name on a work that originates from their cultural past are taking on the traditional role of a tribal storyteller, a member of the community who appropriates communal stories and traditions and "performs" them in a creative way for an audience that now includes both Indians and non-Indians alike. That the performance is written and not recited alters the medium but not the fact that the "author" is utilizing communal stories for a particular occasion, and thus we come to understand that contemporary Indian writers frequently assume the mantle of the traditional tribal storyteller in their works. Momaday emphasizes this point when he comments that the dichotomy between oral texts and contemporary works by Native authors "is more apparent than real, that the one expression informs the other and that the voice is the same. The continuity is unbroken" ("The Native Voice" 15).

Another distinctive feature of Native American oral narratives is their brevity and lack of substantial descriptive and informing details. Kroeber has applied the term "minimalizing" to describe the bare bones texts that are common in Indian stories. There is a decided lack of details that most western listeners or readers are accustomed to learning from an author. A narration is often marked by a paucity of links between sections, descriptions of people and places, and contextualizing background that help position a reader to be able to understand a story. This is a problem only for non-Indian readers or listeners, since members of a tribal community who share a common repertory of stories already know the material and therefore mentally fill in the gaps as the story proceeds. Wolfgang Iser's concept of a reader concretizing the indeterminacies is a western critical theory which serves well to explain what is happening in traditional Indian narratives told in a tribal setting. The community *already* knows the story and already knows the ending, and so what they are listening to is a *rendering* of a specific tale told at a specific time for a specific function. They mentally fill in the gaps of the story, for they know its meaning, its context, and its mythological base. Iser notes that, when "blanks" occur in a story, the reader is forced to try to connect the various parts. He argues:

> They [the blanks or indeterminacies] indicate that the different segments of the text are to be connected, even though the text itself does not say so. They are the unseen joints of the text, and as such they mark off schemata and textual perspectives from one another, they simultaneously trigger acts of ideation on the reader's part. Consequently, when the schemata and perspectives have been linked together, the blanks "disappear." (183)

Even though he is describing a reading process, there is application as well to the context of tribal storytelling; for what he is describing is a mental process that textual gaps trigger in a reader/listener. The point is that the gaps are more easily and naturally filled in by readers/listeners who share a common history, worldview, repertory of stories, and similar identity with that of the author/storyteller. Thus, these gaps, in Native American literature in particular, leave a nontribal member struggling to make connections and to create a mental picture of a story that is given to them devoid of elaboration.

Related to the minimizing feature of Native American oral narratives is the feature that stories are told in various segments, usually brief in length, that often seem unrelated to each other and for whom the connecting elements are simply omitted. Kroeber describes these units as "interdependent segments" (*Retelling* 77) that accrue their meaning once the segments are understood to be part of a larger context. Kroeber is quick to point out that these story segments are not the same elements that structuralists like Claude Lévi-Strauss and Vladimir Propp isolate as recognizable subunits in Native stories, where, for Propp especially, fairy tale units predictably occur and always in the same order. What Kroeber and others describe as individual segments in a story are the very elements that traditional storytellers adapt and change to fit the context of their particular rendering. Therefore, the basic units of any story may be freely utilized to fit a storyteller's specific purpose. Kroeber's insights are again helpful, for he explains, "Segmenting assures that a story may at any time—within a given reading or hearing or at any subsequent reading or rehearing—produce new meanings and effects by aiding the addressee to reconceive the point of the tales' structure" (*Retelling* 78).

Because Native stories are composed of bundles of narratives whose connecting links are not always apparent, they seem to constantly shift the point of view and narrative emphasis in their telling, or as Allen puts it, "The stories out of the oral tradition, when left to themselves... tend to meander gracefully from event to event; the major unifying event, besides the presence of certain characters in a series of tales, is the relationship of the tale to the ritual life of the tribe" (*Sacred* 153).

Vizenor, in his interview with Coltelli, explains the multiple points of view from a slightly different perspective when he describes how storytellers construct stories out of visual references which are the "recollection of multiple senses of an experience so that actually when you call upon an experience in memory and when you decide to tell a story from memory you can tell it from a number of points of view; I mean you see it and hear it and feel it, and you can just step in and talk about it and it takes on a different shape or a different bit of humor" (156). Traditional Indian narratives continually shift the foci in the stories so that each element builds on the others in order to present a primary idea from several different angles. These story segments and shifting foci serve to allow creativity on the part of the storyteller who adjusts the stories' length and moral to fit the need of the particular storytelling session.

Shifting points of view is certainly not a feature of storytelling that distinguishes Native American literature alone. The best modernist writers like T.S. Eliot, James Joyce, and William Faulkner subverted traditional narrative structures through shifting points of view and through a breakdown of a story's traditional linear continuum. Eliot's poetry is marked by fragments that mimic the chaos he viewed as a condition of the modern world. Joyce destroyed conventions of unity, clarity, character development, and traditional story patterns with his radical rendering of Leopold Bloom's mythic wandering through the streets of Dublin. Faulkner's shifting points of view and jumps in temporal sequences violate western narrative form but replicate many features of traditional Native American storytelling structures. It is an interesting footnote in the tradition of literature that writers as diverse as Eliot, Joyce, and Faulkner practice literary techniques that are common to traditional Indian storytellers and to the contemporary Indian storytellers like Vizenor, Welch, Silko, Momaday, and Erdrich who ground their work in an oral tradition. This nonlinear way of representing life stands in contrast to the more traditional method authors use to tell their story, where writers establish an indisputable beginning, middle, and end. The implications of the convergence of these two traditions is fascinating and one that warrants further exploration.

Stories are conveyed through spoken words, and the importance of language in traditional and contemporary Native American literature is its concluding distinguishing feature. I noted this crucial condition of Indian writing in chapter one, but the way in which spoken words function as conveyors of culture merits additional discussion. Vizenor poetically captures the essence of words for Native Americans when he relates to Coltelli in an interview, "We touch ourselves into being with words, words are that important to us" (158), and Simon Ortiz echoes this sentiment in his interview with Coltelli when he says, "Our language is the way we create the world" (107). For Native Americans, traditionally to name was to create, and this power of the spoken word to situate identity still pervades the work of Indian writers today.

Words serve, as Lincoln beautifully describes to "translate the world we experience by aural or visual signs. Words embody reality" (24). In a culture where stories are the sole embodiment and purveyors of culture, they must be chosen carefully. They must convey to all listeners a worldview, for words in the stories define them as a people. Just as the Inuit language contains multiple words for snow, so does the Hopi vocabulary include many names for corn. These intricately defining features of culture mark a people and their distinctive adaptation to life. When the spoken word expresses a tribal epistemology, it must be chosen with extreme care and reverence.

Momaday points out in his introduction for "The Native Voice" in the *Columbia Literary History of the United States* that in the oral tradition, words are of greater importance than in a written tradition where they are often taken for granted; for print provides a permanent access to anyone who wishes to utilize them. He posits the sacredness and powerfulness of the spoken language, where words can control the elements, heal the sick, conquer evil, woo a lover, and create anew in ceremony the mythical dimension in peoples' consciousness. For contemporary Native American authors, their written words continue as carriers of culture and markers of an identity that decidedly contrasts with non-Indian worldviews and cultural traditions.

Lincoln remarks, "In our common language, story once meant history" (223), and Native Americans honor stories as crucial culture markers. As western scholars appropriate these stories for their scholarly domain, the intersection between western scientific theory and tribal culture produces some peculiar results. Analyzing folklore and how folklorists apply their theories to Native American oral texts reveals the extent to which western scholars have often marginalized and misunderstood the function of Native stories in their endeavor to interpret them within categories that they have defined and promoted. Therefore, a look at folklore's foray into Native American stories provides one western view of the function of tribal stories and helps highlight some commonly held areas of misinterpretation.

How Folklorists Have Studied the Function of Stories

The very word "folklore" conjures up images of wicked witches, towering giants, and benevolent godmothers. As Alan Dundes points out in the introduction to his book on folklore, a definition that is agreed upon by all practitioners in the field is not to be found. He illustrates that some scholars concentrate on the "folk" aspect; therefore one must define "folk." Are they primitives, non-literates, or peasants? Is it possible to have folklore among literate urban people? What is "lore"? Can it be dances, traditional symbols, and customs? Are folklore and folk literature the same thing?

Scholars in the field have debated over a definition ever since it emerged as a scholarly endeavor in the beginning of the nineteenth century when the Grimm brothers set about collecting German folktales. Francis Lee Utley summarizes best the consensus of definition at which scholars have arrived—folklore encompasses materials from an oral (verbal, unwritten) tradition (transmission) of people in primitive cultures and of people in subcultures of rural and urban areas (10).

Trained ethnologists set about trying to gather materials that would help them understand cultures and to conclude from these studies the commonalties among cultures. As Utley notes, they often displayed more enthusiasm than accuracy (22), and the results proliferated into varied appropriate and not so appropriate applications of the materials. People in different countries applied different and even contrasting techniques to understanding what was not familiar to them, and rifts developed as to how to best deliver up folk materials in a scholarly way. These divisions exist to this day and have a great deal to do with how scholars research Native American oral materials for, as Robert Georges pointedly notes, the various kinds of research were done "primarily as a means of achieving predetermined ends, [and so] story research has made little contribution to knowledge in the twentieth century" (315).

In addition to the internal divisions concerning how best to interpret oral texts, there exits blurred distinctions between folklorists, folk literaturists, and anthropologists who may or may not be the same and who often approach the material from different theoretical bases. What is muffled when the different disciplines apply their varying techniques to Indian narratives is the degree to which these stories, communicated in a tribal voice, are an integral part of a tribal culture. Moreover, these stories do not derive any benefit from being decontextualized as scientists apply their methodologies searching for meaning they can interpret. The meaning of the stories for Indian peoples is their culture, their worldview, their identity, which is often disrespectfully compromised when scholars reduce traditional tales to conventional parts.

Folklore scholars have taken an astonishing variety of approaches to oral narrative. Charles Seeger would divide scholars into two camps, the structuralists who studied the varying parts of stories as a reflection of the whole society and the functionalists who studied the purpose of the various stories in a culture. These two camps with their diverse offsprings take into account the major approaches in the field to stories.[2]

When Franz Boas, the pioneering anthropologist, became the president of the American Folklore Society in 1900, he changed the direction that folklore studies had taken heretofore. He paid close attention to the role of folklore in a society, and he and his followers edited *The Journal of American Folklore* from 1908–1940. Folklore was important to Boas's work, for he saw it as a mirror of the culture.[3]

Dan Ben-Amos authored another book *Folklore Genres* which categorized stories into various types: ballads, folktales, and oral epics. He positions this approach as one holding prominence, for it foregrounds the research, university courses, and articles in the field. It developed out of a need to categorize the voluminous amounts of material folklorists/anthropologists collected and drew from psychological and anthropological approaches that examined the social dynamics within a culture. Genre studies were utilized "as a methodological paradigm that enabled them [folklorists] to formulate problems and to propose solutions" (Ben-Amos xii). Even though not all stories can be easily and neatly stuffed into defining forms, this approach has been influential in folklore studies in recent decades.

There remain even more approaches to folklore. Richard Dorson surveyed the field in a 1963 article, and he cited "the comparative, the national, the anthropological, the psychological, and the structural theories as dominant in folklore research" (Ben-Amos and Goldstein 1). Nine years later he added to his list the contextual approach, which emphasizes how stories are communicated and performed in a given culture.

This approach borrows many of its methods and practices from the field of sociolinguistics, and Ben-Amos and Goldstein insist that this approach "owes a direct debt to Hymes' idea of 'the ethnography of communication'" (3). The nascence of sociolinguistics as the reigning model in folklore studies is connected to the prominence of semiotics in literary studies as well as in anthropology as new questions arise concerning the role of discourse in human communication. Dorson and others began to concentrate on the story as a communication event, and he, as well as William Jansen, Robert Georges, Richard Bauman, and Dell Hymes established this division of folklore studies. These scholars approach the stories in a context, and they emphasize the role of the storytellers as well as the stories themselves.

Folklorists take for their subject "simple" oral societies (Rosenberg 25) and apply various methodologies to their stories in order to understand the particular culture. Their concern is to reconstruct the past based on the stories which they view as, in Georges' words, "cultural artifacts" (313). Folklorists approached their study using the various modes noted earlier, because they were in essence a conglomerate of disciplines doing similar work—looking at stories—but from different methodologies and from intrinsically different approaches that precluded a consensual finding. Dundes, in his Preface to John Miles Foley's *The Theory of Oral Composition: History and Methodology* notes how over time the emphasis of the folklorists shifted; the nineteenth-century practitioners approached the field diachronically as they attempted to reconstruct a historical past from the stories, while the twentieth-century folklorists use a synchronic approach as they investigate the form and function of stories. Twentieth-century folklorists, in other words, are more interested in the actual performance, the impact of the storytelling on an audience, and the composition of the piece, whereas their predecessors concentrated on the stories' origins.

How does the study of folklore with its multidimensional approaches inform a study of Native American storytelling? It first of all reminds one of the Indian joke that explains the composition of a traditional family unit; there are five members: mother, father, two children, and the anthropologist. Native Americans have been scrutinized, romanticized, vilified, quantified, and marginalized by scholars who seek to interpret their culture and stories based on either preconceived models or on preconceived ideas. Indian oral texts have been broken into morphological units, studied by typologies, compared to other cultures, analyzed in terms of their environment, postulated as underlying social norms, examined as psychological relics, and predicated as exact mirrors of the particular culture. As one example of an extreme position taken by various practitioners, Boas assumed that the field work and subsequent recordings he and his contemporaries made of the Kwakiutl and other Indian tribes constituted a *complete* repertory of folktales from the North American continent.

My point is not to diminish the contributions that anthropologists and folklorist have made in understanding Indian cultures and narratives. Instead, I hope to emphasize through a juxtaposition of "scientifically" acquired conclusions with Indian notions about the function of stories that a cautious approach must be taken when assuming that either group offers a complete rendering of the "truth." Folklorists and anthropologists seek to create models from oral narratives that can be empirically tested and applied to various cultures. Native Americans, on the other hand, experience stories as reflecting tribal consciousness, an ambiguous and spiritual notion which defies scientific testing. Folklorists/anthropologists often don't account for enough with their studies while Native Americans ground their collective tribal history, memory, and being in their stories. One must conclude that an approach to studying the function of Native American stories by a rigid scientific model will result in an incomplete conclusion at best and an inaccurate one at worst.

How Orality Theory Provides a Fuller Context for Erdrich's Work

Not all theoretical approaches to Indian oral texts, however, are shortsighted. Orality theory, a related field to folklore, approaches oral narratives with a theoretical frame that furnishes a better understanding of oral tradition and specifically how stories are composed. While the folklorist/anthropologist's approach often proves too limiting, orality studies offer insights that provide invaluable information. Native American texts have not been atomized by this theory; and, indeed, there has been little practical application of this approach to Indian tales. I find the application of orality theory offers impressive insights concerning how stories are transmitted and composed in an oral society, as well as providing a contextual base which situates Native American storytelling within a worldwide storytelling tradition. The way in which contemporary folklorists have enhanced their field because of the growth of orality studies, which look at traditional stories from a different but not an altogether contrary approach, provides an interesting footnote to the development of both disciplines.

One of the limitations of folklore studies had been that practitioners approached the stories from different perspectives and methodologies. Folklore experienced an identity crisis, and what was needed for the field to perceive itself as a distinctive discipline was its own theory. As the bastard child of anthropology, history, linguistics, and philology, it had, depending on the practitioner, borrowed its legitimacy from various parents. It remained for a unifying theory to directly focus its goals, methodologies, and objectives, and oral narrative theory offered just that. Alex Orlick, a Danish philologist and medievalist, was the first person to explicate an embracing theory for folklore studies. However, his seminal work, which was published only in Danish in 1921, remained unavailable to English speakers until Kirsten Wolf and Jody Jensen translated it for the Indiana University Press in 1992. His work, *Principles for Oral Narrative Research*, proffered a badly needed comprehensive folklore theory, yet only his concept of "epic laws"[4] was available to scholars until this decade. Ben-Amos emphasizes that Orlick's ideas "are not a doctrine but an agenda for research, requiring repeated testing under various circumstances" (Foreword, *Principles* viii). However, Orlick's work, according to Ben-Amos, finally places folklore in the scientific realm with theories that can be tested, agreed with, or disputed.

In the absence of this work that would later serve as a nexus for the different folkloric approaches, scholars focusing on folklore searched other sources for a rationale that could direct their burgeoning discipline. In Milman Parry's Oral-Formulaic Theory, they found the greatly needed theory for their field; for Oral-Formulaic Theory places its emphasis on the text rather than the context of the story in a specific historical continuum, reflecting the change in approach from the nineteenth- to the twentieth-century folklorists. Parry, a classicist, developed this theory when examining for his two doctoral theses in 1928 the age-old question of who Homer was and how could one account for the fact that his great works were composed in an age that did not have writing. By examining compositional elements (especially noun-epithet phrases) in the *Iliad* and the *Odyssey*, Parry made the startling discovery that these bedrocks of western literature were composed of formulas and were, "The collective creations of many generations of bards working not individually but within a poetic tradition [which] developed its own diction, a specialized poetic language consisting of substitutable "formulas" that enabled a poet to make his verses extemporaneously without having to depend on rote memorization" (Foley, *Oral Tradition* 3). These formulas precluded the need for a verbatim memorization of stories, and so Parry concluded that what the great Bard had done was he "stitched together prefabricated parts. Instead of a creator, you had an assembly-line worker" (Ong, *Orality* 22). Parry never denied Homer's genius in creatively composing his works from these well-used formulas; however, he did stress that the venerated Homeric poems were largely composed of common phrases assembled by an artistic oral poet. One of Parry's important insights is that a work composed of traditional formulas must come from an oral culture, i.e., Homer was a traditional oral poet working with conventional patterns of diction.[5]

Alfred Lord, Parry's student, extended Parry's studies and made Oral-Formulaic Theory its own field.[6] Lord's major work positioned him not only as the co-founder of the field, but also as the dean of oral literature for over forty years. Lord's research explains narrative inconsistencies as storytellers use different themes or units of ideas which may, when juxtaposed, present details that don't match. He defines how storytellers use the traditional formulas in essential as well and as in creative ways as they present known details and then express or ornament them with their own particular style. He also observes that once literacy and a fixed text appear the result is a memorized performance as opposed to a created performance, which Lord views as very different entities.

John Miles Foley, founder and editor of the journal *Oral Tradition* and a leading theoretician in the field, points out that folklorists grant the Parry-Lord theory as the precursor to their current widely practiced approach of performance theory where the emphasis is placed on the text, in a performance, with the context of an audience interacting with the storyteller (*Theory* x).[7] Since Parry's Oral-Formulaic Theory applies primarily to epics, it remains a general theory that helps inform folklore studies, as opposed to a rigidly defining methodology to which all in the field could adhere. However, Parry's seminal thinking about how oral texts are constructed offered a real grounding for the discipline that had heretofore been lacking.

What is so attractive about Oral-Formulaic Theory and its various scions is the respect it affords the text and its treatment of stories of creations by gifted tellers who through their artistry shape narrative bundles from their oral tradition into a meaningful and original rendition. The application of orality theory adjusts the overzealous, shortsighted approaches of some of the anthropologists and folklorists by pointing out the limitations involved in narrowly conceived approaches that seek to "scientifically" explain non-literature cultures.

Instead, orality theory recognizes the importance of the speaker and the importance of the context. In addition, it acknowledges that the concept of genre is a decidedly western idea which is not always applicable to the multidimensional stories[8]; that the observer is often unconsciously guilty of imposing values through his or her ethnocentrism; that orality still is a vital element in many "literate" cultures today and cannot be dismissed as a relic of the past; that a written work is permanently recorded for an unknown audience which has no face-to-face contact with the author, and this text necessarily has a markedly different impact from that of a story interacting with an audience; and that a mind that does not rely on writing or analytical thought initiated by writing patterns itself differently. This holistic approach to stories marks it as a more useful and relevant tool than many of the ones employed by folklorists to study oral texts.

Some of the informing ideas brought forth by the cadre of orality scholars have made tremendous impact on narrative studies.[9] In particular, Foley explores the ways in which we interpret works of literature that have their base in an oral tradition. He argues that the same critical analysis cannot be applied to an oral narrative as to a written text. This he believes is one of the major faults of literary critics who try to fit oral narratives into the well-defined literary niches. He argues that unless an oral work is kept in its proper contextual framework, one will miss understanding its creative attributes while straining to force it into a contemporary literary mold. He also suggests that "in oral cultures, words are more or less continuous with the rest of life, not so much part of a separate world as they appear in print" (*Oral Tradition* 155); and because of this, oral expressions tend to have an immediacy not always found in literate societies. Foley argues for orality theory to turn itself to an examination of the text's meaning by analyzing its relation to the tradition out of which it arose.

How do theories advanced by orality studies help inform a study of Native American literature? It is by broadening our very ways of thinking about a chirographic literature whose roots lie in an oral tradition and by validating written Indian fiction as a genre whose distinctive characteristics are driven by its oral-based history. Orality studies, more than any other methodology, provides diverse tools for scholars to utilize while analyzing characteristics of a traditional oral-based culture that now manifest themselves in contemporary fiction.

The concept of an oral residue, lingering evidence of a pre-literate epistemology, may be the single most important informing idea from orality theory that helps situate the foundation for Native American writing. Walter Ong's concept of a residual orality in chirographic cultures is evidenced in the work of the major Indian authors who write out of a traditional oral culture and write out of tribal ways of knowing. These oral residues permeate contemporary Indian writing and manifest themselves in varying ways. For example, many of the best contemporary books are tribal novels that describe an individual's process towards harmony. The success of this journey becomes measured by the extent to which he or she accepts a role not as the lonely and isolated twentieth-century individualist but rather as an integral part of the tribal community where their identity resides. Momaday's *House Made of Dawn*, Silko's *Ceremony*, Welch's *Winter in the Blood* and *The Death of Jim Loney*, Vizenor's *The Darkness in Saint Louis Bearheart*, and Erdrich's North Dakota novels and *The Antelope Wife* all show the power of tribal identity and history as healing agents for disoriented contemporary Indian people.

In addition, there are numerous examples of the mythological trickster figure in many contemporary novels. As cited earlier, most of Vizenor's works incorporate this traditional tribal figure who has been transformed once again and now etherealizes as a contemporary character. Erdrich and Welch (*Winter in the Blood*) also resurrect this traditional tribal figure who flashes in and out of people's lives creating havoc and bringing healing. The tribal novels and trickster novels testify to the residing influence of oral culture on contemporary Indian fiction and posit the evidence for Ong's theory of residual orality.

Another notable application from orality studies is Ong's concept of the power of the word, which correlates precisely with Momaday's highly regarded writings on the same topic. Ong examines the magical potency words can carry once they are spoken, especially in names.[10] Names carry power, for if you do not know the identity of a person, plant, animal, or object, you cannot understand who or what they are. Ong points out that our chirographic culture tends to think of names as labels, which is not the same thing. Labels are for sorting while names are for knowing. Once you give a name in an oral culture, you initiate an interaction between you and the named, an unfamiliar concept for a literate society.

David Bynum makes an important contribution when he distinguishes the differences in organization for an oral and a written narrative. While this theory originated from Parry's work with formulas that could be changed in a recitation depending on the creativity of the singer, Bynum extended it to also include clusters of ideas that are held together by overriding thematic considerations. The narrative pattern for contemporary Indian novels tends to have a superimposed circular frame with additive thematic clusters. The most common structure for Indian novels, as previously noted, is the circular, reflecting a concept of life and a way of knowing, and this pattern is most clearly evidenced in the "homing" novels. William Bevis describes how, in American novels, characters are always leaving home in order to seek their fortune and to find a better way of life. He contrasts this with the Native American novels which are not "'eccentric,' centrifugal diverging, expanding, but 'incentric,' centripetally, converging, contracting. The hero comes home" (582). For in Indian novels, when characters come home, they return to their identity, to the particular land that has shaped them, and to their rightful place in a tribal community. So even when the Indian characters journey out, the place of harmony for them is right where they started, at the beginning/ending of the circle, at home.

The other common structural element in Native American fiction relates to Bynum's idea of narrative clusters. The action in these novels tends to be lumped in groups that do not always seem related to what has gone on previously and what follows. Some of these narrative shifts can be attributed to the modernist influence which reflects societal disorder through the use of atemporal sequencing, while other reasons for narrative shift can be attributed to the postmodern ideas of the ephemeral and unstable nature of language which mirrors no firm foundation in the society from which it emanates. However, contemporary Native American writers who utilize disjointed narrative units and clusters of action are also reaching back to their oral tradition. The oral storytellers, as Bynum, Ong, and Parry point out, for purposes of remembering overriding themes, tended to cluster units of action into recognizable groups that could be moved around according to the purposes of the singer. The intervening spaces may be filled with inconsistencies and voids, but the consistency of theme will remain fixed. Contemporary Indian novelists commonly use this technique to tell their stories.

The novels of Erdrich come to mind most readily, especially *Love Medicine*, as a good example of clustering. While June's death begins and ends the novel, completing the circle, the action shifts back and forth in time to groups of stories relating the lives of the Kashpaws, Morrisseys, and Lamartines. Jumps in time, shifts in action and characters, and narrative holes pervade this novel. The novel was constituted from existing short stories which may account for some of the narrative breaks, but Erdrich has assembled the modified stories in a method used for a millennium by storytellers—she clusters her narratives around a common theme. She reinforces Ong's contention that the patterns of oral thinking and expression run deep in the consciousness and unconsciousness of the people who, even when they utilize a written alphabet, tend to exhibit characteristics of oral thinking (*Orality* 26).

Transitional Texts between Oral and Written Narratives

Lord raises the idea of a transitional text between oral and written narratives based on his fieldwork in Yugoslavia. His concept is "not a *period* of transition between oral and written style, or between illiteracy and literacy, but a *text*, [a] product of the creative brain of a single individual" (129). He raises the issue and then negates its possibility, for he believes that the two forms are mutu-

be regained again through writing. He also emphasizes that noetic ways of knowing are so different in oral and written cultures that once you change the medium of presentation, you change the thought processes.[11] His experiences with the guslari he recorded convinced him that once you start thinking of your performance as a fixed text, you dramatically change the way you approach your material.

Several scholars of Native American literature who have explored this idea of transitional texts have reached a consensual opinion that Indian autobiography serves as a bridge from traditional oral literatures to written texts. Kathleen Sands finds autobiographies oral in presentation, drawing upon myth and ceremony, shaped by tribal ways of knowing, and recorded and "reproduced" in print. Since Sands sees that the oral character of autobiography can be captured in print, she posits that this genre possesses characteristics of both the oral and written and as such can be situated as a transition text. Elaine Jahner's article "Intermediate Forms between Oral and Written Literature" reaches a similar conclusion. She characterizes the three autobiographical works of husband and wife team Gilbert (Oglala Sioux) and Montana (Cherokee) Walking Bull as an intermediary form between oral and written texts. Although their works are presented in a written form, oral ways of thinking inform them. Especially noteworthy is the way in which they invest their work with a participatory sense on the part of the audience in much the same way that traditional storytellers do.

Momaday's autobiographical memoirs *The Names* and *The Way to Rainy Mountain* offer additional examples of transitional autobiographical texts. *The Names* contains a genealogical chart as well as the story of the lives of his parents and other important relatives. Momaday expresses in his introduction that he is trying "to write in the same way, in the same spirit "of a traditional Kiowa storyteller as he combines photographs and quotations with memories of his early life near Rainy Mountain, Oklahoma, and his growing up years at Jemez Pueblo. Lincoln finds this work also in the tradition of western literature as he compares *The Names* to James Joyce's *Portrait of the Artist as a Young Man* because of the way in which Momaday, in a stream of consciousness manner, recollects his childhood as he struggles to come to terms with his identity (104).

his childhood as he struggles to come to terms with his identity (104).

The Way to Rainy Mountain is an experiment and an experiential autobiography that combines myth, history, drawings, poetry, and Momaday's account of his personal journey into Kiowa tribal history. In the "Prologue," Momaday describes how the journey he takes into his cultural past comprises a whole memory, one comprised of the legendary, historical, personal, and cultural. He then formats his work by using all three voices in each of his twenty-four vignettes. Kenneth Roemer calls this work a "prose poem" (51) while Jahner points to this work as a true intermediate genre because of the way "Momaday tried to capture the spirit of oral performance by using his personal commentary to complete the matching process that occurs in oral performance" ("Critical" 216). Jahner observes that Momaday uses his voice to tell about the mythic past in the same way that a tribal elder would do, but at the same time by including his own memories triggered by the mythic stories, Momaday represents the community to whom the elder would be speaking. As Jahner puts it, "He is both presenter and audience" (216). Momaday keeps alive the old traditions by rendering them anew in a format appropriate to a chirographic society, while at the same time capturing in print the flavor of his Kiowa oral past.

While autobiographies undoubtedly are a stage in the development of an Indian literature whose roots lay in oral performance, this genre is not the best example of a transitional text. The work of Lord, Ong, Havelock, and Goody establishes that it is not reasonable to look for a type of literature characteristic of both oral and written culture, for orality studies convincingly demonstrate that the epistemologies of the two are not mutually compatible. It is reasonable, however, to regard certain written texts as representative of tribal ways of knowing and as utilizing traditional storytelling techniques, and this approach comes much closer to a truly transitional text, if indeed there is such a hybrid. Some of the work of Silko (*Storyteller*) and Erdrich's novels (especially *Tracks*) I believe are close to being true links between the oral ways of knowing, storytelling presentation, and a written text.

It is common to hear these two names joined together but not always through a comparison of their works.[12] Critics have flamed a Silko-Erdrich conflict to the benefit of neither. It began with

Silko's acrimonious review of *The Beet Queen* which she entitled "Here's an Odd Artifact for the Fairy-Tale Shelf." Silko finds the novel lacking in a strong Indian presence, which she attributes to Erdrich's use of postmodern techniques. These, according to Silko, position the words as more important than their referent, and what gets lost is Erdrich's foregrounding of Indian life and commitment to representing their struggles. Ever since the article's publication in 1986, Erdrich has been besieged with questions from interviewers asking for her reaction to Silko's comments. Erdrich has replied that the reason for Silko's vehemence is that she clearly misread the text and was disappointed in not finding the main characters to be Chippewas, as Silko supposed that they would be. What becomes obscured as critics concentrate on their differences is how in some respects they format their novels similarly to reproduce the traditional storytelling situation and, in doing so, come closest to positioning their work as truly representative of a transitional text.

Traditionally, the storytellers were the bearers of the traditions, the repository of myths, legends, and stories of the tribal people. What Silko and Erdrich do in their fiction that is different from the work of other contemporary novelists is to assume the role of the traditional communal storyteller as they creatively approximate the storytelling situation in a written format. Silko's *Storyteller* and Erdrich's novels actualize a transitional text from the oral to the written that Lord does not find possible. In his often quoted article on the storyteller Nikolai Leskov, Walter Benjamin decries the fact that "the art of storytelling is coming to an end" (83). He attributes this to the rise of the novel which he distinguished from other genres because "it neither comes from oral tradition nor goes into it" (87). I disagree. While Silko's *Storyteller* is not a novel,[13] Erdrich's books clearly are. The focus of these works is to tell the story of their peoples' lives directly, through the communal tribal voices, and this approach had not been the underpinning structure for any other Native American novel before their books. The mythic (*The House Made of Dawn*, *Ceremony*) and the legendary (*Winter in the Blood*) have been dominant motifs for the best of contemporary Indian fiction, but the communal voice had been silent until Silko and Erdrich beautifully incorporated it as the voice in their works.

A communal voice is a true polyphony, and there is no one point of view just as there is no final version of a story. Stories are heard, interpreted, and retold by various members of the community who pass along their version. As Silko explains in *Storyteller*: "all of us remembering what we have heard together ... create[s] the whole story... (7).

Erdrich and Silko are both receivers and bearers of their tribal stories. They tell the portion that they remember, and so keep alive and in process the ongoing energy in the everlasting circle. There is no one absolute definitive version of a story, a feature found in traditional storytelling. What is remembered are different versions which get retold in order to recreate the "truth" of the event. Silko attributes the stories in her collection to many different people at Laguna who remember the stories: Great-aunt Susie Marmon, Great-grandmother Maris Anaya Marmon, Grandma Lillie Marmon, Grandpa Hank Marmon, her father Lee Marmon, Simon Ortiz, and herself. Likewise, Erdrich uses multiple narrators to tell the stories of her people: *Love Medicine* has six narrators, *Tracks* has two, *The Beet Queen* has six, *The Bingo Palace* has one plus the community, *Tales of Burning Love* has four, and *The Antelope Wife* has four (which includes a storytelling dog) and an unnamed storyteller who is the meta-narrator.

There is no distinct authorial voice for the stories in these works, a common feature of oral stories. Instead there is the voice of the community composed of fragmented individual perspectives who express through recounting their lives the very life of the community. No one voice is privileged over others, and no one truth reigns; and so diverse voices combine to become a communal voice and to tell a communal story. In this way, Erdrich and Silko seek to give the appearance of traditional storytelling by using several communal narrators.

Silko constructs *Storyteller* by narrating how she heard the tribal and family stories and myths in the same way that Erdrich manipulates the various voices of the Chippewa and German immigrant descendants. Erdrich juxtaposes these individual voices alongside an omniscient voice interspersed throughout, acting as the arbitrator of the versions, filling in missing significant details, and explaining other points of view. Erdrich's fictional form is a rendering of a traditional storytelling session in which differing people tell distinct versions of events and history for all to hear; and it positions her as a tribal storyteller, one who mediates and communicates varying versions of a communal truth. What has changed is the medium, from oral recitation to books, and the audience, from tribal to an unknown reading public.

Communal storytelling is a new form for Native American fiction. It incorporates the many voices of a tribal people, not just the historic, not just the legendary/mythic, but most of all the lives of the people who tell their stories. Lincoln has commented, "Indian storytelling, old and new, is drawn from living history. Its angle of truth derives from a belief in families telling their lives directly. Its sense of art turns on tribal integrity" (222). Likewise, Silko notes how communal storytelling acts as "A self-correcting process in which listeners were encouraged to speak up if they noted an important fact or detail omitted. The people were happy to listen to two or three different versions of the same event or the same humma-hah story. Even conflicting versions of an incident were welcomed for the entertainment they provided " ("Landscape" 88).

Silko and Erdrich tell family stories, stories that would be heard when people share a meal together, when they converse with one another about things they have just heard, when family members tell example-stories for the younger children so that they will learn a lesson and learn some history, and even when people gather to gossip about other people in the community. Silko has said that she does not like the term "gossip stories" because the inference is all wrong (Hirsch quoting from a *Sun-Track* interview), however gossip is certainly a component in the stories told and heard. Silko's story about old man George and a younger woman fooling around in the cornfields, and the story about the lascivious young woman who locked herself in an outdoor toilet when her five or six boyfriends confronted her are definitely communal gossip told as juicy tidbits and told as lessons in moral behavior. Likewise, Erdrich's stories often retain the flavor of a juicy piece of gossip just heard, particularly when people talk about the amorous carryings on of Lulu Lamartine with her three husbands and numerous lovers. As Lulu herself declares, "I always was a hot topic" (LM 233).

Silko and Erdrich use different mediums to try and render as closely as a written work can a communal storytelling situation, for as Silko emphasizes, stories are communal property. Silko utilizes poems, myths, photographs, family stories, personal remembrances, and stories of friends as she serves as the storyteller for her community, telling the versions and bits that she remembers in a similar fashion to that of a traditional tribal storyteller. Bernard Hirsch has noted the circular design in this work (2) which echoes a tribal way of seeing as well as seeming a remnant from oral performances. Silko's multitextual approach resembles a traditional storytelling session where dance, song, multiple levels of voice intonation, gesture, and expression act together to perform a story. Silko's *Storyteller* is a performance with a written text that is neither an oral rendering nor a contemporary novel, but rather a creative embodiment linking old and new ways of storytelling.

Critics have made comparisons between *Storyteller* and Momaday's two autobiographical works because of the experimental approach to the text that both authors practice.[14] Clearly there is a similarity in their use of poetry, photographs, and personal memories as the two writers try to create a living history of their people. What distinguishes the work of each from the other is the meta-narrative voice relating the diverse materials. Momaday, as in his other works, presents a very strong male voice that is both serious and highly literate. He is telling the story of his people, and the meta-voice is clearly his own. Krupat comments on this aspect of the text, "His writing offers a single, invariant poetic voice that everywhere commits itself to subsuming and translating all other voices" (*Voice* 180). This is in marked contrast to Silko's voice, which, as I have pointed out, is a communal one. She submerges her voice so that it blends in with the other voices of her family and community. She is the voice of the nurturing female who is concerned with the well-being of the entire tribal family. In her powerful novel *Ceremony*, she speaks with both male and female voice as Thought-Woman tells the story of Tayo and his mythic healing through Ta'eh the mountain spirit. I quote again from Krupat who so precisely summarizes how the memoirs of the two authors differ, "Silko's autobiographical writing is as firmly oriented toward dialogue and polyphony as Momaday's is toward monologue" (*Voice* 182). While their autobiographical works present a common format and can clearly be identified as transitional works, Momaday speaks primarily through his own voice while Silko approximates a communal voice.

Erdrich's novels are another attempt to approximate storytelling sessions through the use of multiple narrators, different versions of stories, and community anecdotes. Allen has pointed out that, although the novel is a fairly new form for Native Americans, it is really nothing more than a series of long stories "that weave a number of elements into a coherent whole and, in their combinings, make significance of human and (for Native Americans, at least) nonhuman life" (*Spider* 4). She further explains that the folklorists have categorized this element in traditional novels as "cycles," where a number of stories with the same characters "cluster" around a prevailing theme (4). Dorris applies the same term when he comments on *Love Medicine,* "It is a story cycle in the traditional sense" (Coltelli, *Winged Words* 44, Chavkin and Chavkin, *Conversations* 22), thus situating the text within a particular set of assumptions: that stories are communal assets; that stories never have one version; that different versions of a story are the attempts by community members to amend, revise, or refute another person's version of an event; and that one story is only the beginning of many other stories. Thus it is possible to have many different stories with the same characters revolving around a few key events that comprise what is now known as a novel. The concept of story cycles is an appealing one, and one that I explore in the final chapter. Since story cycles represent a distinct genre within the twentieth-century American literary tradition, it is interesting to reflect upon the degree to which Erdrich utilizes this genre as well as her traditional Chippewa storytelling.

Erdrich's Novels as Storytelling Sessions

The communal voice is heard throughout Erdrich's novels, just as it is the narrative voice in *Storyteller*. Stories are the property of the community and as such are available for anyone to use for a particular purpose, and different families in different generations seek to understand their history as well as a communal history through stories. Erdrich formats her North Dakota novels and *The Antelope Wife* as a series of voices in what Dee Brown calls "a chorus of differing characters speaking in different cadences… " (5). What distinguishes her work from the more mythic work of Momaday, Welch, and Silko in *Ceremony* is that the grounding of her stories is not in a legendary past, but rather in a present that tells the story of a tribe of Chippewa people living on an unnamed (but presumably Turtle Mountain) reservation and the German immigrants of the region who are trying to live with integrity and purpose against what at times appears to be overwhelming odds.

As in *Storyteller*, the strongest voices in Erdrich's novels are of family incident, of communal anecdote, and of juicy gossip. Sands was the first to note this latter aspect in *Love Medicine* (it remains an informing voice throughout the novels). She relates, "The source of her storytelling technique is the secular anecdotal narrative process of community gossip" (14), a comment Dorris found to be one of the most perceptive in the reviews (*Conversations* 39).

A. I. Hallowell relates that the Ojibwa use two distinct narratives that have arisen from the oral tradition: one is the mythic dimension, the sacred stories, and the other is what he terms news or tidings or the anecdotes referring to events in the lives of the people.[15] These stories can range anywhere from the everyday occurrences to those that are more legendary.[16] Erdrich is clearly following traditional Ojibwa oral patterns when she adopts the latter category in her novels with her mingling of family and community voices that tell the story of her people.

Erdrich has confirmed in many interviews that she writes out of a background where people commonly sit around telling stories, and the extent to which her novels are a storytelling event has been the subject of numerous articles and a few dissertations. The feature of her works that critics repeatedly note is the degree to which her novels replicate a traditional storytelling situation with a teller and an audience.[17] Nancy Peterson analyzes the storytelling markers she finds most obvious in *Tracks*, the novel most directly replicating a traditional storytelling session: the narrator (Nanapush) does not name himself; the listener (Lulu) is not named except to establish her relationship (granddaughter) to him; there are numerous repetitions, and he uses traditional tribal names and phrasing, not Anglicized wording (985). Louise Flavin points out that by having Nanapush address his remarks to his granddaughter Lulu, Erdrich establishes the traditional storytelling situation of the grandparent instructing the grandchildren (2). In this case, the topic is of extreme importance, for Nanapush is attempting to affect a reconciliation between Lulu and her mother Fleur, to try make Lulu understand the history behind the recent events that have affected her so much and to try and persuade her from making a disastrous marriage with one of the trashy Morrisseys.

In *Tracks*, there are two narrators: Nanapush talking to his granddaughter and the religious zealot Pauline Puyat. Pauline in the time-honored tribal tradition tells her version of events that Erdrich juxtaposes against Nanapush's, and the reader, as would a member of the community, is left with different versions, different truths, and different justifications.

Erdrich also establishes a storytelling situation in *Love Medicine*, which critics have noted. In this case the speakers, Nector, Marie, and Lulu relate their stories for their grandchildren Lipsha and Albertine who as bearers of the family stories and tribal histories are now more positioned to make informed decisions in their life. Lisa Schneider notices how Lipsha and Albertine seem to be the ones most actively seeking the family stories (10), and she observes how narratives related in the third person speak for characters (June, Gordie, Henry, and Eli) who have lost the ability to speak for themselves (11).

The narrators in *The Beet Queen* seek understanding and acceptance by the new families they have formed. There is no traditional family unit, because the parents have either abandoned their children or died. There is no traditional storytelling situation, because there is no interaction of grandparents and grandchildren. Instead, the characters Celestine, Mary, Karl, and Wallace seek to establish the truth of their lives for the child Dot who is the receptacle of all their love. The voice of Sita is the voice of one who deliberately negates her family ties to this Dot-centered matrix,[18] and she is the one who loses her ability to speak. Without an audience, without a bearer who will tell her story, she becomes forever silent.

This novel focuses on the lives of the Anglo and mixed-breeds in the town adjoining the reservation, and Erdrich makes the point through her storytelling situation that without families who hear, acknowledge, and pass on the story of the lives of their respective members, the truth of a life may never be heard. The best one can do without a family is to create new units, and the characters in *The Beet Queen* who bond through their common love of Dot are the ones who endure. The novel ends fittingly as Dot tells her story for the first time. She is grown up, she has been molded by the devoted love of her family unit, and now it is time that she step into her place in the continuum of history; and so she tells her story in order for it to be passed on to future generations.[19]

The voice of the community is nowhere stronger than in *The Bingo Palace* where the narrator for the opening and closing chapters (twenty-five and twenty-seven) is the voice of the community. Erdrich signals this by such remarks as, "We know her [Lulu's] routine—many of us even shared it—(BP 1), or in chapter twenty-five "the rest of us" (BP 261), "us old ones" (BP 263), and "us ordinary Chippewas" (BP 263). The many eyes and many voices see and relate all. As the novel opens, they see Lulu in the post office sending a summons to Lipsha to come home. They give the opinions on the various community members who have been major characters in the North Dakota novels: Lulu, Lyman, June, Albertine, Lipsha, Shawnee Ray, and Gerry, and they try to understand the whole of the story that was happening, "We were curious to know more, even though we'd never grasp the whole of it. The story comes around, pushing at our brains, and soon we are trying to ravel back to the beginning, trying to put families in order and make sense of things. But we start with one person, and soon another and another follows, and still another, until we are lost in the connections" (BP 5).

Lipsha is the only first person narrator, and on several occasions he directly addresses an audience to whom he says that he is telling his story: "my story doesn't turn out to be . . ." (BP 11), "Hold on now, the tangle, the plot, the music of homecoming thickens" (BP 20–21), "You want to know what this place is. I'll tell you. Okay. So it's a motel ..." (BP 68), and "I know you'll say it, you'll wonder, you'll think ..." (BP 254). With these signals, Erdrich is clearly indicating that Lipsha is now the storyteller for the community. As a member of both the Kashpaw and Lamartine families and the one to whom the "power travel[ing] in the bloodlines" (T 31) is strong through his Pillager heritage, Lipsha is positioned, in this final novel of the reservation community as the inheritor of the traditions: the traditions of the families, the traditions of the spirits, and the traditions of the community. Her people will endure as long as there is Lipsha and those who follow him to tell the stories.

Four out of five of Jack Mauser's wives tell their stories of Jack, a German-Ojibwa man raised off the reservation and living in Argus, North Dakota. Reworking the traditional frame story of Chaucer's *The Canterbury Tales* and Boccaccio's *Decameron*, Erdrich situates Jack's four wives in a stranded car during one of North Dakota's freak snowstorms where they tell stories to stay alive. Eleanor (second wife) suggests they "Pretend this car is a confessional" (205) and Dot (fifth wife) makes the rules, "Rule one . . . no shutting up until dawn. Rule two. Tell a true story. Rule three. The story has to be about you. Something that you've never told another soul, a story that would scorch paper, heat up the air" (206). And so begin the "tales of burning love."

What is interesting to note is the dominant narrator, Dot, and the absent narrators, Jack and June. As the first of Jack's wives, June's presence lingers between the words and in the minds of all connected to Jack. She has no voice as in the reservation novels (*Tracks, Love Medicine, The Bingo Palace*), but her memory and her story not only open the novel but permeate it as well. Especially during the snowstorm when the wives' car becomes encased in snow, the horror of how June froze to death in a freak Easter snow storm suggests a fate which, too, might await all of them.

Jack is told about, but he never tells his story directly. His former wives and an omniscient narrator tell his life story. The voices are about "him" and not about "me," allowing the reader to only see him through the eyes of others. As Eleanor suggests, "Jack probably showed a separate facet of himself to each one of us. Or we brought it out in him. Made him as different as we are different from one another" (200). Erdrich limits our understanding of Jack by silencing his voice.

Before the snowstorm, the only first person narrator is Dot, practical, direct, headstrong, and honest. Just as in the off-reservation novel, *The Beet Queen*, her presence and personality dominates and subsumes all the other voices. *Tales of Burning Love* is a continuation of Dot's story begun in *Love Medicine* and *The Beet Queen*, and it is her voice that predominates and assumes narrative authority.

In *The Antelope Wife*, Erdrich moves from North Dakota's reservation and surrounding towns to Minneapolis. With the change of location comes a change of characters, and a new group of Chippewas tell their story of living in *Gakahbekong* (Minneapolis). There is also a shift in the narration pattern as an omniscient narrator establishes the storytelling situation, "I relate it here so that it not be lost" (3), closes the story, "All that followed, all that happened, all is as I have told" (240), and directly addresses "you" (11) in the established storytelling pattern. The traditional teller narrating the tales allows for individual stories to arise from people in two intertwined families who need to tell their story in order to make sense of their life: Klaus Shawano who has kidnapped Antelope Woman; Rozina Whiteheart Beads, a Roy woman with two biological mothers, an alcoholic husband, a lover, and a dead child; Cally, Rozina's daughter and surviving twin who tries to interpret her history and her life as a contemporary urban Indian; and Almost Soup, the Windigo storytelling dog who narrates the story of his descendants and who replaces the pink elephant as the discourse partner of the drunken Klaus.

Erdrich's multiple narrators and the replication of storytelling sessions situates her books deep within the heart of traditional storytelling, and this chapter provides a context for readers to be able to position Erdrich's work along the continuum of the Native American storytelling tradition. As Sands notes in her review of *Love Medicine*, one of the most remarkable qualities in the novel is how the author "manages to give new form to oral tradition" (23), and James Ruppert, in a review of the same novel, comments that he feels Erdrich "is trying to explore the mid-ground between the oral and written tradition through personal storytelling" (47). Lord didn't think that a transitional text could be a reality, but Erdrich, Silko, and Momaday create texts that transfer the oral traditions of their people into a contemporary chirographic format and prove that the oral tradition can be rendered afresh for readers, the newest audience for cultural, tribal, and family stories.

CHAPTER 3

LOUISE ERDRICH, A CONTEMPORARY TRADITIONAL STORYTELLER

LOUISE ERDRICH'S SUCCESS as a contemporary American storyteller derives from her poetic ability to thread stories of the Anishinaabeg and Anglos residing in north central North Dakota and Minnesota into a saga that recounts the triumphs, failures, and interconnectedness of their lives. Her novels reach back to the late 1800s when the people of the Woodlands who had moved onto the Plains battled the United States Government for their land. It spans the prereservation and reservation formation period for the Turtle Mountain Band of Chippewa while describing the realities of living through the Depression for the reservation people as well as for Anglos in neighboring towns. She tells of life in the Twin Cities where Chippewas, removed from their home reservation, form sustaining communities. It celebrates the triumph of a way of life that continues to be vital for Chippewa people, who have had the formidable weight of the United States Government thrown against them in a concerted attempt to eradicate their culture, remove them from their homelands, acculturate their children in boarding schools, marginalize their language, eliminate their traditional religion and ceremonies, impose on them an Anglo concept of individual ownership in direct contradiction to their view of land as a sacred communal gift, and change their pattern of living from a subsistence base to that of an agricultural economy. Erdrich in her novels celebrates the lives of her people, contemporary survivors in a culture war that has been waged against her Indian people for centuries.[1]

Her voice, however, is not the strident political one found in the writing of Vine Deloria, Jr., Dee Brown, and Gerald Vizenor, although she reflects in an interview that almost every time a contemporary Indian writer discusses the history of their people, there are implicit political overtones in subject matter.[2] Instead, her fiction draws upon traditional storytelling techniques to paint a broad canvas of her people's lives during the last century. In her fiction she assumes the role of the traditional communal storyteller who through relating significant community events, tribal policies, and lives of reservation families and urban Indians helps to contribute to a cultural continuity.

Her novels function in the same way that a traditional winter count does as symbols of the year's most significant events (a battle, disease, natural phenomena, or government action) painted on a tipi or hide. Working out of this tradition, she inscribes cultural markers through stories primarily of her Chippewa people in the twentieth century that serve as a record for the tribe and for an Anglo audience who has been invited to share her tribal story. Emphasizing the most important events in the tribal life is a practice preceding the arrival of Europeans in America, and one of Erdrich's gifts as a writer is her ability to draw upon these old tribal ways of knowing and understanding how events shape a people. As a contemporary Native American, she positions herself within a traditional tribal way of marking time and transforms the tradition in her fiction. Her novels are a modern winter count, and the stories of the Turtle Mountain Chippewa and urban Minnesota Chippewa and their struggles over the last century serve as symbols for the evolving life of her people in the same way the winter counts on hides symbolize stories in tribal life.

The storytelling voice of Erdrich becomes the meta-narrative voice throughout the novels, and this voice specifically draws upon her Native American background and the practice of tribal storytelling. To read her novels in the spirit of traditional storytelling positions readers within the context out of which they originated, and this chapter examines ways in which she transforms well-known traditional conventions in her fiction. The ensuing discussion of her background and specifically how she mingles the voice of the tribal storyteller with her own helps position her as a modern/traditional storyteller. The Chippewa tradition out of which she writes has been the subject of numerous articles,[3] but there has been no significant discussion of the way her combined novels represent the story of her people, full-bloods, mixed-bloods, and Anglo immigrant descendants in the last century. This will be the chapter's focus, as I discuss Erdrich's life and the tradition out of which she writes, describe her creative use of the tradition, and then finally relate how as a contemporary storyteller, she inscribes a living history of her people to serve as a record of their lives in the twentieth century.

Erdrich's Life and Work

Erdrich's background reflects a tribal reality for many contemporary Indians, that of a mixed heritage, a factor of fundamental significance in understanding the inclusion of *The Beet Queen* and *Tales of Burning Love* in her North Dakota series. She is an enrolled member of the Turtle Mountain Band of Chippewa Indians, whose reservation lies amidst a hilly oasis in the otherwise flat and expansive plains of north central North Dakota. As noted in chapter one, in order to be on the roles for her tribe, one needs to have a blood quantum of at least one-fourth. Her mixed heritage qualifies her to be on the roles even with her modest amount of Indian blood, and it reinforces the concept also discussed in chapter one that being an Indian is often a matter of identification with a worldview and a way of life rather than a classification based on an actual amount of Indian blood.[4]

Erdrich's maternal grandfather Patrick Gourneau was an important model for the family, serving as tribal chairman from 1953–59 and publishing a history of the Turtle Mountain Band of Chippewas. He simultaneously practiced his traditional religion alongside the Catholicism with which he had been raised, and Erdrich admired the degree to which he "had a grasp on both realities, in both religions" (Bruchac 99). His intelligence, worldliness, and outspoken political stances evoked great respect amongst family members who regarded him as "a kind of a legend" (Bruchac 98). Erdrich pays tribute to the great admiration and love she felt for her grandfather by using him as a model for grandfather Nanapush, the traditional Chippewa elder in *Tracks* who seeks to strengthen a fractured community through his medicine, his stories, his power as tribal chairman, and his love.

Her maternal grandmother was part Chippewa and part

French American, a common heritage found on the Turtle Mountain Reservation, which makes her mother less than a full blood. When Rita Joanne Gourneau married Ralph Louis Erdrich of German American background, their seven children, of whom Louise was the oldest, inherited something over one-fourth Indian blood.[5] Erdrich's parents lived off the reservation where they served as teachers in a boarding school run by the BIA in Wahpeton, North Dakota, a community located in the Red River Valley in the eastern part of the state. The family lived on the campus in the small town, where German-Americans, Norwegian-Americans, and Native Americans all mixed in one pluralistic community. The reservation served as a second home to her, a place for family visits and for renewal of cultural ties to her Indian heritage. As she relates to Joseph Bruchac, "When you go on Indian land, [you] feel that there's more possibility, that there is a whole other world besides the one you can see and that you're very close to it" (98).[6]

Her passion for words and stories emerged early, and she was reading avidly at a very early age and writing with the encouragement of her parents, who paid her a nickel for her work. Stories for her were not only those she found in books but also those told by family members, and she grew up nurtured with tales about her family and relatives. She relates to Michael Schumacher how her family, especially her father, loved to tell good stories, and that they would "make everything into a story.... People just sit and the stories start coming, one after another. You just sort of grab the tail end of the last person's story: It reminds you of something and you keep going on. I suppose that when you grow up constantly hearing the stories rise, break and fall, it gets into you somehow" (175).

Her literary talents earned her acceptance to Dartmouth College in 1972, which she entered as one of the women admitted to the very first co-educational class in the college's history. Reverend Eleazar Wheelock founded Dartmouth in 1769 from an Indian School he began in Connecticut in 1750, and, as such, it is an institution committed to Indian education. In its long and illustrious history, though, only twelve Indian students had graduated from the university (Cryer 82). Dartmouth's consciousness of its original mission has prompted the institution to recommitting itself to Indian students and studies, and Erdrich was admitted in that first wave of renewed mission. It was there that she met Dorris, who had come to the college the same year in order to establish a Native American Studies Program, of which he was chairman and half of the department.

After her graduation, she returned home to North Dakota to work in a program sponsored by the North Dakota Arts Council, where she traveled to a different site each week teaching poetry to hospital patients, inmates, and classes of elementary children. Her isolation from a writer's community drew her back to the East Coast where in 1976 she entered the graduate writing program at Johns Hopkins University. Her immersion into an academic community where she taught writing and received feedback and support for her own work proved to be a needed impetus for her creative talents; and upon her graduation, she devoted as much of her time as she could to her work, which was at this stage almost exclusively poetry. She supported herself with various jobs: editor/writer for the Boston Indian Council newspaper, waitressing, life guarding, editing textbooks for Charles Merrill Co., and serving as researcher for a television movie.

In 1979 she was asked to give a poetry reading back at Dartmouth, where she renewed her acquaintance with Dorris and began the now legendary practice of sharing her work with him, albeit at that time by mail. Her literary talents continued to receive recognition, and in 1980 and 1981 she resided as a fellow at New Hampshire's Macdowell Colony, as a fellow at Yaddow Colony, and then in 1981 as a visiting fellow at Dartmouth, where she worked as the writer in residence. It was here that her relationship with Dorris bloomed, and they soon married and began their unique collaborative writing relationship. Until this point, she had received many rejection slips, even while her talent was acknowledged. She credits Dorris with changing her work in a way that publishers found more appealing, and she began shifting her primary emphasis from poetry to fiction where she found so much more room to tell the stories that continued to assert themselves in her poetry.[7]

Her breakthrough into the established literary world is both dramatic and legendary. In late 1981, she and Dorris acted on Michael's aunt's suggestion that they enter the newly established Nelson Algren fiction contest. With less than two weeks to submit, with Dorris recovering from back problems and prone on the floor, and with a houseful of holiday company, Erdrich and Dorris managed to mail in "The World's Greatest Fishermen," which won out over two thousand other entries and propelled the couple into literary acclaim. When they recognized that this one story contained within it many other stories, they expanded it by telling it from different points of view and by including important historical background on the major characters. *Love Medicine*, published in 1984, became the first novel in the North Dakota series that launched Erdrich into fame.

In addition to these North Dakota novels (*Tracks* 1988, *The Beet Queen* 1986, *Love Medicine* 1984, *The Bingo Palace* 1994, and *Tales of Burning Love* 1996) which tell the stories of people living on and near the Turtle Mountain Chippewa Reservation, Erdrich extended her geographical territory to include *The Antelope Wife* (1998), a story of urban Chippewas living in Minneapolis. She retained her love of poetry and published two volumes, *Jacklight* (1984) and *Baptism of Desire* (1989), but there have been no new poetry volumes since 1989. She has also published a non-fiction work about motherhood entitled *The Blue Jay's Dance: A Birth Year* (1995). In the 1990s, she made her foray into adolescent literature with *Grandmother's Pigeon* (1996) and *The Birchbark House* (1999). She and Dorris co-authored two books that carry both their names: *Route 2* (1991), a short account of a family trip in 1985 traveling from New Hampshire to Washington State visiting reservation relatives and sight seeing, and *The Crown of Columbus* (1991), a book over ten years in the making which relates two Dartmouth professors' search for the long lost diary of Christopher Columbus. Given the already established commercial success of the two authors, HarperCollins gave them 1.5 million dollars for the heavily promoted work that came out during the Columbus quincentenary. The literary reviews were mixed, with critics and reviewers insinuating that literary values were of secondary importance to commercial success for the authors.[8]

Another less successful collaboration by the two was a series of romantic stories written for women's magazines in a time of greatly needed cash at the very beginning of their literary marriage; one of these stories for love-starved housewives appeared in *Redbook*, with the rest published in the overseas market. The two authors used the pen name Milou North, the former being a combination of their first names, but this venture yielded little financial success. Erdrich's most successful writing, artistically and commercially, came when she turned for her subject matter to her Chippewa heritage and their traditions as well as to her strong sense of place growing up in North Dakota. This subject matter has proved to be extremely lucrative, so that she and Dorris were able to devote themselves to full-time writing careers.[9] Dorris's suicide in 1997 accompanied by allegations of sexual abuse of their children has altered the public's perception of their "idyllic" writing relationship. Erdrich currently lives in Minneapolis with her three daughters, where she continues her career as an author.

In an interview with Laura Coltelli, Erdrich asserts her role as a storyteller (45), and in another interview with Kay Bonetti, she stresses how she felt, as a contemporary survivor of her Indian tradition, compelled to tell the story of her people:

> I think both of us feel, in writing from our background, that we're really spurred by this feeling that we have to tell the story. When both of us look backward we see not only the happiness of the immigrants coming to this country, which is a part of our background, but we see and are devoted to telling about the lines of people that we see stretching back, breaking, surviving, somehow, and incredibly, culminating in somebody who can tell a story. (98)

There is a great need to tell these stories, as Indians today face an intrusion of Anglo values and culture that continues to challenge, erode, and devalue their traditional lifestyles and culture. As more and more young Native Americans do not learn the traditional language, have not integrated the ceremonies into the fabric of their lives, leave the reservations, and adopt Anglo lifestyles, the need for cultural continuity becomes a primary concern for Native American tribes. Kenneth Lincoln calls this "the threat of discontinuity that challenges Indianness today" (187), and stories become a primary vehicle for serving as translators of tribal identity. Stories embody culture, and the need is acute to retain a sense of Indian identity in a larger culture that through the centuries gradually has eroded the underpinnings of a minority culture.

Elizabeth Cook-Lynn in a speech for a 1993 Great Plains Writers Conference poses the question: "Who Gets to Tell the Stories?" Her premise is that Anglos telling the stories of Indians through popular movies like *Dances with Wolves*, books like *The Education of Little Tree*, and "other assorted outrages" (61) provide the populace at large with an Anglo image of Indians rather than with a picture written by Indians about the Indian way of life. This, she believes, is the challenge and the obligation facing Indian writers today who need to renew their efforts "to tell the honest stories, not for ourselves, not for an audience of idiots ... but, rather, as our ancestors always have ... *for the sake of the tribes*" (63). Thus, Native American writers today balance themselves between two roles: one to speak to and for their tribe, and the other to create a work which will be commercially successful so that non-Indian audiences can read and appreciate tribal stories.

Thus, the need to tell the stories is of extreme importance today for the tribes and as well as for the sake of the young Indian people who struggle with their Indianness. John Stansfield believes stories are "history telling" ("Reclaiming" 16) and as such function to situate a person within a framework larger and more complete than their individual lives. Native American writers today face the enormous challenge of framing their work within the context of two cultures. While their Indianness determines their point of view and value structure, their language and audience is most often that of the larger Anglo world. The challenge is to mediate between the two worlds, encode cultural values in an appealing fictional situation, and retain a sense of Indian identity while writing for the world at large. Even with Erdrich assuming the stance of a tribal storyteller in her fiction, the audience has changed. Many young people no longer are gaining insights and understanding through grandparents' stories, and a larger audience than the tribe is now the recipient of stories from Native American writers like Erdrich.

Erdrich has successfully merged her role as the communicator of tribal culture and surrounding communities with that of a successful fiction writer for a larger audience. Her fiction is a record of her people over time, and her stories, according to Cook-Lynn, must be told. In this way, contemporary Native American fiction serves as a vehicle opening up new opportunities for talented writers to assume the traditional role of storyteller by telling tribal stories for the Indian people and to the non-Indians who are interested, and thus they play their part in helping ensure cultural continuity. If the stories are told and remembered, then the life of a people will not be lost to time. Lincoln sees Native American literature functioning today as "literature and culture in translation" (25), and Elaine Jahner suggests that the good novelist transforms traditional structures (specifically the oral tradition) to "function within new structures" ("Critical" 223).

This is what Erdrich does in her work, and her novels are a fictional rendering of five generations of her Indian people and the communities people establish for themselves in the neighboring towns. Nanapush as the traditional storyteller in *Tracks* tells his granddaughter Lulu that the pattern to lives is revealed only when one looks back over a great distance, when events have settled into memory and the threads of a person's life and a people begin to form a fabric of life. It is the knowledge of the pattern that must be passed on to future generations in order for the heart of tribal culture to survive, and this is the function that stories have always served for Indian people and continue to serve today, albeit in a different form. Louis Owens writes that "The knowledge of the inextricable interrelatedness of all things, and the need to articulate the patterns of things through stories—[are] both qualities integral to Indian cultures and central to Indian literature" (*Other* 215), and Erdrich successfully transforms the role of traditional tribal storyteller so that her fiction becomes a tangled, complicated, and poignant story of her people. Erdrich's retelling and reshaping of stories of generations of Indian and Anglo people residing in a certain geographical area increases the possibility for their history to be understood by a larger world and for the pattern of their lives to unfold. This story demands to be told, and Erdrich in her novels compassionately and poetically narrates a tribal history that must be remembered and learned.

As a contemporary mixed-blood author, Erdrich has a wealth of traditions upon which to draw, the primary ones being a storytelling tradition and Indian culture out of which she writes her novels. Whether she is telling about her Native American or her German-American ancestors, she is always writing out of this distinctive communal voice, and this meta-narrative voice marks a change for Native American fiction. Ursula Le Guin was one of the first critics to recognize that Erdrich's use of different voices marked a new approach to narrative, something she had "not met within a novel before" (6). As noted in chapter two, the communal aspect of tribes and the communal as a reinforcement of the individual identity is foregrounded in Momaday and Silko's non-fiction work; however, contemporary Indian fiction has tended to appropriate more of the western tradition that favors the struggles and growth of an individual as opposed to the story of the life of a community. The struggles of Tayo in *Ceremony*, Abel in *House Made of Dawn*, Ephanie in *The Woman Who Owned the Shadows*, Jim Loney in *The Death of Jim Loney*, and the nameless narrator in *Winter in the Blood* all evolve around the individual's effort to regain a balance with an Indian self that has been diminished by the outside Anglo world. Erdrich's fiction of her Indian and Anglo ancestors returns to the communal aspect of self as she positions her characters as articulations of a combined collective voice. Dorris comments to Coltelli that this is a fictional device Erdrich deliberately chose, "This is a world that is encompassed by that community, and it isn't so much the outside world of discrimination or wealth or anything like that, but rather this is how a community deals with itself and with the members of itself" (46).

The manner in which she tells her story of community engenders a sizable body of critical work. In recognizing the uniqueness of her voice, critics carve out their own special niche examining Erdrich's narrative strategies. The foreword reviews the critical work in this area, primarily the extent to which traditional oral conventions structure her fiction, especially *Tracks*, the clearest rendering of the traditional storytelling situation.[10] The critics' contributions in this area help to define various aspects of the oral tradition Erdrich draws upon in her work. However, no comprehensive study exists for how she uses the storytelling tradition throughout her novels. Additionally, two important traditional manifestations in her work have not received much critical attention: her use of the autobiographical voice in the novels and her use of story cycles to frame her work. These two elements, as much as the traditional oral markers, signal she is writing out of a storytelling tradition.

Erdrich's Use of the Autobiographical Voice in Her Novels

Erdrich's contemporary rendering of communal life draws upon a very old and respected Indian practice of telling one's life story in relation to the community, that of the autobiography. As A. LaVonne Brown Ruoff points out in her article "Old Traditions and New Forms," "American Indians have always had a tradition of creativity in story and song. As they were introduced to the written word, Indians used it as a tool both to help preserve their oral traditions and to share them with others" (168). In her novels, Erdrich reworks the personal narrative by transforming traditional autobiography into the forged voice of a contemporary Chippewa community or mixed-blood/non-Indian community.

Autobiography stands as a form of personal narrative, and Paula Gunn Allen summarizes the major features of this genre: "A distinctly personal mode, the first-person narrative weaves history, traditions, beliefs, and life ways of individuals living in tribal societies into unified works that allow the reader to share the cultural and literary perception and expression of a people" (*Studies* 75). Kathleen Sands further characterizes the genre as one where a person selects particular facts, and she cautions readers to be aware that "The autobiography, while seeming to be wholly factual and straightforward, is an imaginative work of literature" ("Autobiography" 60). Autobiography is always a product of a person's selective recollections; and precisely because the genre depends upon memory, it is purely discriminatory as persons highlight different incidents shaping their lives. The emphasis, Sands explains, is on event, and the connecting threads in the life story are often omitted. A tribal member would understand the context of the particular story, while an outsider is often left puzzled at gaping narrative holes.

It is interesting, as well as instructive, at this point to briefly consider the differences between the Euro-American autobiography and the Native American one. Arnold Krupat's insights on this subject in his chapter "Native American Autobiography and the Synecdochic Self" in his book *Ethnocriticism* provide a useful analysis of the differences between the two emphases in autobiography. He points out the degree to which an understanding of the self differs in the Anglo and the Indian culture. For, as he notes, "the centrality of the self to western autobiography has no close parallel in Native American autobiography" (201). He explains that the western concept of self is tied directly to the notion of the individual and "interiority" (204), and the Euro-American autobiography has for its form and theme the story of an individual who struggles to find his or her individual place in the world. Krupat emphasizes that the privileging of "the sacred inviolability of the self setting ... in opposition to society or culture, [is] standard western practice..." (206).

In contrast, the Native American autobiography speaks not of the "me" but rather of the distinctive place *within* a tribal world that an individual holds, for as noted in chapter 1, an Indian person's definition of self is tied to his or her place in a particular family, community, and tribe. Thus, a traditional Native American autobiography includes such things as coup stories and visions, both of which serve the tribe as a whole; and this Euro-American genre became for Indians a means of expressing tribal beliefs and culture and their place within a larger tribal world.

Autobiographical voices telling their stories is one way to approach reading Erdrich's novels. Her fictional characters relate their recollections and incidents from a collective tribal memory. Sands in her article "American Indian Autobiography" stresses that "the subject, no matter how dominant within the culture, is a participant in his or her own family history and in the events of the tribe" (57). In other words, unlike Anglo autobiographies emphasizing an individual's personal accomplishments, Indian autobiographies describe a person in relation to their culture as well as being a product of it. Indian autobiography according to Sands is "both personal and cultural narrative" (57), and Erdrich's novels emerge from this autobiographical/communal voice so distinctive to Indian narratives.

H. David Brumble, Arnold Krupat, Andrew Wiget, Kathleen Sands, Gretchen Bataille, and A. LaVonne Brown Ruoff are prominent scholars who chronicle how the American Indian autobiography developed from people recounting an important event in their lives, such as men relating details of battles where they counted coup, stories depicting aspects of specific hunts, and events told to reinforce an important lesson for tribal members.[11] The scope of such stories evolved from specific event to recounting an entire life story, and early autobiographies by literate Indians used the format to relate the facts of their lives positioned in a rapidly changing America. William Apes's (Pequot) *Son of the Forest* (1829), George Copeway's (Ojibwa) *Life, History, and Travels of Kah-ge-ga-gah-bowh* (1847), Sarah Winnemucca Hopkins's (Paiute) *Life*

Among the Paiutes (1883), Francis La Flesche's (Omaha) *The Middle Five: Indian Schoolboys of the Omaha Tribe* (1900) and Charles Alexander Eastman's (Santee Sioux) *From the Deep Woods to Civilization* (1916) are five of the best known early Indian autobiographies. This genre owed its early popularity in part to the tremendous interest in the lives of Americans, ranging from the spiritual confessions of the Puritans to captivity narratives to Benjamin Franklin's autobiography to the slave narratives.

With the advent of ethnologists and anthropologists who sought to record the "vanishing Red Man," a new era in Indian autobiography began. Up until this time, Indian autobiographies were written by literate Natives, most of whom had been Christianized and used their life story to exemplify why Indians should embrace the new Anglo religion and renounce their old ways. When anthropologists set about collecting life histories of Native Americans, a new form of Indian autobiography emerged, the "as-told-to" accounts of Indian lives. With the assistance of Anglo transcribers, some remarkable records of the turbulent and changing lives of Native Americans emerge. Some well known 20th-century personal narratives are Luther Standing Bear's *My People, the Sioux* (1928) assisted by E. A. Brininstool, Sam Blowsnake's (Winnebago) *Crashing Thunder* (1926), transcribed by Paul Radin, Maria Chona's *The Autobiography of a Papago Woman* (1936), transcribed by Ruth Underhill, John Stands in the Timber's *Cheyenne Memories* (1967), transcribed by Margot Liberty, and the best-known of all Indian autobiographies, *Black Elk Speaks, Being the Life Story of a Holy Man of the Oglala Sioux, as Told through John G. Neihardt* (1932; rpt. 1961).

The problem, of course, with "as-told-to" accounts is that recorders by their very function also act as interpreters. Given the different realities of the individual Indian's worldview (an emphasis on one's tribal community, the cyclical non-linear nature of stories, and the omnipresence of a tribe's mythic tradition), transcribed accounts often reflect the particular biases and personal interpretations of the recorder at the expense of the accuracy of the subject's life. It was not until recently that Native American writers began to appropriate their traditional genre and to tell their stories with a different veil of interpretation, erasing the Anglo's nuances of judgment that often crept into the transcribed accounts of their ancestors' lives. John Joseph Mathews (one-eighth Osage) was offered a Rhodes scholarship which he turned down in order to enter Oxford's Merton College where he took a second undergraduate degree. His *Talking to the Moon* (1945) recounts his life story. *The Names* and *The Way to Rainy Mountain* are two autobiographies by another highly educated Native American, N. Scott Momaday.

Other Indian stories told in their own voice are emerging, and Bataille and Sands examine the importance of Native American women in the autobiographical tradition in *American Indian Women Telling Their Lives*. Their book canvasses the tradition, both Anglo and Indian, out of which women's autobiographies emerge while examining how the changing role of Indian women is depicted through the telling of their life stories. Women have always played a vital role as keepers of family and community values, and beginning with the "as-told-to" narratives given to field workers, women's voices have emerged as important cultural keepers. Whereas their stories follow a basic autobiographical emphasis on event, tribal values, and cultural continuity, the women's stories especially place the family and community's welfare above their individual concerns. The woman's traditional role in the community was always honored by her ability to give life and to ensure the life cycles, as she is expected to pass on knowledge and values to her family. Allen points out that "women's traditions are largely about continuity, and men's traditions are largely about transitoriness or change" (*Sacred* 82). Allen also notes how the woman's voice and place of importance in the tribe gradually diminished over time, as tribal councils were changed to reflect more of an Anglo organization where certain people, mostly males, were responsible for decision making at the expense of the traditional balance of men and women working together (*Studies* 135). The emergence of women's autobiographies addresses this hole in the fabric of Indian life and reasserts the role of woman as storyteller and cultural preserver.

It is out of this tradition that Erdrich registers the lives of resolute women who by the strength of their individual wills keep together family and culture. Erdrich's use of women's autobiographical voices stands as one of the distinctive features of her novels. This is clearly seen in the characters of Marie and Lulu, two very different women who are fiercely protective of their respective families; and the juxtaposition of their influence against that of the weak and ever vacillating Nector, who has been tribal chairman, serves to point out the degree to which twentieth-century Indian family units survive through the woman's strength. As the older generation of men (Nanapush, Eli, and Nector) dies out, and with no male to speak for preservation of the old ways, it falls upon the women to carry on the traditions.[12] When their efforts no longer center on raising their families, Marie and Lulu turn to running the tribe. By the final book of the Indian novels, *The Bingo Palace*, set at the closing of the twentieth century, they dominate the senior citizens' complex and are involved in forcing tribal decisions that promote traditional values; Lulu, especially, fights for the old ways that have become submerged under the weight of Anglo culture. Lulu works to return allotment land sold questionably to white farmers, she wrangles to return buffalo to the land, and she serves as a potent reminder to the younger generation of the importance of traditional values.

In the off-reservation novels, Dot binds together her family and the community which has formed around her. In *The Beet Queen*, pleasing Dot becomes the *raison d'etre* for people in her self-formed family. Wallace, Mary, and her mother Celestine have stories to tell, but they all focus in one way or another on Dot. It is these stories about Dot that comprise the whole of the novel, which ends with her voice, the strongest of them all. Then again in *Tales of Burning Love*, it is Dot's strength which keeps Jack Mauser's business afloat and it is she who makes major decisions concerning Jack with his three former wives. Her voice is the dominant one in both novels, and it is Dot's story and her strength of character that lie at the heart of the novels.

The stories of Roy women dominate *The Antelope Wife*. Grandmothers Zosie and Mary, elusive figures throughout, should be the traditional storykeepers, yet their daughter Rozin and her daughter Cally struggle to learn the family and tribal stories from them. Zosie and Mary are trickster figures suddenly disappearing and unexpectedly reappearing. They pop in and out of their family's lives in the city and divide their time between their reservation community and the city. There is no longer a traditional community where storytelling serves as the integrating communal fabric, for these grandparents are not often available to tell the stories, and, indeed, Zosie and Mary do not narrate any of the chapters. Instead, the city scatters people and the stories. It is only on the occasion of communal or family gatherings like Rozin's wedding or Christmas that stories get told and family/tribal questions become answered.

Erdrich additionally uses the autobiographical voice to relate the stories of other tribal members: the men, once the proud warriors, and the mixed-bloods or Métis in Erdrich's tribe, the people whose stories are an attempt to confirm their identity, either in the tribal community or in the Anglo world. Male characters reflect a diminished strength, as their role of food provider through hunting and protector through battles has been changed to that of farmers, governmental pawns, and city workers. Nanapush is the only traditional male who speaks with his own voice, and his role as storyteller is to ensure tribal continuity and family solidarity during a time when sickness and government policies have sucked the life out of his people. Lipsha is the questor who seeks to learn who he is and how to access and utilize his traditional medicine powers. He is both the inheritor of the old ways and reflector of the price of acculturation. He will take on the mantle of healer and storyteller that Nanapush has left, but he is still in process, and it is only through the strength of knowing who he is that he begins to emerge as the traditional community healer. His narrative is a question to himself as he struggles to grow into his potential.

Lipsha's role in the community is positioned against that of Lyman, whose goal to make money for himself and the tribe compromises traditional values. He dances in powwows only for money, and he would sell out traditional family properties in exchange for the economic rewards of establishing a bingo palace. Nector, the consummate politician, goes with the strongest force around him, and his moral and emotional weaknesses are conspicuous. Things have always been handed to him, and as a traditional leader and family provider he is merely adequate because he lacks moral fortitude and resolve. He doesn't serve as the repository of traditions and memories for his family since, in his later years when he should be the bearer of traditions for the younger generation, he has lost his memory, the victim of self-deluded importance and selfish intents. The voices of both Lyman and his father Nector are those of the bureaucrat whose tribal allegiances are always secondary to their personal gain.

The urban Chippewa males do not fare well either. Jack Mauser in *Tales of Burning Love* is a mixed-blood raised off the reservation and raised white. Even though he is from "the old strain" of Chippewas, he uses his Native American heritage only when it is advantageous in business. He is bright, sentimental, tender, hard working, and morally weak, a psychological brother to Nector. He finds women who shore up and put up with his weaknesses, and his potential gifts become dissipated due to his lack of community and a sense of identity. His wives tell stories about him, but he has no voice.

On the other hand, Klaus Shawno in *The Antelope Wife* tells his story. As a trader traveling through the West working the powwow circuit, he is happy and content. However, once he kidnaps Antelope Woman and forces her to live in Minneapolis, his life begins to unravel as a consequence of violating cultural mores. Antelope woman is taboo, a descendant of the mysterious Antelope People. Kidnapping her causes him to lose his job, his money, his sobriety, and his dignity. Only after becoming sober and letting his Antelope wife return to her home is he able to pick up the pieces of his life.

Pauline and Albertine are the voices of the mixed-blood women in the community. Pauline wishes herself white, and her reality becomes the grounding of her being. Her entry into the all-white convent on the reservation comes about through a denial of her Indian blood, and her life mission becomes freeing the Chippewa people of their old gods and getting her people to accept Christianity as the one true religion. A generation later, Albertine is caught between two worlds. Her mother Zelda has turned her strength to serving the tribal agent with her meticulous organization, and her grandfather Nector, who traditionally would tell her the stories of her people by the time she wants to understand them, has lost his memory. She lives in the Anglo society where she is studying medicine in order to be a healer and returns home to traditional dances, her family, and her elders, which help affirm her Indian identity. Albertine strives to maintain the delicate balance required for one who walks in two different cultures.

Some critics have viewed *The Beet Queen* and *Tales of Burning Love* as questionable inclusions in an otherwise all Indian saga,[13] but this stance overlooks the significance of Erdrich's mixed heritage. Her German-American background is highlighted in *The Beet Queen*, and here Erdrich retains the autobiographical rendering of the people's lives within a specific community; but she ever so slightly changes the format in order to represent the more traditional western autobiography. Thus, the stories of Mary and Karl Adare and Sita Kozka, all of whom are Anglos, begin with their early lives and continue into their adulthood, in the most traditional form of western autobiographies. Another important narrator is Wallace, but he does not define the story in the same ways that the other characters do; rather he serves as a link among family members, the person who depends upon Karl and Dot to give meaning to his life, and as such his stories center around them and their importance to his life. Another major character Celestine is a mixed-blood who narrates the significant moments of her life in a more traditional Indian manner, while it is left to the other Anglo characters to fill in the details of her early life. Her story does not originate with early childhood memories and proceed through to her adult life. Instead, she narrates her life story focusing on key events that have shaped the course of her life, and her life is bound by her daughter's life, her traditional family (Russell), and her nontraditional one (Mary, Karl, Sita, and Wallace).

Similarly, Erdrich casts the tales of burning love, stories Jack Mauser's wives tell about him, in a more western autobiographical form. Their community unexpectedly forms after being trapped together during a winter storm, and Dot, Eleanor, Candy, and Marlis assume the role of contemporary communal storytellers as an act of survival, in much the same way that traditional tribal stories serve to ensure the cultural survival of their people. Their stories tell of the strength of love in all of its various guises to heal those broken in spirit. These strong female voices, all of whom are Anglo except for Dot, an urban mixed-blood, reside in the autobiographical woman's format established in the other novels.

What becomes interesting is the degree to which Erdrich mixes western and Native autobiography depending on the speaker. If the narrator is Indian, the autobiographical account is cast in the traditional tribal manner. Non-Indians whose own stories influence off-reservation tribal members naturally employ a western autobiographical form. Erdrich's juxtaposition of traditional western and Indian autobiographies acknowledges the primacy of Anglo narrative forms off the reservation. As a contemporary tribal storyteller, Erdrich gives voice to the stories of non-reservation tribal members as well as more traditional reservation members. It is the traditional autobiographical personae Erdrich privileges that confirms her writing as emanating from a tribal frame.

Erdrich's appropriation of the autobiographical format for her fictional work marks a new and creative use of traditional materials. Her Native American voices speak as representatives of a community undergoing rapid and often devastating cultural changes. As people speak for themselves and highlight the significant events of their lives, a picture emerges of a group of people in transition. Listening carefully to each voice allows readers to understand the fabric of a community and how it adapts and changes over time.

In her chapter on teaching personal narrative and autobiographies, Allen provides a list of questions for readers working with these materials; and several of the issues she raises provide a useful approach for readers struggling to contextualize Erdrich's "fictionalized auto-biographical segments" (Ruppert, "Patterns" 47). Allen asks: What is the purpose of the narrative? Was it solicited or spontaneous? How reliable is the narrator? What oral techniques are evident in the work? What is their effect? How are other literary genres incorporated into the text? What characteristics identify the American Indian personal narrative as a distinctly Indian literary form? (*Studies* 77). A careful reader who considers these issues within the context of Erdrich's autobiographical voices gains an understanding of the richness of her narrative voice and can appreciate the degree to which she creatively uses and transforms the traditional autobiography.

Erdrich's Use of Story Cycles to Frame Her Novels

Using autobiographical voices as a structuring fictional device is only one of Erdrich's skillful remakings of traditional materials in her novels. The other major tradition she modernizes and reworks is that of the story cycle, transformed and reformatted in her novels. Allen explains this term: "a number of stories that cluster around a more or less central theme and often feature particular characters and events" (*Spider* 4) and further points out that the Indian novel is basically one long story made up of many short stories (*Spider* 20). The story cycle serves as the structuring device for the novels, as Erdrich selects specific characters and specific events that best reveal in a fictional form the life of her people in the last 100 years. Dorris remarks to Coltelli that what Erdrich does best is first-person narratives that she weaves together in "a story cycle in the traditional sense" (44). Her novels consist of people telling their lives directly in the autobiographical tradition and as a collection of stories about a particular group of people. Reviewing the life of the Chippewa, especially in the last century, identifies events which Erdrich reworks for her story-telling cycle. This historical background places characters and their actions in a larger tribal reality, and it is the underlying foundation upon which Erdrich builds her Indian novels.

Allen maintains that "Native writers write out of tribal traditions, and into them" (*Spider* 5), and Erdrich specifies in her interview with Bonetti that "It is a Chippewa tradition, that forms the work" (98). Erdrich clearly identifies herself as a Native American writer, one who feels compelled to tell the story of her people. The story she tells in fictional form is a dazzling account of the tenacity and will of a people to endure against overwhelming odds.

The Historical Ojibwa

The story begins a long time ago when the Algonkian people, living in the East long before Columbus "discovered" America, were driven out by the more powerful Iroquois. They migrated to the Great Lakes region around 1200 A.D. where they gradually split into groups: the Ottawas, Crees, Potawatomis, Menominis, and the Ojibwa. According to Stanley Murray, some time around 1600 the Ojibwa group began moving westward and split again into groups occupying areas around Lake Superior. "Those to the south of the lake now commonly are known as the Chippewa, and those on the north side came to be known as the Northern Ojibwe" (15), a distinction of importance when relating the history of the Turtle Mountain Band of Chippewas. The Northern Ojibwa eventually moved into the Saskatchewan region and intermixed with their Cree kinsmen, while Chippewa bands began moving into northern Wisconsin and northern Minnesota. The first Anglos to come upon the various Algonkian peoples were the French fur traders, who in the late 1600s encountered the people occupying areas around Sault Ste. Marie and the Upper Peninsula of Michigan, and the ensuing French influence from the missionaries and fur trading posts plays an important part in the economy, culture, religion, and language of the Northern Ojibwe and Chippewa peoples.

These early French trappers encouraged the Northern Ojibwe and Chippewa, who were hunters and gatherers before contact, to extend their hunting and bring them fur bearing animals, primarily beaver pelts, but by the early 1800s, the depletion of game forced some of the people to again move further west. Whereas most of the Chippewa remained in Minnesota (after they had driven out the Lakota) and Wisconsin,[14] small groups of Chippewa from Leech Lake and Red Lake and Northern Ojibwe moved into the Red River Valley of Eastern North Dakota around 1820, where three different fur companies: the Northwest Fur Company of Montreal, the XY Company, and the Hudson Bay Company had established a trading center at Pembina (Murray 15). The presence of a major post in the region assured a secure trading partner, and soon the Ojibwe and Chippewas joined their Cree relatives, the Assiniboine, and the Métis to hunt a new fur-bearing animal, the buffalo. This newly amalgamated group of people spent part of their year in the Turtle Mountains of north central North Dakota, and it is their unique history of which Erdrich writes in her North Dakota novels. *The Antelope Wife*, in contrast, relates stories of the Minnesota Chippewa.

Traditional Ojibwa Beliefs

The newly formed North Dakota group came to be known by many names, including Bungi, Plains Ojibwa, Saulteaux, Chippewa-Cree, Plains Cree, Little Shell Band, and Turtle Mountain or Pembina Band of Chippewas, and from their assorted backgrounds emerged a distinctive people complete with its own language (Michif) and culture. However, many important cultural elements and beliefs of the Ojibwa ancestors were carried across the plains and prairies and continued to hold a significant role in the life of the people. Of prime importance was the Midéwiwin or the Grand Medicine Society performed in the spring and the fall, which, according to legend, was brought to the people by the Great Bear. The Midéwiwin Ceremony, according to Basil Johnston, commemorated the gift of healing through ceremony and celebrated the lives of medicine men and women who led upright lives in conferring their gift of medicine (83). The ceremonies would last up to a week, and they included reciting the Society's origin myths, soliciting the supernaturals, and performing ritual activities. As the newly formed group slowly acculturated to Plains life, the Sun Dance began to emerge as another important ceremony in which the buffalo was honored as the source of their new economy, and the spirits were called upon to send the rains. Alanson Skinner reports in the early twentieth century that these two religious ceremonies, the Sun dance and the Midéwinin, seemed to play an equally important role in the life of the people (317).

Other residual Woodland beliefs become the bedrock for significant cultural attitudes in the reservation novels, including the place of the underwater manitous, the importance of Nanabozho, visions and hunting, the clan system, the fear of witchcraft, and the importance of the family. The people of the Woodlands lived amidst the heavy forests and numerous bodies of water, and quite naturally one of their important spirits (manitous) evolved as the underwater spirit who so capriciously could take the lives of people caught out in rough waters. The underwater creatures were termed *micipijin*, and this could refer to lions, cougars, or pumas whose copper bodies and malevolent intentions inspired great fear among the Chippewa (Barnouw 133–34). Christopher Vecsey reports slightly different information; he believes that the underwater manitou was a composite of the lion and the horned serpent and, while dangerous, it could also provide great power to those people who claimed it as a guardian (74). A detailed discussion of the underwater spirit and how it serves the Pillager family follows in chapter 5. What is important to note here is that when the Ojibwe-Chippewa migrated to the hills and lakes of the Turtle Mountain region, they brought with them a belief in powerful underwater manitous who now reside in the waters of North Dakota.

Nanabozho is a culture hero, for it was he who was sent into the world to teach the Ojibwa and to give them the gift of hunting and healing.[15] Because he was the son of a mortal woman, he was not considered a god in the same category as the Great Spirit (Kitche Manitou) or the powerful spirits of the air, the Thunderbirds. Rather, according to Johnston, Nanabozho served as the intermediary between the power spirits and the people, and, as such, had the power to transform himself at will in order to perform his tasks (159–60). He is most often identified as the Great Rabbit or the White Hare (Coleman 56–57). Nanabozho is also the traditional trickster figure identified by Radin, for while he could be capable of great courage, generosity, and kindness, he could also be cunning, unreliable, and inept. His transformation in *Tracks* into grandfather Nanapush positions him as a figure of highest importance and significance; he is one whose stories must be taken with caution, though he is to be regarded with great reverence for the many ways he attempts to once again save the Chippewa people.

One of the most important experiences in the life of the male Chippewa was the fasting for a dream or a vision at the time of puberty in order to evoke a spirit that would appear in an animal form. Life was very difficult, and the presence of a spirit guardian helped a person to survive and to understand his life's purpose (Johnston 120). This spirit then served the person as a source of power throughout his life. The boy would make himself appear pitiful so that the manitous would have pity on him and grant him a vision. Once this was done, the young man entered into a relationship with the spirit in the same way he would with humans, and for this reason the spirit granting the vision was often referred to as "grandfather" (Vecsey 134). Shamans and good hunters were thought to have great powers because of their extraordinary abilities, and a young man could additionally seek visions asking for help in locating game for hunting once he had established a relationship with a manitou. These visions could provide the seeker with the whereabouts of game, and if properly asked through supplication and ritual (blackening one's face, assuming a position of humility, drumming, and singing), the once scarce animals would make themselves available to the hunter.

Lipsha, the heir of the Pillager magic, seeks a vision in *The Bingo Palace*. Although his original intent is to impress his girlfriend Shawnee Ray with his belief in traditional ways, he receives, in spite of himself and because of the great power in his blood, a potent vision from a manitou skunk who admonishes him not to allow sacred Pillager land to be requisitioned for a bingo palace. A hunting vision is granted to Nanapush in *Tracks*; he purifies himself by smearing his face with charcoal, and he calls on his spirit helpers to aid Eli who is hunting for the two of them. It is only the powerful magic of Nanapush/Nanabozho that can accomplish the feat of transferring his vision to Eli and thus allowing a moose to sacrifice itself so that the two of them can eat. Nanapush then brings Eli home safely through the snowy woods with the help of his drumming and his song.

The Woodland Ojibwa organized themselves into patrilineal exogamous clans which originated when, according to legend, the Great Spirit ordered the crane to fly down from the sky and find a suitable place for the people to live. When she saw the Great Lakes, she settled down at Sault St. Marie in upper Michigan and called out for help. The bear, catfish, loon, moose, and marten answered and came to live with the people (Bleeker 31–32). According to William Warren, an educated nineteenth-century mixed-blood Ojibwa, these great original clans with their several offshoots made up about eight-tenths of the entire tribe (86). Vecsey points out that these special animals became the totem animal for individual families, their personal family mark, and, as such, served to identify a person in the society and to regulate whom he could marry and whom he could not marry (78). The predominant clan is the bear, and a full account of its significance follows in chapter 5. The clan totem for the most powerful family on the reservation, the Pillagers, is, not surprisingly, the bear.

The mighty members of the Midéwinin had the ability to turn their gift of healing into malevolent forms, and fear ran rampant among the people that these powerful medicine people might direct their medicine to destructive ends and witchcraft. Ruth Landes maintains, "The availability of purchasable magic—like madness-inducing love medicines or spells for hunting, midwifery, war, and friendship—implied and encouraged the practice of all the sorcery imaginable" (58). The fact that a powerful medicine person could and would use his or her powers for evil purposes promoted terror and a strong belief in not only the possibility but also the probability of such witchcraft. Certain herbs could unknowingly be placed in a victim's food, or various entities from the body—hair, nail parings, and even excrement—could be used by the sorcerer to fix their evil spell on a person (Landes 60). Additionally, a witch could bring great harm by influencing game to stay away and therefore bring about starvation for the victim. However fearsome these spells were, there loomed an even more frightening possibility described by Vecsey, "Particularly fearsome to the Ojibwas were witches who posed as bears, either by wearing the skins of bears or by metamorphizing into bears. These bear-walkers owed their powers to their personal manito, the bear, and traveled in disguise at night, causing disease among their victims" (148). This image immediately brings to mind the numerous mentions throughout the reservation novels of Fleur assuming the spirit of the bear, of Fleur transforming herself into a bear, and of Fleur leaving the tracks of the bear. A detailed discussion of the relationship between Fleur and the bear follows in the Fleur chapter.

The family serves as the most important unit in the Woodland economy, primarily because the people originally broke off from the main group to hunt and gather maple syrup and rice in family bands. "Tribal families were the basic political and economic units in the woodland and the first source of personal identities" (Vizenor, *People* 13). Hereditary leaders from the large families assumed leadership roles and as such made the important decisions for their relatives. The Bureau of Indian Affairs (BIA) disrupted this traditional pattern of leadership by establishing councils and elected officials, often favoring those individuals who would acquiesce to government proposals and policies. This pattern is reflected in the Kashpaws in the persons of Nector and Lyman, who best serve their own interests and the interests of the BIA, often at the expense of traditional tribal values and unity. Nector passively allows the Lamartine land to be allocated for a BIA venture, the tomahawk factory, while his son Lyman serves as the administrator for this ill-fated government project. When this venture fails, Lyman turns his formidable energy to requisitioning prime Pillager land for use as a bingo palace. What family leadership remained into the twentieth century was not in the hands of the men, who according to Vizenor seem to have lost their pride (*Everlasting* 58), but rather in the hands of the women and grandparents who keep alive traditional cultural practices.

The grandparents (the term is used as a sign of respect and

does not always denote a blood relative) were the ones designated by tribal custom to give a child a name, and this act also brought with it the obligation on the part of the elders "to teach the child and impart to him their wisdom" (Johnston 141). Johnston further notes that a name was more than a means of identifying someone, it also embodied the future character of the child, and as such was considered a respected gift (141). Grandparents continued throughout a child's life to play a vital and respected part; and the children were expected to honor and assist grandparents, who would care for the children if the need arose through the parents' death or their general inability to raise the child.

The role of grandparents in the Indian novels is the strongest and most enduring family tie outside of those families blessed with the strength of Lulu and Marie's abiding maternal love. Nanapush names Lulu and serves as her grandfather as well as respected father to her mother Fleur. Marie takes in and raises the abandoned "throw away" children from troubled family members. Her niece June is dropped at her door, and Lipsha, June's son, also is rescued by Marie's love and caring. Albertine finds her identity through being a member of the Kashpaw family even more than she does as the daughter of Zelda, for it is in the collective embrace of the family at large that Albertine can feel security and acceptance. Since Nector has lost his ability to serve in the traditional grandfather role, she learns the stories from Marie. Albertine's voice along with Lipsha's represents the promise and assurance of cultural continuity through the younger generation whose nurturing by grandparents has bestowed upon them a tribal and personal identity providing the strength for the younger generation to carry on in the face of overwhelming cultural loss.

Grandmothers Zosie and Mary do not play as traditional a family role in *The Antelope Wife*. They are constantly on the move and mysterious by choice. They are healers, traditional beaders, gifted as namers, and powerful visionaries. As tricksters, however, they are unreliable and not accountable. Everyone in the Minneapolis Chippewa community thinks they know them and their whereabouts, yet they flash in and out of people's lives. In reality, people are not sure which sister is which, and the question of which one of them is Rozin's mother is unanswered for most of the daughter's life. Zosie and Mary are certainly nontraditional grandparents who reflect the realities faced by many urban Indians who live outside their traditional community.

Ancient Woodland beliefs persisted among the group of Chippewas who migrated to North Dakota and transported the structure of their society and their worldview into the new homeland with relatively little modification; however, additional patterns and practices gradually worked their way into the fabric of Ojibwa life, inspired by the new identity structured from a blended group of tribal peoples. The history of the Turtle Mountain Chippewa is a fascinating study of divergent groups joining together for a common cause (the buffalo hunt) and ending up forming a new society. The works of Stanley Murray, James Howard, David Delorme, Mary Jane Schneider, Alanson Skinner, Gregory Camp, and the Indian Claims Commission (Horr) provide a comprehensive critical background on the history of the tribe. What is important to know as background for Erdrich's novels is the composition of the Turtle Mountain Band and the significant events shaping the course of their lives.

The Formation of the Turtle Mountain Band

Since the blended identity of the Turtle Mountain people and the extent to which this blendedness factors heavily in the North Dakota novels has received little critical attention, it provides the best point to begin the discussion. A group of Chippewas from Leech Lake and Red Lake began pressing across Minnesota in the later part of the 1700s, where they encountered fierce resistance from the Lakota people. In order to combat this powerful tribe, the Chippewas aligned themselves with the Cree and Assiniboine and were successful in driving the Sioux out of the territory. The Chippewa-Sioux Sweet Corn Agreement assured the rights of the Chippewa people in the area, and they soon extended their occupation into the lands across the Red River and into northeastern North Dakota. By 1800, these people were hunting in the Turtle Mountains and were recognized as the Plains Ojibwa (Horr, *Chippewa Indians VII* 328). Once on the plains, they joined with their Cree kinsmen from the Saskatchewan area, and groups of Northern Ojibwe from the Rainy River country (Southern Canada) as well as the Assiniboine. An alliance among these various groups assured not only a productive hunt but also safety from their Lakota enemies. The Cree, Northern Ojibwe, and Chippewa intermarried, thus producing full-blooded Algonkians whose specific tribal identities began to blur.

Around the late 1800s, these full-bloods joined forces with the Métis, whose history is a remarkable account of what happens when two peoples from totally different cultures merge. Delorme explains, "The intermixture of Caucasoid and Mongoloid blended to produce a physical type that drew from both races, but did not approximate either of its progenitors: divergent societies clashed and compromised to create a disparate culture—new language, religion, social order, and economy" (124). In this case, it was the fur traders, particularly the French but also the English and the Scots, who, encouraged by their company, married Indian women. These unions provided stability in the new country for the Europeans and produced a new class of people, the Métis or mixed-bloods. Patrick Gourneau points out, "The 'Mechifs' are descendants of traders, le voyageurs, the canoe paddlers of the fur trade period and wagonmen, the Red River Cart drivers of the same period" (9). The trappers most commonly married Cree and Northern Ojibwe women, and the English and French surnames immediately marked the offspring as different from the full-bloods.

The Métis' close association with the fur companies provided them with a natural entry into the economy, and Murray relates that they were encouraged by the merged Northwest and Hudson Bay companies to become full-time hunters (16). They aptly adapted to this role; and when the fur-bearing animals became depleted in the region, they turned to hunting larger game, the buffalo. Murray describes how, around the beginning of the 1800s, "the buffalo hunt created a cultural and political unity among the Métis (18). By 1850, the Métis became the dominant group in the region, numbering more than 5,000 (Murray 16). Because the Métis proved to be such successful hunters, the Cree, Northern Ojibwe, and Chippewas soon joined them, and the blending of the various groups accelerated. This group, which hunted all the way from Minnesota to Montana, illustrates a successful transition from one way of life, traditional Woodland hunting, to another, hunting the buffalo herds on the plains.

The Métis became an integral part of this new community; Murray reports that by 1870, they were the dominant people in the community centering around Pembina and the Turtle Mountain region (19), and Delorme estimates that the total number of Métis in the United States and Canada at this time was around 33,000 (125). The new culture developed distinctive cultural traditions from those of the full-bloods, notably the jigs, reels, fiddle playing, log cabins, and Roman Catholic religion. What the two groups did share was a common language. According to Howard, "Cree was a sort of *lingua franca* in the Northern Plains during the latter half of the nineteenth century, and was spoken by the Assiniboine, Blackfoot, and Dakota, as well as Plains-Ojibwa and Métis" (7). Cree emerged as the language of trade, while the group united through hunting developed their own pidgin dialect, Michif. Delorme explains the jargon as a mixture of French, Cree, and Chippewa, with its roots stretching back to an "obsolete French of the type still to be heard in Normandy" (126).

Several different languages are still spoken on the Turtle Mountain Reservation today, including English, Michif, Canadian French, and an Ojibwe dialect termed "Cree." Howard explains, "Sometimes, when speaking English they [the elders] may refer to their dialect of Ojibwa as 'Cree,' or to themselves as either 'Chippewa' or 'Cree,' which has led incautious Whites to draw incorrect conclusions regarding their identity" (7). C. J. La Framboise, museum director of the Turtle Mountain Chippewa Heritage Center in the early 1990s, explains that the Cree language is the traditional language, pointing out that, in fact, many of the hereditary chiefs like Little Shell spoke Cree. The dictionary of the traditional language for the reservation is the *North American Indian Cree Dictionary*, which its author Edna Martin Cloud presents as the "oral language of my tribe" (3), and it is barely distinguishable from a similar Michif dictionary by John Crawford entitled *Michif Dictionary: Turtle Mountain Chippewa Cree*. Gourneau relates that the Michifs named the newly amalgamated language Cree, which included French, Cree, Plains-Ojibway, and English; but, asserts Gourneau, "it differs greatly from the real Cree" (9–10). He further distinguishes the three reservation Indian languages as "'Mechif [Michif] Cree, the real Cree and Plains-Ojibway" (11). The language of the Turtle Mountain band before the infusion of the Métis was not solely Cree; it was a combination of Cree and Chippewa, reflecting the merged past of these two Algonkian tribes. The point of this discussion concerning the languages is to highlight the fact that the community began as a mixed group, linguistically, culturally, and socially, and that today while the cultures have blended, echoes of a traditional Ojibwe past still remain.

The reservation today is comprised of Métis, Ojibwe-Cree, and Chippewa from Minnesota, and they are also grouped as the full-bloods (Chippewa from Minnesota, Northern Ojibwe, and Ojibwe-Cree), the Canadian mixed-bloods, and the mixed-bloods who consider themselves U.S. citizens.[16] The roots of friction in the combined community arose at the time the U. S. Government removed the people from most of their lands in North Dakota and set aside a reservation area in the Turtle Mountain region for their homeland. The first treaty concerning the Turtle Mountain people occurred in 1863 when the group ceded the Red River Valley, but as long as the area remained free from Anglo settlers and the buffalo herds continued to supply trade, clothing, hides, and meat, the loss of this land was not devastating. In less than two decades, however, the Gold Rush brought hordes of settlers onto the Plains, and the extermination of the great buffalo herds was nearly complete. The Indian people, recognizing the need for an established and permanent land base, began negotiations with the U.S. Government.[17]

The problems with land rights were exacerbated by the fact that the Métis outnumbered the full-bloods, and the mixed-bloods wished to accept the land in severalty, while the more traditional elements held out for a reservation area to be kept in common. Chief Little Shell, living in Montana, returned to North Dakota to fight for a common reservation area, and in 1882 President Chester Arthur "designated a twenty-four-by-thirty-two mile tract in Rolette County as a reservation for the Chippewa" (Murray 23). Nevertheless, the agent Cyrus Beede sent by the government to make recommendations and to fix the reserve site found himself negotiating with two different groups, the thousand or so Métis who wanted individual tracts and the approximately 300 full-bloods who continued to push for a common area. Subsequent government agents "found" that many of the people on the tribal roles were in fact Canadian mixed-bloods who had no claim to North Dakota lands, and this misinterpretation resulted in hundreds of tribal members being stricken from the roles. This gave the government an excuse to again reduce the land base, and in 1884, "the original twenty-two township reserve was reduced to two townships" (Murray 23) with the best land remaining available to white settlers.

The government continued to erode the land base of the Turtle Mountain people. The McCumber Agreement of 1892 "divested the Turtle Mountain Indians of their rights and title to almost 10,000,000 acres for the consideration of $1,000,000. This 'ten cent treaty' was amended and approved by Congress on April 21, 1904" (Delorme 133). These were lands still being claimed by the tribe when the government summarily opened them for Anglo settlement. The reservation was reduced to 275 quarter sections that needed to be divided among 326 families (Murray 32). The ensuing result was a dispersion of the people to lands off the reserve, with some people settling on public domain lands near the reservation, in the Trenton and Walhalla communities in North Dakota, and on Graham's Island, a peninsula of Devil's Lake (Murray 32). Because the Dawes Act of 1887 gave women and children the rights to land, some people were allocated property as far away as Montana on the Rocky Boy reservation. With the best farmland in the hands of the whites, the tribe dispersed, government-supported lumber companies encroaching, the buffalo herds depleted, the assault of disastrous flu and smallpox epidemics, a national depression between 1893–1896, and questionable property taxes levied for the people of the band receiving land off the small reservation area, the beginning of this century found the fortunes of the Turtle Mountain people bleak indeed. The 1910 census found 229 full-bloods and 2,546 mixed-bloods (only 569 of which had received allotments) (Camp 30) living on one of the smallest reservations in the U.S.

There have been some favorable developments in this century. Based on the Wheeler-Howard Indian Reorganization Act of 1934, 33,435 acres near the reservation were purchased for tribal use (Mary Jane Schneider 131), and in 1979, the Indian Claims Commission awarded the tribe $52,527,338 as compensation for the unfair seizure of tribal lands under the "ten cent agreement." In 1994, each tribal member was awarded an additional $3,000 check. Belcourt remains the administrative center for the tribe, and the town contains many businesses owned by tribal members, a tribally-owned shopping mall and Junior College, St. Ann's Catholic Church where the majority of the people worship, schools, and as of the late 1980s a bingo hall. In 2000, Doreen Bruce, director of the Turtle Mountain Chippewa Historical Center reported 28,021 people on the census rolls with most of them enrolled with one-half Indian blood and 15,000 tribal members living on or near the reservation. Given the long and arduous struggle for recognition and rights alongside crippling epidemic diseases, it is little wonder that Erdrich feels compelled to write the story of a people who survived into the twenty-first century against tremendous odds.

Two other points require mention before examining how Erdrich depicts these events in the reservation novels. One is the curious absence of a name for the reservation. The events and people clearly point to the author's Turtle Mountain Chippewa Reservation as the model for her fictional world, yet it is never designated as such. One could conclude that her choice to eschew the specific in favor of the general points to a desire to paint a portrait of reservation people who might reside on any reservation throughout the country. Erdrich positions her novels in a fictional world bearing resemblance to, but not a copy of, her reservation homeland. She chooses to invent her own mythical homeland in much the same way that William Faulkner created Yoknapatawpha County, and as such, gains a freedom to invest her people with the shared attributes of a reservation community and to describe a homeland and a tribe continuing to thrive today.

Erdrich's Non-Reservation Novels

The other issue meriting examination is the inclusion of *The Beet Queen* and *Tales of Burning Love* in an otherwise predominantly Indian story. Given the fact of Erdrich's combined Indian-Anglo heritage and the high percentage of mixed-blood tribal members on the Turtle Mountain Reservation, it is not surprising that she chooses to include in her mythical world people living off the reservation whose lives brush and mingle with those of tribal members. The characters in *The Beet Queen* struggle against the same natural forces as do their Indian neighbors, and the Anglo commitment to the land and the area simply records another side of the picture of the often harsh life on the uncompromising North Dakota Plains. *Tales of Burning Love* is primarily the story of two mixed-bloods, Jack and Dot, who were raised off the reservation and who do not regard themselves as Indians. Since nearly half of the enrolled Turtle Mountain population lives off the reservation, their lives reflect a tribal reality. Jack and Dot negate their Indian heritage and live comfortably in the Anglo world.

For Native Americans, a people who for countless generations have lived, worshipped, hunted, and been buried in a certain space, the land achieves a nearly mythical status. It is named Mother Earth by Indian people who revere her for her bountiful gifts and as the source of all life. She imprints the people living in a particular area so that people and place merge into one being. The land forms the identity of the people living there as a reference, a security, and a reality. Erdrich specifies, "In a tribal view of the world, where one place has been inhabited for generations, the landscape becomes enlivened by a sense of group and family history" ("Where" 1), and a tribal person's sense of history depends as much on their blood ancestry as it does on the land that nurtured clan and family.

Just as the geography of north central North Dakota forms her Indian people, so does it shape her Anglo relations residing there. The sense of place for them is as firmly established as it is for their Indian neighbors. The vast expanse of the sky, the rolling hills, the arid and intensely hot summers, the bitter winter winds, and the uncertainty of the powerful forces of nature—blizzards, tornadoes, sleet, and hail—form resolute and intense character. Only the strong survive, and as Russell Banks points out in a review of *The Beet Queen*, "Erdrich has quite as much compassion for the white inhabitants of the small town of Argus, North Dakota, and environs as for the Chippewas" (461). These immigrant people also form her past, and *The Beet Queen* and *Tales of Burning Love* are a tribute to Anglo survivors in the same way that the rest of the North Dakota series celebrates the lives of the Indian survivors.

The Anglo settlers began moving into the area in 1882 when the McCumber Agreement opened up 9,000,000 acres. The area was heavily settled by immigrant farmers, creating the state's unique character of rural foreign settlers and Native Americans. E. B. Robinson reports that by 1920 over half of the state's population was bilingual (Germans, Russians, Scandinavians, and Canadians) and over 85% of the residents lived in the country or in small towns (548–49). Even though the whites received the most fertile land, it was still an area of dry farming, because two-thirds of the state averages less than 17 inches of annual rain. The semiarid environment accounts for the dispersed population, the exodus of young people, and the importance of wheat and cattle (Robinson 9). Wheat reigns supreme, for it only needs a 100-day growing season and less than 30 inches of annual precipitation, and Russo-German settlers in the 1870s brought to North Dakota varieties of drought-resistant crops such as goose wheat and speltz "from their homeland in the semiarid regions of the lower Volga" (Hargreaves 84).

Nature's capriciousness exacerbated an already marginal existence for many, and a drought lasting from 1929–1939 combined with a grasshopper plague and the Great Depression wrecked havoc on the lives of the people. From 1930–1944, around one-third of the people lost their farms because of their inability to pay taxes, and only the advent of a war-time economy rescued the state from its plunging fortunes. By this time, large segments of the population had gravitated to areas of greater promise, and the depopulation from rural counties matched that of the thousands who left in hopes of finding a better life in another state.

The Beet Queen opens in 1932 in the fictional town of Argus when economic conditions in the state had reached a low point, and it ends at the close of the Vietnam War. Again, Erdrich does not specify a historical town in favor of encompassing general aspects of Anglo life in rural North Dakota. Thus, the North Dakota novels detail both sides of Erdrich's heritage during the last century, since the exclusion of the Anglo element would disrupt the historical flow as much as it would disrupt the chronological one.

The events in *Tracks* take place from 1912 to 1924, and while the novel primarily concentrates on Indian affairs, already the children of the Indian and the Anglo settlers begin to mingle their lives as Fleur and Pauline go to Argus and work with Pete Kozka and Dutch James. The stories of Indian life, except for a flashback to 1934 recounting how Marie and Nector meet and mate and Marie's relating how June came to her in 1948, pick up again in *Love Medicine* in 1957. *The Bingo Palace* takes place in the present and continues the stories of the reservation families, while *The Beet Queen* supplies the necessary counterpart to the lives of twentieth-century Native Americans by relating an equally important story of the lives of second-generation rural whites struggling to endure throughout years of extreme hardship. It also continues the story of how the lives of reservation people and the lives of the people in the surrounding towns interface. The Kozkas and Pfefs are survivors of drought, depression (human as well as economic), and mass exodus from the region. Their story mingles with the lives of the Adares and Kashpaw descendants (Russell, Celestine, and Dot). *Tales of Burning Love* continues stories of contemporary mixed-bloods and German immigrant descendants living in Argus and Fargo. The collective stories of reservation Indian, off-reservation Indians, and immigrant descendants supplies a comprehensive history of strong-willed survivors in North Dakota.

The Indians endured epidemic diseases and enormous land losses, and the Anglos survived the ravages of fickle weather along with the national Depression. Erdrich points out to Wong in an interview that "the four books [she had not yet written *Tales of Burning Love* and *The Antelope Wife*] are about a region, a small area" (*Conversations* 32) affirming the idea of complementary novels. The North Dakota novels relate the story of life on the northern plains, and while the Indian side of Erdrich's heritage is foregrounded, the lives of her German ancestors complete the picture of twentieth-century North Dakota life.

Erdrich's Incorporation of Tribal and Anglo History

A communal Indian voice relates the story of the Plains Ojibwa people over the last 100 years. Erdrich builds the novels around certain events where stories stand as metaphors (winter count images) for the major episodes in tribal life. She creates her own myth about the life of her people. In doing so, she utilizes the storytelling cycle to recount her story in the Indian way. Readers do not learn Chippewa history from anthropologists, missionaries, nuns, and sociologists. Rather she appropriates the role of the traditional tribal storyteller to serve as a receptacle and bearer of culture. Stripes believes that "Erdrich's novelistic interventions in history are not unique; many writers of tribal descent reflect historical themes and employ complex rhetorical figures" (31). Even so, Erdrich and James Welch (from *Fool's Crow* all the way through *Indian Lawyer*) remain unique among Native American authors who are able to encompass so much tribal history in their novels.

Tracks presents a historical perspective and reveals the extent of what has been lost. The smallpox epidemic combined with the severe 1886–87 winter has decimated the population. Nanapush is the sole remaining traditionalist, one who has guided a buffalo hunt and who practices the old ways. He exemplifies traditional culture and old ways of knowing. He buries Fleur's Pillager family in traditional grave houses scratching in their clan markers. He smokes a pipe and offers tobacco to the Father while admonishing their spirits to be at peace. He can speak the old Anishinaabe language, and his ability to seek a vision and employ hunting songs to lure game saves his life during times of starvation. He has the powers to cure and is responsible for saving the lives of Moses, Fleur, and Lulu, the entire Pillager clan. He is the traditional culture hero who ensures that the old ways will be passed on, and when he merges his fate with the Pillagers, the promise of tribal survival is assured.

The novel is about the Chippewa's fight for their land and culture. Already the Catholic Church has made inroads against the traditional Chippewa religion, and Pauline is only an extreme example of the extent of their influence. The two narrative voices in the novel, that of Pauline the fanatical religious mixed-blood pitted against the traditionalist and culture hero Nanapush, dramatically underscore the fight taking place at large in the culture between the mixed-bloods and the full-bloods. Pauline denies her Indian heritage while Nanapush labors to continue Chippewa culture, and the juxtaposition of the traditional voice with a proselytizing Christian one serves to remind readers of the very different identities Indians have adopted since the initial contact with European trappers and missionaries.

The government's allotment policy was primed to promote disunity in an already fragmented tribe. Nanapush laments that Anglo settlers are making "wholesale purchase of our allotment lands" (T 98) and waiting expectantly for Indian lands to fall "underneath the gavel of the auctioneer" (T 99). Tribal members are pitted against each other when unexpected fees for their land come due; Margaret and Nector sell off the Pillager land by defaulting Pillager and Nanapush fees in favor of Kashpaws, and thus keep their land, but sell their tribal integrity. While the Dawes Act provided that women and children be given the rights to land, with the dearth of available property, the older Kashpaw children are assigned land on the Montana reservation, far from their tribal homeland and family.

The friction between the mixed-blood families—the Morrisseys, Lamartines, Puyats, and Lazarres—and the traditional full-blood families—the Kashpaws, Pillagers, and Nanapushes—reach a climax over property rights. Bernadette Morrissey becomes the Bureau of Indian Affairs' agent's secretary and asserts her influence in sending out tax notices, and so lands pass into the hands of the mixed-bloods who have gained government favor and influence. The best farmers, including the Morrisseys, seize prime lands for themselves, but other mixed-bloods also position themselves to take over defaulted lands. The Lazarres swarm onto Nanapush's land and into his house within weeks of his losing it because of dubiously assessed late fees. Nanapush bemoans the fact that the Lazarres seem so ready to usurp traditional homesteads, "It seemed they were everywhere now, multiplying and dividing, taking up the cracks and cervices between the clans, the gaps the illness had left. No house stayed empty, no land unclaimed. There was always a Lazarre..." (T 184). To exacerbate the land problems for the traditionalists, lumber companies were ready to pounce on ill-gotten allotment lands. The Turcot Lumber Company easily bought lands from mixed-bloods who were quickly eroding the original reserve which the government had set aside for the tribe. The Lazarres and the Morrisseys signed purchase agreements with the company and urged others to do the same. Trees fell, and lands passed into the hands of white farmers, and tribal property continued to shrink while the factions raged on.

The Métis influence asserts a strong cultural role, and fiddle dances, the French language, and the Catholic church and schools are omnipresent. Whereas the two cultures blended their music, language, and religion over the years, the bad blood over land issues continued to simmer and finally erupted into a feud that divided the people. The affair between Eli Kashpaw and Sophie Morrissey is the catalyst in the battle for power between the Métis and the full-bloods, and Clarence Morrissey and Boy Lazarre use this as an opportunity to humiliate Nanapush and Margaret. They tie him up, rape her, and cut off her braid. Nanapush and Fleur take revenge, but both actions accelerate the demise of the already diminishing tribal unity. With full-bloods against full-bloods, full-bloods against mixed-bloods, and the U.S. government in charge of tribal annihilation, the chances for tribal culture and identity to survive grow dim.

To complete this picture of relentless U.S. intervention in tribal affairs, the hope for the Indian future, the children, are sent away to BIA boarding schools where they are forbidden to speak their language and where they are far away from the influence of tribal culture. Traditionally, the young children learned tribal history throughout their growing-up years listening to their grandparents tell them the stories of the people. Away in the BIA schools in uniforms and Anglo haircuts and forced under threat of punishment to speak the English language, the Indian children quickly become estranged from traditional tribal customs. Nector is sent away to school in order to learn how to assume the role of tribal bureaucrat. Lulu, the only child of the most powerful medicine woman on the reservation, Fleur, is sent away and consequently does not acquire the healing powers that should have been passed on to her. Nanapush has to assume a grandfather's role in order to fill Lulu in and try to make her understand how tribal events have affected her life and caused her mother to send her away far from revenging Lazarres and Morrisseys who might harm her. This is the history he tells Lulu in *Tracks*, those stories that were lost to her during her years away. Even so, Lulu abrogates her Pillager heritage, maintains a separation from her mother throughout her lifetime, and only in her later years does she begin to esteem traditional values and work for their continuity. The novel ends as Lulu returns from boarding school to Nanapush, and a faint hope begins to glimmer for cultural continuity.

The Beet Queen is notable as much for what is left unsaid as for the stories told. The novel opens in the midst of the Great Depression of the 1930s in which those city people who lost all their savings in the stock market crash and subsequent bank failures stand in bread lines and work on federal projects like the Works Projects Administration (WPA) to survive. Thousands are homeless, and thousands more die of malnutrition. With the stock market crash coming on the heels of the severe farm depression of the 1920s, the lives of countless urban and rural people alike waver on the brink of disaster. Thus, youths (like Karl) travel in freight cars across the country looking for food and shelter. In later years, removed from the pain and anguish of those times, many families recounted their experiences to their children as a reminder of the fickleness of life, and Erdrich's family was no exception. Both she and Dorris grew up hearing Depression stories that were so real to them that they have subsequently had a great impact on their work (Wong, *Conversations* 38).

The Depression and later World War II and the Korean War remain in the background, however, and assert only a secondary importance in the lives of *The Beet Queen* characters, other than the veteran Russell. Like the other three novels, this is the story of a community and how it deals with itself. While national events certainly affect economic conditions, the lives of these characters are so emotionally thwarted that the outside world has little chance of penetrating their closed world. What becomes of prime importance is their relationship to each other and how they endure. This is the story of the Anglo survivors of the Depression where "it is every man and woman for him- and herself, where emotional toughness ensures psychic survival and losses are continually cut" (Owens, *Other* 233). Karl wanders through life looking for the big job and a place to belong.[18] Only in his later years does he realize that his place is back in Argus, from where he first embarked on his journeys, in the devoted hands of Wallace Pfef.

Erdrich's narrative technique in *The Beet Queen* (and also in *Tracks*) reflects the impact of storytelling in her family where people sat around listening to others and then took up where the teller left off (Schumacher, *Conversations* 175). This created a continuity and an intricately connected web of family tales, and in *The Beet Queen* it is Mary who repeatedly picks up the thread of the storyline and continues with her version of the story. This occurs when an omniscient author describes how Mary and Karl arrive in Argus, and then Mary picks up her story, "I was the girl in the stiff coat" (BQ 5). This happens again when Sita with burgeoning adolescent hormones strips off her blouse in front of Celestine to reveal her budding breasts. Mary watches the event in disgust and picks up Sita's story and continues, relating her truth and her reality. Mary picks up Sita's story again after Sita takes a fatal overdose and wanders out to her yew bushes, where she lifelessly rests against the branches. Mary drives up to find her, and once again takes over the story as her own, as she has done repeatedly throughout her life. She tends to appropriate parts of other people's lives in order to create her own. She becomes favored by her aunt Fritzie over Sita; she wins Sita's best friend Celestine away and forms a lifetime bond with her; and Mary tries to insinuate herself into her niece Dot's life, often at the expense of Dot's relationship with her mother Celestine. Mary is a survivor, and her tough, uncompromising nature underscores the attributes needed to survive in a harsh physical environment.

Wallace Pfef is the community activist. From its modest population of 300 people in 1913, Argus has grown to the point in the 1960s where the town merits a bypass on the interstate, where large supermarkets replace small family businesses like Kozka Meats, and where large-scale housing developments crop up in response to the growing population. Pfef, the son of dour German settlers, homosexual, rose gardener, and collector of Hummels, is the unlikely driving force behind his community's development. From managing the town's swimming pool, a WPA project (one of the few references to the national life), he takes over as head of the Chamber of Commerce and as number one promoter of Argus. His methodical nature and unfulfilled love life culminate in vast stores of energy directed outside himself, and he sublimates the town's future for his own and links them together in a positive way. Beets, the crop of choice for the semiarid and unpredictable North Dakota climate, are brought to Argus as a result of Pfef's driving energies. He builds the town's commercial base and rounds out his life by finding companionship and love when Karl returns to his home.

Sita remains unfulfilled throughout her life, the victim of self-delusions and self-indulgence. She aspires for a finer life than the one Argus offers her, for she finds her parents' butcher shop oppressive and small-town life provincial. Sita finds her identity in her appearance, and subsequently her whole life is devoted to its enhancement and preservation. She tries to mold her environment to fit her image, an attempt which ends in foolish projects like trying to change her husband Jimmy's successful steakhouse, the Poopdeck, into an establishment offering haute cuisine. Her inability to accept the reality of the people of Argus, "heavy people, Germans and Poles or Scandinavians, rough handed and full of opinions" (BQ 68) and to live solely in her Sita-centered fictive world of elegance render her physically and emotionally sterile. When she can no longer preserve her fragile hold on sanity by retreating farther and farther into this world of her own creation, she ends her life. Sita ends up the victim of a demanding environment she was unable to defeat.

This discussion of *The Beet Queen* began with the statement that the story seems to be surrounded by the unsaid, the main events occurring outside the community, highlighting the remarkably insular lives of the people of the area. This is particularly true in reference to the nearby Indian reservation, where the lives of its residents are for the most part encapsulated in their own world. Owens suggests that "Unlike *Love Medicine*, *The Beet Queen* provides only faint glimpses of points of contact between Indian and white cultures in this country, a kind of no-man's land where margins on the map have blurred..." (*Other* 207).

Argus serves as a place for those Indians who wish to deny their heritage and assimilate into a white world to escape to. Pauline Puyat comes to Argus as a young woman repudiating her Indian blood, and she returns later as Sister Leopolda, sent to teach in the convent school after she becomes too deranged even for the reservation convent. Russell Kashpaw and his half-sister Celestine James are the sole reminders of the neighboring reservation. Russell is an Indian of whom whites can approve. He is a remarkable high-school football player, and he volunteers for both World War II and the Korean War, getting so shot up that the town's people wish to honor him first by giving him a bank job, even though he is an Indian, and then by making him "North Dakota's most-decorated hero" (BQ 111). He finds whites applauding his life choices and holding him up as a model Indian. Eventually, he drifts between his Indian world on the reservation and his sister's world in Argus, never achieving a harmonious blend. Russell ends up a disabled, nonverbal husk of a once powerful and brave man reduced to depending on the charity of others to fulfill his basic needs. His entry into the Anglo world results in a shattered body and a lost soul, and it is only when once he is again in the care of his Indian relatives that he finds any modicum of peace.

Celestine, on the other hand, is a mixed-blood who successfully navigates her way in Argus's community. As the daughter of Dutch James, she is offered some acceptance, and she fights for the rest of it with her imposing personality. Standing nearly six feet tall, she is a formidable woman not only physically but also emotionally. She is prone to argument, jealousy, and pragmatism. Even though Mary brings out her worst, she remains bound to her throughout her lifetime, and it is this quality of being able to care for the unlovable people, Mary, Karl, Sita, and Dot, that reveals her true strength of character and human compassion. This is most vividly demonstrated in her abiding and unconditional love for her obnoxious daughter Dot. Celestine never abandons those she loves, and her ability to cherish even the most unlikeable people underscores Erdrich's major theme, the power and gift of human love.

Love Medicine returns the story to the reservation with Erdrich again recording the lives of Indian people. In this novel as in the others, she functions as a traditional storyteller who tells the life of her people through example and metaphor while relating the touchstone stories that will be passed on to future generations. *Love Medicine* is June Morrissey's story; and by the time of her death in 1981, all of the major reservation families are related. The lines have blurred between the Métis and the full-bloods, and the traditional Kashpaw family includes Lazarre children (June) and has merged with the Puyats (Nector and Marie). Other traditional adversaries, the Pillagers and the Morrisseys and Lamartines, are blended with Lulu's marriages. The only full-blood of the third generation is Gerry Nanapush,[19] the traditional Chippewa trickster figure, and even his son Lipsha who inherits the Pillager powers is a mixed-blood through his mother June's Morrissey heritage. It is then little wonder that tribal requirements for enrollment necessitates only one-fourth Indian blood, for the years have found the Indian people slowly assimilating and intermarrying with the dominant culture, thinning their Indian blood and cultural traditions.

Love Medicine reflects reality for tribal members living in the last part of the twentieth century. Economic development is at the forefront of reservation issues, and the ill-fated tomahawk factory once again pits the traditionalists against the mixed-blood assimilationists. Unregistered Lamartine land becomes the target of the BIA and its henchmen's idea for progress. Before it burns, Lulu's house is slated to be torn down so that a factory called Anishinabe Enterprises producing machine-made "original" Indian artifacts can be constructed. Lyman assumes the bureaucratic lead in promoting this idea set into motion by his father Nector in previous years; Nector approved the measure out of weakness, while Lyman promotes the project on the strength of his drive and business acumen. However, what both fail to properly assess is the degree of opposition from the more conservative tribal element, now led by Lulu and Marie, which succeeds in undermining the project.

The demise of this project leaves an opening rather than closing the door. Within a short period of time, prompted by the Indian Gaming Regulatory Act highlighted in the Congressional Record to which he subscribes, Lyman conceives of the idea of a bingo casino. Gambling has been an integral part of tribal life for centuries in hand and dice games, and Lyman's idea is to "make a money business out of money itself" (LM 327). The idea of bringing Indians into the American mainstream through economic success is not a new idea. Stephen Cornell notes that this notion was behind Secretary of War Henry Knox's plan after the Civil War to offer Indian nations "the dream of economic and social progress and individual freedom" (61). Additionally, the idea behind the 1887 Dawes Act was to "allow" Indians to own land in severalty, and the termination policy of the 1950s was based on the notion that the reservation concept hindered individual Indian initiative (Cornell 61). However, these perhaps well-meaning Anglo proposals did not consider the Indians' dreams, and so the American Indian Movement (AIM) was born during the turbulent years of the 1960s, serving as a catalyst for other Indian activist groups seeking tribal sovereignty, treaty recognitions, and return of tribal lands. Bingo became another means to achieve economic success, but tribal members across the country remained divided as to its appropriateness, while at the same time the U.S. government challenges the reservations' right to regulate and control their own gaming in accordance with the National Indian Gaming Commission and state and federal jurisdiction.

The bingo seed is planted in *Love Medicine*, but Erdrich does not explore its implications for the Indian future until her next book *The Bingo Palace*. Lyman is the most prominent spokesman for business development on the reservation, and as he works to bring jobs and money into the reservation, his brother Gerry instills Indian pride with his AIM activism. This would be in keeping with his membership in the bear clan through his Pillager heritage. Warren explains that members of this clan are the acknowledged warriors and "are often denominated the bulwarks of the tribe against its enemies" (49). Warren also points out other traits of the bear clan males: they are fond of fighting; they are a physical presence; and they possess coarse, thick, black hair (49), all traits of Gerry Nanapush. Owens suggests that Gerry is based on a more recent model, since he bears a strong resemblance to Leonard Peltier, an American Indian activist found guilty of murdering FBI agents on the Pine Ridge reservation (*Other* 200).[20]

Gerry fights for Indian rights at a time when traditional culture on the reservation is precariously weak. By the time of *Love Medicine,* Eli is the only one who still speaks the old language and who still knows the old hunting ways. His way of life is fading into a distant past as his relatives intermarry with whites, fall victim to the ravages of alcohol, and become casualties of the U.S. government's latest war, Vietnam. King and Gordie represent those fallen warriors whose loss of pride in themselves and in their Indian heritage plunges them into alcoholic despair. King affects a stab at sobriety under the threat of Gerry's visit, but his weak moral character guarantees a quick return to the bottle when the crisis passes. King and Gordie represent two Native American casualties of drinking. Vizenor points out, "Alcoholic related deaths are four to five times higher [for Indians] than among the general public. Two-thirds of those deaths are caused by cirrhosis of the liver. Alcohol is also related to higher arrest rates, accidents, homicide, suicide, and spouse and child abuse" (*Crossbloods* 305). The Red Road is an Indian organization seeking to make inroads against the ravages of drinking and to help restore Indian pride. Such help comes too late for Gordie, who dies after ingesting Lysol in a frantic attempt to numb himself with any available alcohol-related product.

The list of Indian war veterans in the reservation novels is impressive, but these soldiers often return to a society that does not honor their patriotism. Edgar Pukwan fights with Pershing and returns home a hero. In fact, 25,000 Native Americans signed up to fight in World War II (Vizenor, "Minnesota" 54), and Russell is one of the many decorated Indians who lived to receive his medals. Russell fights in two wars, World War II and Korea, and Gordie also sees action in Korea. Bev and Henry Lamartine serve in the armed forces, and Henry Sr.'s oldest "son" is killed in boot camp.

Another Lamartine war casualty is Henry Jr., who survives nine months of combat and six months of captivity by the North Vietnamese Army; but after his release upon the evacuation of Saigon, the war continues for him at home. As his brother Lyman comments, "I guess the whole war was solved in the government's mind, but for him [Henry Jr.] it would keep on going" (LM 185). Henry's suicide by drowning, a death the Chippewa hold in horror, only accentuates the extent to which the war has shattered his mind and body.

June is another victim. Her wretched childhood is marked by neglect from her alcoholic mother Lucille Lazarre, by sexual abuse from Lucille's boyfriend Leonard, and by little physical and emotional security. When Lucille dies and her brother Geerzhig is no longer around, June survives by eating pine sap. By the time her alcoholic Lazarre grandmother and no-good Morrissey father bring her to Marie, June is a dirty, half-starved, pathetic child of nine. She is never able to completely trust or love anyone in her lifetime, because her sordid childhood leaves too many emotional scars. Even Marie who loves June unconditionally is unable to repair the severe damage done to June and realizes by the time she comes to Marie that "it had been too late to really save her.... Some children you could not repair" (BP 27-28). June is both a survivor and a victim, and her life is marked by her futile attempts to find a wholeness being shattered by her desolate childhood. However, her will to survive and her courage and hope for a better life have a powerful impact on those who love June, and *Love Medicine* is "both elegy and post-mortem as other characters and especially the reader struggle to understand her life and death" (McKenzie 58). She has been blessed and cursed in her lifetime, but the power of the love of Eli, Marie, Albertine, Gordie, Gerry, and at last Lipsha sustains her hope for the future. June is finally able to accept this powerful love in her afterlife, and she aids Lipsha from the spirit world by affirming herself as his mother in *The Bingo Palace* and by saving his father Gerry's life in *Tales of Burning Love*.

This is one of the signs of a hopeful future in *Love Medicine*, which is not about despair and cultural loss entirely. It is the story of a culture in transition, and signs are present that bode well for a Chippewa future. While the government's relocation program of the 1950s scattered Indian families like the Lamartines and

Kashpaws into Minneapolis and Chicago, even they maintain their cultural roots and return to the reservation for funerals and powwows. Others, like Lipsha, leave the reservation, but return when their hope for a future seems more assured in their cultural homeland than in the Anglo cities.

Albertine enters medical school on new schooling opportunities available for Native Americans, and her future promises a dedication to healing her people with western medicine. Fleur and Moses are the most powerful practitioners of traditional medicine, and the lack of a successor to their Chippewa healing gifts seems to spell the end of this vital cultural connection. However, there is a successor, who in *Love Medicine* is beginning to learn his latent powers; and, as Lipsha becomes more comfortable with who he is, his potential as a traditional healer begins to take root.

Other signs of a hopeful future include a Catholic Church now better serving its nearly all-Catholic reservation congregation. The shabby convent on the hill that was once the repository for misfits and religiously warped nuns like Sister Leopolda has now come up in the world. The building is freshly painted and boasts a fresh parking lot, and new and compassionate nuns like Sister Mary Martin de Porres populate the convent. Many of the traditional Indians are comfortable combining their Catholicism with their Chippewa gods, and this merged religious consciousness promises a strong spiritual future.

Lulu and Marie's activism for traditional values signals that the old ways and heritage are not yet forgotten and that there is still a place for them in modern Chippewa life. With their families raised and their husbands dead, Lulu and Marie devote their formidable energies to tribal matters by becoming outspoken agitators for treaty rights, tribal integrity, and the maintenance of a strong cultural tradition. "Heavy into politics" (LM 300), Lulu is a constant thorn in the side of her assimilationist son Lyman, the consummate tribal bureaucrat. Their battle continues into *The Bingo Palace*; but in this novel, the power of the traditionalist activists is beginning to be felt. Lulu and Marie serve as models for other tribal members who are eschewing Anglo culture and beginning to assert their Indianness in dress and hairstyles, and their "battle of the beads" in the tomahawk factory serves as the catalyst to arouse the simmering resentment of the workers against the shabby product they have been asked to produce. The workers "methodically demolished, scattered, smashed to bits, and carried off what was left of the factory" (LM 319), and Lyman drinks himself into a stupor as he surveys the wreck of his government project.

The Bingo Palace is the most hopeful novel in the reservation novels, for it depicts a tribe making a successful transition to a new way of life. The other novels show the struggles for tribal sovereignty and Indian pride; and these ground building efforts result in a tribe entering the twenty-first century blending the old ways with the new, showing a means for economic development through the bingo palace, and assuring cultural traditions through tribal members like Lulu, Marie, Shawnee Ray, Xavier Toose, and especially Lipsha. The novel opens with hopeful signs. Lipsha is being rescued and recalled home from Fargo by his grandmother Lulu for the traditional winter powwow. Attending this traditional gathering are those who have returned home for it, like Albertine, along with the community members: the tribal council, the powwow organizers, the medics, the drum groups, the singers, little old Cree ladies, the fancy dancers, and the shawl girls (BP 9). Traditional dances like the grass dance are modernized and serve the principal social feature at these gatherings. Give-aways are associated with this dance as well as substantial cash prizes. Once the property of the warrior dancing society, the grass dance retains its warrior origins and today is often used to honor returning soldiers. Howard found that, in 1956, the grass dance was in the process of being revived on the Turtle Mountain Reservation due to a renewed interest in its traditional potential; and today in its modern form, it is the principal feature at the main tribal powwows (197–208). The shawl dance, a traditional woman's component of the grass dance, and the jingle dance, original to the Chippewa, are still integral parts of powwows. Lyman is a top grass dancer, and he dances in honor of his brother Henry. Shawnee Ray is the best jingle dancer, and her dancing abilities and sewing talents that produce beautiful costumes earn her top prizes at area powwows.

The sweat lodge, used for purification and as a cleansing for vision quests, is still a part of tribal life. Shawnee Ray, Lyman, and Lipsha all participate in sweat lodge ceremonies conducted by Xavier Toose, a traditional medicine man. Although their motivations for the ceremony range from Shawnee Ray's sincerity to

Lyman's pragmatism to Lipsha's desire to enhance his sagging image, the fact remains that it is still a part of tribal life. Lyman and Lipsha seek visions; and although Lyman claims to have received a traditional vision, it is never specified. What is detailed is Lipsha's "little vision" given by a skunk. Lipsha doesn't understand the meaning of his vision, but it is traditional that other, older community members interpret a vision for a seeker. With the loss of most of the traditional elders practicing the old ways, Lipsha is left to ponder his vision's meaning; and his feeble grasp of its implications is a factor that helps head him into the role for which the community and Fleur have been waiting, that of the traditional healer. Fleur by this time is so old that people call her a half-spirit and speculate that she cannot be killed. In fact, Fleur cannot die until there is someone to take her place, and she is waiting for a successor, someone who will carry on her knowledge but in a different way since she has not trained anyone in her traditional healing methods. The community and Fleur all know that her successor will be Lipsha, but he is not yet aware of the full potential of his gifts, and so he dawdles, squanders his talents, and lusts after Shawnee Ray.

Authoritative women now are powerful forces in tribal life. Zelda has a "deep instinct for running things" (BP 14), and Lipsha believes that "She should have more children or at least a small nation to control" (BP 14). Zelda holds an administrative position in the tribal office, and as such she has the power to affect people's lives, as when she gets Redford, Shawnee Ray and Lyman's son, registered as a full-blood on tribal rolls. Lipsha acknowledges Zelda's power over his life as well as over community life because of her strength of will and iron determination. He muses, "When women age into their power, no wind can upset them, no hand turn aside their knowledge; no fact can deflect their point of view" (BP 13). This statement applies to Marie and Lulu especially who now work tirelessly for the tribe's welfare. Marie has taken charge of the senior citizen's home, and all acknowledge her role as an old time traditional and community benefactor. The community voice proclaims that Lulu's "day's business [is]... running the tribe" (BPI 1) with her intended goal "to reclaim the original reservation, no less. It was once six times bigger" (BP 129).

Lulu's other goal is to protect traditional values and Indian pride symbolized by her son Gerry and to help his son Lipsha come into his proper tribal responsibilities. Gerry has been scapegoated by government officials, who implicate him as the one pulling the trigger that killed an FBI agent on the Pine Ridge reservation. Lulu works tirelessly to secure his transfer to a less restrictive prison compound than Marion, Illinois, where Gerry spends heavily guarded and solitary days. Citing the terms of the 1978 Indian Religious Freedom Act, Lulu wrangles for her son to be closer to his medicine people, and Gerry is flown to Minnesota where he escapes a plane crash fatal to the other occupants. His intuitions tell him his luck is changing, and Lulu is the powerful force setting these events in motion. The last image of her in the reservation novels in which she has been such an engaging character and compelling force is one of federal marshals, after implicating her in Gerry's escape, dragging away Lulu in her full powwow regalia, carrying an eagle fan and beaded pouch, and trilling the old-lady victory yell in front of rolling news cameras.

Lipsha is the engaging, soul-searching, Holden Caufield-like narrator of the novel, for it is his story that is most directly connected with the destiny of the tribe. He is the promise for the future as soon as he figures that out. This novel explores his journey to find his past and his future and how that journey is anxiously watched and carefully guided by community members and family members like his grandmothers Marie and Lulu. Even his mother June returns from the afterlife to aid him by lending her support and acknowledgment that he is her son. With Lipsha linking his fortunes with Shawnee Ray, who "is the best of our past, our present, our hope of a future" (BP 13), an assurance exists that traditional Chippewa values will continue to endure and be passed on to the community. With money rolling in from bingo, Erdrich ends the reservation novels on a guardedly optimistic note.

Tales of Burning Love is remarkable for the degree to which it picks up threads of stories from the four previous books and mingles the lives of the Chippewa with the German immigrant descendants. Jack's first wife is June Morrissey Kashpaw, and Dot Adare Nanapush is his fifth wife. Jack's second wife, Eleanor, is devoting herself to chronicling the life of Sister Leopolda, and her father, Lawrence Schlick, runs the funeral parlor in Fargo, where Mary and Celestine took Sita when she died. The idling car Lipsha steals at the train station in an attempt to spirit Gerry away turns out to be Jack's car with his son in the backseat, whom Jack has just kidnapped. Then, when Jack follows the car in a snowplow and ends up walking off into the field looking for the car he has just seen, it is June who comes to him in a wedding dress and leads him to Lipsha and the baby. Lyman saves Jack from financial ruin by hiring him as the project manager for the bingo palace to be built on the reservation, since the tribe wants to make the entire project Indian built and run. As Erdrich tells us in *The Bingo Palace*, "One story hinging into the next" (48), the stories which connect in often mysterious ways the people of this particular area of North Dakota.

June's story lingers in the air, and the novel is as much her story, although she is voiceless, as it is the story of the four narrators. The novel opens with the same scene that opened *Love Medicine*. There is familiar dialogue ("You got to be... You got to be different," she breathed); but in *Tales of Burning Love*, Jack is going under an assumed name. After her death, her presence haunts him, who knew her only a few hours, just as it haunts the lives of her family throughout the reservation novels. "Jack knew what he had done [married June] but kept telling himself that he was not the one. He was not the one. Still, he saw her constantly, wherever he looked, in his mind's eye" (10), and "He lived that one-night marriage every night" (382). Each of his subsequent four marriages is an attempt to redress the wrong he did June by letting her walk off into the snowstorm and not immediately reporting it to the authorities. "In spite of all his other wives, he's stayed married to a ghost" (381), for "Here was a truth he knew: he couldn't hold on to a woman even since he let the first one walk from his arms into Easter snow" (13).

Dot is his fifth wife, although she is still legally married to Gerry, who is back in prison. *The Bingo Palace* reunites the lovers June and Gerry. Gerry believes Dot has divorced him (incorrect) and remarried (correct). When June in her blue Firebird leads Lipsha and him off the highway and into the field during a blizzard, Gerry leaps into her car, a victim of a surge of feelings for his former lover. However, as a trickster, Gerry does not follow June to Chippewa heaven, for he reappears with Dot and their daughter Shawn. June remains to lead Jack through the snowdrifts in order that he can rescue his son Jack Jr. and her son Lipsha. Dot and June, two dominant figures in the North Dakota novels, remain as intertwined in June's death as they were in life. They both have loved the same men, Gerry and Jack, but June is finally able to let the living return to their lovers, Gerry and Dot, Jack and Eleanor.

All the stories in *Tales of Burning Love* revolve around the person of Jack Mauser, as told by his wives, present and former. It is a true communal tale of four women who love or have loved Jack. Eleanor Schlick, his second wife and true love, is spoiled, sensual, neurotic, and brainy. Her father's passionate love for her mother has spoiled her for life as she seeks to replicate with Jack and others that same intensity and depth of feeling in her own life. Candice Pantamounty, wife number three, is Jack's old high school girlfriend and now a prominent family dentist. Unable to have children because of a perforated uterus and subsequent hysterectomy, she adopts Jack's baby with his fourth wife, Marlis Cook, and becomes her lover. Marlis, who lived off accident payments and had been living under her ex-sister-in-law's trailer, is as unpredictable and flighty as Candice is predictable and solid. Her relationship with Jack is brief and stormy, but long enough for them to marry and for her to get pregnant. Her complicated relationship with Candice, who is her child's adopted mother and her lover, brings her stability and brings Candice unremitting joy.

Just as the reservation novels end with a great guarded hope, so does *Tales of Burning Love*. Lovers reunite—Dot and Gerry, Eleanor and Jack, Candice and Marlis, and Lawrence follows Anna to be with her in death. Jack's Indian self finally emerges. Going to the reservation to work on the bingo palace means reuniting with a part of himself he thinks dead. "He had the sense of a swift undertow, pulling from beneath the glazed Formica table, tugging. Home" (408). Thus, one more acculturated tribal member reconnects to his Indian community.

It is no accident that *The Antelope Wife* focuses on the lives of urban Chippewas living in Minneapolis. With Erdrich currently residing in the Twin Cities, the lives of urban Native Americans becomes a natural subject for her fiction. These are the Chippewa who remained in Minnesota, first on the reservations and then migrating into the cities when part of their numbers splintered off to hunt and live in North Dakota. These urban Indians differ from the Chippewa residing outside the reservation in the North Dakota novels, who have left both the reservation and their Native American identity behind. These Chippewa in *Gakahbekong* have formed their own community, and the Shawno, Whiteheart Beads, and Roy families function similarly to the Kashpaws, Nanapushes, Lamartines, and Morrisseys on the North Dakota reservations. They intermarry, they feud, they celebrate and mourn together, and *The Antelope Wife* is the story of their contemporary urban reservation.

These urban Indians are the product of the 1950s and the U.S. Government's effort to "terminate" Native Americans from federal support and protection. House Concurrent Resolution (HCR) 108 and Public Law (PL) 280 served as official notice of the government's abrogation of Indian stewardship and led to federal efforts to relocate Native Americans into the cities where better educational and employment opportunities existed. In 1954, the BIA established Relocation Branches in most of the major U.S. cities and were responsible for shepherding more than 30,000 Native Americans off their reservations and into nearby cities (Trigger and Washburn 242–43). Although the effort at first saw a majority of these relocated Indians returning to their home reservations due to an inability to adapt to city living, this marked the beginning of the migration off the reservations and into the nearby cities. Grandmother Zosie and Mary come from this older generation of tribal members born on the reservation, raised with communal values, speakers of the tribal language, and alternating living between their reservation and the city.

The second generation urban Indians may have been born on the reservation, but they are definitely at home in the city. This group still retains certain Indian values and orientation and prefers Indian communities, yet Arthur M. Harkins and Richard G. Woods in *Attitudes of Minneapolis Agency Personnel Toward Urban Indians* describes this group as a basically stable, employed, middle-class, married Chippewa population residing in Minneapolis (27–28). Richard Whiteheart Beads and Klaus Shawno both work for the first Native American Disposal Service in the United States and, until their drinking binge, live comfortably in the city. Rozin Whiteheart Beads is a teacher, and her lover Frank Shawno owns and runs his own bakery.

The third generation urban Indians (like Cally Whiteheart Beads and Cecille Shawno) represent a fairly assimilated group.

They were born and raised in Minneapolis, do not know the tribal language or culture, and have little contact with their home reservation. While Cally spends time on the reservation after her twin sister's death, both she and Cecille are acculturated Chippewas. Cally's stay on the reservation from her eleventh year to her eighteenth year fills in a cultural void that living in the city created. Even so, she is unfamiliar with many Chippewa traditions, and her grandmothers, unlike the traditional grandparents, only pass on stories and traditions when Cally presses them to do so. Cecille, on the other hand, has no desire to learn the stories, language, or traditions. She runs a Kung Fu studio, dyes her hair blond, and is an Indian only by heritage. Nevertheless, even for these assimilated Anishinaabeg, their Indian community centers their lives. They live in the same part of town and gather in a traditional manner for celebrations like Rozin and Frank's wedding. These communal occasions reinforce their Chippewa identity and culture and illustrate that living in the city is not a negation of traditional values but rather is only an adaptation to economic circumstances that have forced them away from their home reservations.

In *The Antelope Wife,* Erdrich completes the story of Chippewa people in the twentieth century. From the forming of the North Dakota reservation in the late 1800s to the exodus off the reservations and into the cities at the end of the 1900s, the story of the Chippewas is that of a people who survive despite disease, attempts of cultural and physical annihilation by the U.S. government, and the acculturation lure of the dominant Anglo culture. Erdrich's fictional stories of her Indian ancestors through the last century are her tribute to their adaptability and amazing powers to endure in a world that alternates between seeking their extermination to encasing them in a governmental bureaucratic web.

Vizenor writes in *The Everlasting Sky* that "Stories are the circle of believable dreams and oratorical gestures showing meaning between the present and the past in the lives of the people. The stories change as the people change because people, not facts, are the center of the Anishinabe world" (69). Erdrich is a contemporary-traditional storyteller who draws portraits in order to construct a living history, a record of her people in the last century. Stories of people and stories of significant tribal events, like winter counts, are fictionalized in her offering of Chippewa history and the history of immigrant families settling in North Dakota. Her technique includes her use of first person narrative derived from traditional autobiography, her rendering of tribal life through the voices of different community members, and her utilization of the traditional story cycle (stories centering around a central theme and pointing up particular people and events) to frame her various narrative voices. All these techniques are signs of cultural continuity. Her contemporary fiction signals a renewal of Indian values and ways of knowing as she transcends the old forms to render anew the story of her people.

CHAPTER 4

THE POWER OF LOVE AS MEDICINE:
LOUISE ERDRICH'S FAMILY STORIES

IN HER NORTH DAKOTA/MINNEAPOLIS NOVELS, Louise Erdrich writes out of and in to her Chippewa heritage. As a mixed-blood, she foregrounds her Indian heritage by appropriating it as the contextual base of her novels, and chapter 3 examines how she integrates traditional materials such as autobiography and story telling cycles. Another way she uses her Chippewa tradition is to emphasize families throughout the novels. Arnold Krupat, a prominent scholar of Native American literature, notes this importance of families in Indian culture and stories. Responding to Frederic Jameson's question of whether the majority of traditional stories of a third-world culture could contain a single dominant theme, Krupat suggests a tentative "yes." Kinship relations, he asserts, pervade all genres in tribal narratives (*Voice* 222–23).

Erdrich's novels reflect this tribal focus on kinship. Each book thematically revolves around families, and even in the off reservation North Dakota (*The Beet Queen* and *Tales of Burning Love*) and Minneapolis (*The Antelope Wife*) novels, the mixed-blood and Anglo characters principally concern themselves with the way in which people construct family units, albeit in non-traditional ways. The loss of tradition and culture fosters new adaptations to the basic human need to belong. Taken as a whole, each novel contributes a piece to a picture of Chippewa life during the last century. The format of interlocking novels allows Erdrich to accumulate layers of complexity by presenting conflicting versions of events and to span a wider view of contemporary Indian life. Although the novels can be read singly, when regarded as a series, the complex history of tribal families reveals its complicated pattern. The novels stand as Erdrich's composite version of the reality of her Indian people's lives, and, as such, the individual volumes accretionally impart the saga of the trials and triumphs of tribal families.

Erdrich's novels concern themselves with relationships within families and the specific traits that constitute each family's particular identity. Families are at the heart of the books, and an understanding of how they do or do not function and the implications of their stories on community life lies at the heart of Erdrich's work. While critics are quick to point out that *Love Medicine* revolves around family matters,[1] until Peter Beidler and Gay Barton's 1999 *A Reader's Guide to the Novels of Louise Erdrich* was published, no comprehensive study of families in the novels existed. This chapter will complement the Beidler and Barton study by considering the novels as Erdrich's rendering of family narratives through a discussion of both the specific meaning of family to Ojibwa people and the degree to which family stories lie at the heart of each book. A study of her family groupings and the touchstone stories and traits defining those families, as well as a reflection on the power of love as a thematic element, is the subject of this chapter.

Defining "Family"

As we know, families are complex and often contradictory entities; even so, they are the first way in which we perceive ourselves. As Renate Bridenthal notes, "Here is where we experienced our first emotions and ambivalences: love and hate, joy and pain, giving and taking" (225). To add to the inherent complexities of family life, since the 1960s the very configuration of families has undergone a tremendous transformation as a result of record numbers of working women, an alarmingly high divorce rate, and a subsequent increase in one-parent households. George Masnick and Mary Jo Bane in their classic study *The Nation's Families: 1960–1990* find that there is a "trend away from traditional households and toward more varied living arrangements" (11). What then constitutes a family? Since the "traditional" nuclear family of two parents and their children, a working father, and a mother who stays at home to raise her children is receding farther and farther into a nostalgic past, a new definition of the concept of family is emerging.[2]

In this respect, Masnick and Bane make a distinction between household and family, noting that a household is comprised of people living together who may or may not be related, whereas a family includes individuals related by blood ties or through marriage (11). Jane Howard eschews an exact definition by concentrating on the effect of binding relationships: "Call it a clan, call it a network, call it a tribe, call it a family. Whatever you call it, whoever you are, you need one. You need one because you are human" (260). Similarly, Howard maintains that people are often bonded together through chance or through "connections of choice," and that far from dying, families are, in fact, "changing their size and their shape and their purpose" (15). She further asserts that people have a need to maintain themselves in some type of a "family" unit, however conventional or unconventional it may be, because "The trouble we take to arrange ourselves in some semblance or other of families is one of the imperishable habits of the human race" (15).

The rapidly changing family unit has generated great consternation, countless articles, and chart-laden books by contemporary psychologists and sociologists, and the figures and tables quantified in the studies confirm new realities for the once sacred traditional American family. However, as Native American nuclear family units change in response to the problems of lack of employment opportunities on the reservations, substance abuse, and relocation off the reservation, the family units tend to rearrange themselves and not to dissolve, since the Indian definition of family is much broader than the one commonly used in academic studies. For Native Americans, family is bound with tribe and clan and therefore encompasses a larger nuclear unit than the Anglo family limited to close blood relations. Family, tribe, and community are synonymous. Krupat notes this fact: ("To live is to live familially, tribally" [*Voice* 230]), and so does Kenneth Lincoln: "To Indians tribe means family, not just bloodlines but extended family, clan, community, ceremonial exchanges with nature, and an animate regard for all creation as sensible and powerful" (8). Krupat additionally observes that in the best known Native American novels—*House Made of Dawn, Winter in the Blood, Ceremony,* and *Love Medicine*—the tribe is the family (*Voice* 231).

Erdrich's Use of Families in the Novels

Michael Dorris notes in an interview with Laura Coltelli that family connections have always been at the core of the Chippewa tribe; and in *Love Medicine* as well as *Tracks* and *The Bingo Palace*, Erdrich undertakes a conscious effort to make this book different from other Native American novels (45–46). This difference resides in an emphasis on families, their connections, and their history. Bill Moyers in an interview with Erdrich and Dorris astutely observes, "So many of your characters are bonded across time and space by ties of kinship and community. In fact, it's very hard to single them out as separate from their community or from their extended family" (Chavkins and Chavkins, *Conversations* 138). Moyers's comments go directly to the heart of the matter—Erdrich does choose to explore a different theme from other Native American novelists because her intent is to show families as the collective reality of the tribe. An individual's story then becomes a family story and thus a tribal story, as Erdrich in her novels links together the family chain of tribal being. The family in Erdrich's novels stands in synecdochic relationship to the tribe; the family is the tribe. Gerald Vizenor, ever the consummate wordsmith, speaks of "a communal discourse in a tribal narrative" (*Narrative Chance* 10), thus reflecting the sense of individual voices together relating a tribal story.

The Circular Narrative Structure of Erdrich's Family Stories

A family's story frames each novel, and the reverberations of its history upon the life of the community encompass the heart of each book. Erdrich draws upon the Indian notion of circularity to structure each book; thus, each novel begins and ends with the same characters or theme. Paula Gunn Allen explains, "The circular concept requires all 'points' that make up the sphere of being to have a significant identity and function, while the linear model assumes that some 'points' are more significant than others" (*Sacred* 7). This decidedly Native American way of focusing on the blending of all elements that make up the whole differs from stories of "key" moments in Euro-American literature. In Erdrich's novels, all points are equally significant, because they constitute the narrative threads from different tribal families, intermingling and writing the story of the tribe. These individual family stories become the

The Power of Love as Medicine

vehicle by which Erdrich mirrors the story of her people in the twentieth century.

Tracks opens and closes with Nanapush and Lulu. In the novel, Nanapush gives Lulu his last name in order to satisfy Father Damien's registry, thereby assuming the role of grandfather to a granddaughter who has hardened her heart against her mother, Fleur, who has sent her away to boarding school. *Tracks* is the story of Nanapush explaining her family history to Lulu in the tradition of the grandfather instructing the younger family members. At this point, she is a young woman who wishes to enter impetuously into marriage with a traditional family enemy, the Morrisseys, and Nanapush strives to create a larger tribal context for Lulu so that she can grasp the implications of her intended marriage. Since Nanapush's rendering of the story of her family is tied into the history of the tribe, he begins in 1912 when consumption has nearly decimated a tribe already ravaged by smallpox and war. He then explains to Lulu the events that led to her being sent away to boarding school, and he tries to make her understand that it was to assure Lulu's personal safety from revenging Lazarres and Morrisseys that Fleur allowed herself to be separated from her beloved daughter.

The novel ends with Nanapush and Lulu together, after she returns home to her tribe and to Nanapush who, in Fleur's absence, must now stand to defend and protect his granddaughter. The events after Lulu's return to her people are within her recent memory, but the events leading up to her being sent away are unknown to her. Thus, Nanapush and Pauline, as another viewpoint, relate tribal events that have had a profound impact on Lulu's life. Without her knowledge of the interconnectedness of the lives of the Puyats, Lazarres, Morrisseys, and Kashpaws, Lulu stands to make an inappropriate marriage. The story of *Tracks* begins and ends with a grandfather and his adopted granddaughter, and their individual story can only be understood within a larger tribal context.

The Beet Queen, the next novel chronologically, begins and ends with children and their mothers. It is the absence of a mother that drives Mary and Karl to Argus in hopes of finding a new family, since their mother Adelaide has flown away with the Great Omar and has abandoned her three children to fate. Subsequently, the plot in *The Beet Queen* centers around the effort to create a family unit, and Mary forges her own prickly bonds with her cousin Sita and her friend Celestine after her adored aunt Fritzie and her husband Pete retire and move away. Mary, always described as solid and practical, implants herself in Argus and in the Kozkas' life, so that her new home as a young girl remains her residence for the rest of her life. Karl, on the other hand, leads a peripatetic life until he, too, finally comes home to Argus to settle with his "family"—not his sister, not his wife and daughter, but his lover Wallace. As an adult, one is able to commit themselves to the relationships which are the most personally satisfying, and in Wallace, Karl finds the unconditional love and acceptance he has been seeking.

The novel begins and ends in Argus, and with the most essential of family relationships, that of a child and its mother. Mary, Karl, and their baby brother are abandoned by their biological mother at the beginning of the novel which nevertheless ends on a hopeful note with a reconciliation of a mother and daughter. Dot flies away in Tom B. Peske's airplane in order to escape the humiliation of the common knowledge that her "uncle" Wallace rigged her Beet Queen title. Noting the similarity of her action to that of her grandmother Adelaide, Dot initially flees her problems, yet she quietly returns to a mother who has patiently and lovingly waited. The ending thus constitutes a reversal of the childhood fates of Mary and Karl, who innocently waited for Adelaide, who did not return to them. Celestine is the mother who does not abandon her child, and Dot's recognition of the power of her mother's love makes her "want to lean into her the way wheat leans into the wind" (BQ 338), an image very close to the one that concludes *Tracks*. Lulu, returning home from boarding school, rushes into Nanapush and Margaret who brace themselves and hold on to each other in the fiercely blowing wind. In Erdrich's work, abandoned children find new homes and create new families, thus satisfying the most basic of human needs, to belong. While Mary and Karl find substitutes for Adelaide, the ending of *The Beet Queen* affirms that the relationship between a mother and her child is still the strongest and most enduring of all human ties.[3]

Love Medicine also begins with a mother who abandons her child, but its hopeful ending has the abandoned child Lipsha reconciled in spirit to his mother June and returning her spirit (in the

The Power of Love as Medicine

form of a car bought with her insurance money) home to her tribal community. June Morrissey Kashpaw is the principal character in *Love Medicine*, and the novel revolves around her familial relationships and the effect of her life and death on all those who loved her. She is a part of all of the reservation families portrayed in the novel except the Lamartines, so her death engenders a kind of communal dirge. Her mother Lucille is a Lazarre/Morrissey, and her father is a Morrissey. June is taken in by Marie, who is a Puyat, before June decides to seek the comforts of Eli Kashpaw's home. She marries Gordie Kashpaw and also has a child by Gerry Nanapush/Pillager. She remains an ephemeral character in life and in death, for no one person can penetrate her emotional defenses and hold her in a binding relationship.[4]

Even so, June is greatly beloved. Marie loves her with such a ferocious and protective passion that June runs away to the taciturn and undemonstrative Eli, who raises her as his own. Her husband Gordie starts drinking again when she dies, and in his drunken state he calls back her spirit, which returns to him in the form of a deer. Her niece Albertine loves her aunt June for spoiling her and treating her like an adult and for giving her the conscious attention she does not receive from her mother Zelda. Her lover Gerry escapes from prison and slips into her son King's house in order to be near someone who has a connection to June; and, most importantly, Lipsha, the dubious inheritor of "the touch," is told by his grandmother Lulu that June is his mother. This is the information he has been dreading to find out, for his "real" mother abandoned him and threw him into a slough to drown, and Lipsha calls Marie and Nector who raise him his true parents. However, Lulu gives Lipsha the true details of his early life and confirms his identity as the love child of June and Gerry, information which she acknowledges will either make or break him. The novel ends with Lipsha and the spirit of June returning home to the reservation where June was trying to go when she was caught in a Chinook. Mother and child have bonded over time and space, and her son lovingly brings June home to the reservation hearts who care for her in life and in death.

The Bingo Palace begins and ends with the communal voice, Erdrich's most direct indication that the well-being of the tribe is the primary concern of the novels. The communal voice, here represented by the tribal elders living at the Senior Citizens' home, is an omniscient presence. They see all; they comment on all; and they ponder the future for all. They move through Erdrich's roster of characters in this novel with a sweeping glance. They see Lulu running family and tribal business; they disdainfully acknowledge Lyman's role as a tribal bureaucrat; they mourn June's death; they worry for Albertine's headlong rush into life; they thankfully marvel at the sweetness and goodness of Shawnee Ray; they muse over Fleur and wonder at her attempts to pass on her powerful medicine; and they express disgust over Lipsha's wasted potential. These are the major characters in this novel, and Erdrich positions them immediately as vital links in the chain of tribal well-being.

The novel's central theme is the critical role of cultural continuity as indicated by the communal regard for its young people. This concern is more than just a bemused interest in their lives; the community is vitally connected to the lives of each of these young people, for they represent the tribal future and continuance. It is the mother's nurturing their children to be good tribal members that will insure a tomorrow. They say, "The red rope between the mother and her baby is the hope of our nation. It pulls, it sings, it snags, it feeds and holds. How it holds" (BP 6). Albertine and Shawnee Ray hold out hope for a strong tomorrow, while Lyman and Lipsha, the tribal nation's best and most promising males, are so wrapped up in themselves that they display little regard for communal well-being.

This final reservation novel ends in the same way that *Tracks*, the first reservation novel, begins, with Lulu and Fleur's story. Lulu is carried away by federal marshals, but her grandson Lipsha's joining with Shawnee Ray promises that the traditional Chippewa spiritual link will not be broken. Fleur returns to the sacred Pillager island in Lake Matchimanito where she is transformed into a still powerful protective spirit. The community sees all and knows all, and as their voice fades away, it is with the promise of a strong tomorrow for the Chippewa people.

Tales of Burning Love, like *The Beet Queen*, is set outside the North Dakota reservation in Argus and Fargo where people's families are less nuclear and more "connections of choice." *Tales of Burning Love* is the story of Jack Mauser's "family" of wives and their connections to each other. While he is the matrix around which the stories of his wives revolves, it is really their story of making Jack, the sentimental, hard-working, fast-talking, mixed-blood Chippewa mud engineer, into a responsible human being and faithful lover. Each wife evinces one of Jack's personality deficits and forces him to come face to face with his "pride, his too-lofty ambitions and misplaced energies" (139). Growing up in Argus with his German relatives, no father and a crazy mother living on the reservation, he eschews connections to people unless they can be useful to him. His "family" of wives changes all that.

June, his first wife, is the presence throughout the novel who haunts him. He has married her in a drunken and painful state (six teeth needing root canals) and then does not prevent or follow her as she walks into a raging spring snowstorm. This act of irresponsibility in 1981 with its attendant lingering guilt accelerates his need to love and to be loved, which propels him from one wife to the next. Eleanor, his second wife, brings out the tender side in both of them, and his faithfulness to her needs in and out of marriage is what finally settles him into his manhood. Candy, his third wife, connects him back to a respect for the animal world. They remeet (they had been sweethearts in high school) when he is preparing to shoot his dog. She rescues the dog and awakens his need to respect animal life as witnessed when he wounded a buck and went to extraordinary efforts to track it and put it out of its misery. Marlis, his fourth wife, is the mother of his son, John Joseph Mauser, whose birth stirs paternal instincts, love, and responsibility Jack heretofore has not experienced. She also teaches him humility. Thomas Matchie observes, "What distinguishes Marlis, however, is the direct way she responds. She treats Jack like none of the others: she not only tells him but shows him what he is like" (117). She graphically demonstrates to him what it is like to be a woman helplessly abused and abandoned by him. Again Matchie notes, her "method is unique" (118). She ties him up with duct tape, shaves his legs, plucks his eyebrows, pierces his ears, then leaves him. With the power she gains over him with this act and by depositing his large loan check from the bank into her own account, she forces him into much needed humility. Dot, his fifth wife, temporarily keeps his construction business alive with her business acumen and practical nature. She forces him to be sexually responsible by refusing to sleep with him unless he marries her, and she brings him to a realization that all his misspent love and passion were really a journey to connect him back to Eleanor. Erdrich ends this novel with a message about the enigmatic power of love: "We are conjured voiceless out of nothing and must return to an unknowing state. What happens in between is an uncontrolled dance, and what we ask for in love is not more than a momentary chance to get the steps right, to move in harmony until the music stops" (452).

Jack's "family" of wives allow him to grow spiritually and emotionally. The novel circles from Jack to each of his wives and then back to Jack, who is now redeemed by his declaration of faithful love to Eleanor. Jack had felt he "had come full circle at last" (14) by marrying Dot, who connected him back to Argus and to June, but it is ultimately June and her memory, which begin and conclude the novel, as well as Eleanor who open up Jack's heart and allow him to finally effectively connect to another human being.

The unlikely progenitor of one of the major families in *The Antelope Wife* is Private Scranton Theodorus Roy, a romantic Eastern Quaker. His actions in a "spectacular cruel raid upon an isolated Ojibwa village" (3) begin the human story which becomes the actualization of a mythic Anishinaabe tale. Excited by the chaos and blood letting of the raid, Roy participates in the butchery by bayoneting an old woman, thus setting in motion a chain of events which will link his story and his descendants with the people in the violated Ojibwa village. His adoption of the Indian child sent out of this ravaged village by its mother to an uncertain fate on the back of a dog begins a history that eventually merges the Roy, Shawno, and Whiteheart Bead families. Who could have predicted the power of atonement that drives Roy into not only adopting and raising the Indian child as his own but also finds the murdered old woman materializing as a manifestation of his guilt. Returning to the village to expiate his sin, Scranton brings beads and his grandson Augustus, who barters precious whiteheart red beads and all he has for the beautiful and bashful Zosie Shawno. Generations later, the descendant of Scranton Roy and Blue Prairie Woman, the woman who had sent her daughter to safety on the back of the dog a generation before, becomes the teller of the story. *The Antelope Wife* is the story of Chippewa who have left the reservations and ventured into "Gakahbekong,"[5] and their story is told through the new designated tribal storyteller, Cally Whiteheart Beads. Her

The Power of Love as Medicine

determination to give voice to her family's stories connects all members of this urban reservation, the Roys, the Shawnos, and the Whiteheart Beads. She is the recipient of the larger tribal stories, and her journey to unlock the secrets of the past from her mysterious grandmothers Zosie and Mary is the heart of this novel.

Cally is the surviving twin who struggles to reconstruct a new sense of family and meaningfulness once her sister dies and her nuclear family disintegrates, and she accomplishes this when she understands the pivotal role her human drama plays in her larger family and tribal history. Her tribal name, given in a dream to her grandmother Zosie by Blue Prairie Woman, is Blue Prairie Woman, the one who endures; this "name was old and exquisite and had belonged to many powerful mothers" (13). With this understanding of her role in the larger tribal and sacred story, Cally begins yet another reenactment of the mythic story with the need for the beads which will complete her narrative. Just as the mythic twins battle with each other, gamble all their possessions, and contemplate infanticide in order to retrieve prized whiteheart beads, so does Cally become possessed by the thought of possessing the blue beads for which Zosie had gambled the life of her twins. These beads, called northwest trader blue, symbolize the blueness of time and the human desire to hold it. As the amalgam of Roys, Shawnos, and Whiteheart Beads, Cally is the one who must tell the story, the one "sent here to understand and to report" (220). It is through her part in the reenactment of the mythic story of the twins risking all to possess the beads that Cally brings together all of the family stories in the novel. The beads she covets are possessed by Antelope Woman, her relative and another descendent of Blue Prairie Women. Just as the single beads represent the individual Anishinaabe who have been scattered and pulled away from the original design, so too does Cally represent the new beader who carries the tradition and the desire to sew the beads back into a new pattern found in the urban Chippewa community.

This bead motif that frames each section evolves from the mythic Anishinaabe story of the twin sisters, Matchikwewis and Oshkikwe, and their contest to find the exact bead which will complete their mythic design. Daughters of Nanabozho and Madjikiwis, a human woman, these sacred twins are central to Chippewa mythology. Sometimes they are twins, and sometimes Matchikwesis is a year older, but always they represent women's rituals, and their stories are used as example stories for young girls. Allen explains that Oshkikwe and Matchikwewis are the sacred beings in women's stories among the Chippewa/Ojibwa/Anishinaabe people. Women tell these stories for instruction in the ritual ways of woman and for spiritual development (*Spider Woman* 43). Matchikwewis resembles her father Nanabozho who is excitable, impulsive, curious, seductive, and volatile. Her changeable disposition and tendency towards violating interdictions can represent the darker side of ritual power. On the other hand, Oshkikwe, the younger one, is reserved, steadfast, and practical, and it is her stories that are more often associated with women's stories and rituals. Cally is not only an actor in the larger human story, which the mythic twins foreground, but she is also a representative of the powers these twins possess. Her story becomes the example story to the Chippewa of the ability of urban Indians to keep culture and tribal identity. She will be the one to pass on the stories and the traditions to the next generation, especially to those Ojibwa who find themselves struggling to construct an Indian identity and to retain family connections in an impersonal and heterogeneous urban environment.

Although *The Antelope Wife* relates Cally's role in unraveling and interpreting her family's secrets, she is but an echo of the traditional storyteller who opens and closes the novel with the sentence, "What happened to him [Stanton Roy] lives on, though fading in the larger memory, and I relate it here in order that it not be lost" (3) and "All that followed, all that happened, all is as I have told" (240). This storyteller frames her story by contextualizing it within the mythic story of the twins beading the story of our human lives. Their struggles for the "precise" bead that forms the "perfect" pattern becomes actuated in our human drama. This storytelling voice is notably different from the one Erdrich engages for *Tracks* and *The Bingo Palace*. In *Tracks*, Nanapush recounts for Lulu the story of her family in the traditional way grandparents pass on information and lessons to their grandchildren. *The Bingo Palace* is distinguished by the communal voice of the elders who interpret and comment on tribal people and events. However, in *The Antelope Wife*, the storyteller is a metanarrator, one who is non-human and all knowing of human, tribal, and mythic stories. The storyteller in *The Antelope Wife* beads the human and mythic stories into one intricate, complex, and delicate design. The effect of this powerful narration is to contextualize our human drama within a larger mythic story and to affirm the connectedness of history, ancestors, all sentient beings, stories, and time.

Touchstone Family Stories

Family stories, the foundation of the novels, affect the lives of tribal members, so that a collective history and a collective sense of being constructs tribal consciousness. The "touchstone" stories are those reverberating through time and thus forming the basis of tribal history. These are the important events in a storytelling cycle that Erdrich highlights as she relates the story of her people. Many of these stories echo throughout the North Dakota novels, thus registering the most significant moments of tribal life in the last century. A review of the touchstone family stories in the series serves as a recitation of major narrative threads.

Tracks provides the foundation for the North Dakota novels, and events in this novel set in motion actions and consequences that profoundly affect tribal life decades later. It is not always clear as to what actually happens in certain instances, since Erdrich cultivates narrative indeterminacy by carefully playing narrators and different versions of stories off of each other. She demands that the reader figure out the novel's complex chain of events by relating the relative versions of the truth. Hence, *Tracks* is narrated by two people whose stake in the truth propels them into a kind of messianic need to tell their story. As many articles point out, Nanapush is the traditional Chippewa trickster figure who serves as the carrier of traditions. His need is to tell the story of his people so that there will be a story to tell. With numerous kinspeople and tribal members fallen to the ravages of disease and starvation, Nanapush as a survivor feels he must be the bearer of the old traditions as the grandfather who passes on tribal stories to the younger generation.[6] He is emphatic in his need to tell the story, and as a respected tribal elder and healer, the reader wants very much to position him as the bearer of the truth. However, it must be remembered that Nanapush is the trickster figure and, as such, cannot be counted on to always tell the truth. Since Trickster is prone to lying and self-aggrandizing, Nanapush's words must always be listened to with caution.

Nanapush's mission is to save the story of the Chippewa people; in contrast, Pauline Puyat, who becomes Sister Leopolda, is on a different kind of mission. She wants to save the (not her) Chippewa people from their superstitious beliefs in the old Manitous and to bring Christ into their lives. She sees herself as Christ's agent among the Indians who must gather souls, and her ultimate mission is to subdue the lake spirit Misshepeshu with the cross of Christ. She is a religious fanatic whose words must always be questioned. The reader never catches Nanapush in a lie, but Pauline tells obvious lies. For example, she tells Bernadette Morrissey that she has returned to the reservation from Argus because Regina beat her; she tells the nuns at the convent that she does not have any Indian blood; and she denies the power of the Pillager look to harm people. She is responsible for the death of four people, Lily, Tor, Fleur's baby, and Napoleon; she tries to abort her baby, and when unsuccessful, she attempts to prevent its birth and suffocate it in the birth canal. In addition, there are countless others she infects with germs from the dead, because she does not wash after she leaves the death houses.

The truth of events lies somewhere in between the versions of these two narrators, and it is only on a few matters specifically relating to Fleur that they both agree. Nanapush and Pauline both mention that Fleur has "died" three separate times by drowning, that Fleur enters the lake in the winter, that Fleur curses Boy Lazarre, and that Fleur is the source of great power. In addition, each narrator accurately characterizes the other, Pauline stressing how much Nanapush loves to talk while Nanapush proclaims that once Pauline opens her mouth, she cannot contain her words. These facts the reader can be fairly sure are truthfully told.

The other touchstone stories in *Tracks* are offered to the reader with varying versions of the truth, and all that is certain is that they profoundly affect the lives of the people. Fleur goes to Argus and comes back after a devastating tornado with a black umbrella (Fritzie's gift) and money to pay every Pillager allotment; she may also be pregnant. Once she returns, the spirits become restless, as if to acknowledge the presence of her power once again. Pauline focuses her mission to Christianize the Chippewas by testing her

THE POWER OF LOVE AS MEDICINE

powers against those of Fleur, and almost all of the Puyat's actions can be seen as a direct challenge to Fleur's traditional skills. It is through Pauline's pitting her power against Fleur that the Morrissey/Lazarre and Pillager/Nanapush/Kashpaw feud begins. Pauline's jealousy of Fleur's intimate relationship with Eli causes Pauline such pain that she approaches Eli and makes herself available to him. His disdainful rejection of Pauline sets in motion a chain of events that ends up dividing the tribe. Pauline seeks revenge on Eli and Fleur and sets up a gullible Sophie to offer herself to Eli. After the seduction, the Morrissey family, already in collusion with the Lazarres to sell allotments to the Turcot Lumber Company, takes revenge by raping Margaret Kashpaw and cutting off her braid and by tying up Nanapush so he is forced to helplessly watch. Nanapush and Fleur work their revenge, and so the tribe clashes against one other, weakened by the lure of money and a fanatical nun who stands against traditional Chippewa families and cultural values.

Two other stories continue to reverberate through the North Dakota novels, and both of them revolve around Fleur. She is pregnant with Eli's child and lifts large tin kerosene cans of water to wash the filthy Pauline, causing her to begin to miscarry. Pauline's ineptness, fear, and secret fascination and delight at Fleur's pain results in the baby's death, and Fleur goes on the death road and returns only when the dead threaten Lulu's life. Margaret saves Fleur, but the baby is lost and buried in Lulu's shoe box high in old oak trees. The final touchstone story in *Tracks* comes about as the result of Pauline's scheming, the Kashpaws' vested self-interests, and the Métis' positioning themselves to buy up any allotment of the full-bloods available due to unpaid taxes. The Turcot Lumber Company moves on to Fleur's land when Nector and Margaret pay Kashpaw fees and back fines only and leave Nanapush and Pillager fees unpaid, leaving their lands available to the public at large and to the lumber company specifically. Fleur unsuccessfully tries to drown herself when she finds out this news, and when she fails, she exacts her revenge by cutting through the base of the trees around her cabin. A strong wind traps the encroaching men, horses, and wagons from the lumber company in a barrage of trees. This is Fleur's final assertion of her power before she leaves the reservation, and she trudges off in a cart with her most sacred possessions in order to gather once again the necessary money to buy back Pillager land.

The next novel chronologically, *The Beet Queen*, weaves together the lives of the Anglos in the neighboring town with some of the reservation people. One of the first encounters between them occurs when Fleur, peddling to farmers and Métis families, rescues Karl from the embankment where he has landed after jumping from the train. Fleur cures his pneumonia, mends his broken feet, and deposits him at a place of safety, the convent on the reservation. Russell, Eli, and Fleur populate the largely Anglo world of *The Beet Queen*, and the stories of the people of the region continually impinge upon each other.

The Beet Queen reads like the history of many small rural towns in the twentieth century that experienced tremendous growth as the result of a local industry. The story features six different narrators, Mary, Sita, Karl, Celestine, Wallace, and Dot, whose stories cover the years from 1929 through 1972. Their different voices are those of disenfranchised souls populating a small town on the vast North Dakota Plains, and it is their longing to form a family unit that brings them all together. Sita and Mary are cousins; Karl and Celestine are nominally husband and wife; Karl and Wallace are lovers; and Wallace and Mary are devoted to Dot. It is a strange and highly unconventional arrangement, but it satisfies the most basic longing of its members, that of belonging to someone or to someones.

The touchstone stories of this "family" comprise the heart of the novel. First, and most importantly, is the story of Adelaide flying off with the Great Omar. This act results in Karl and Mary's coming to Argus on the freight train, Karl's subsequent flight, and Mary's subsequent planting of her roots in Argus. The next important story concerns the manifestation at Argus, when Mary zooms down a frozen slide only to crash her head into the ice below. The nuns, especially Sister Leopolda, see the face of Christ in the ice, and the playground becomes a shrine until the ice melts. Another touchstone story revolves around The Beet Festival, the extravaganza created by Wallace Pfef to celebrate his town's new growth and to show his love for his adopted niece Dot by making her the Beet Queen. All of the "family" assembles for this major event; and at its conclusion, the members arrange themselves according to where they wish to be (or not) in a relationship. Dot is with her mother Celestine, and Karl returns to Wallace. Mary is alone, and Sita has just killed herself with an overdose of pills. This unconventional grouping of people have come together by chance and by choice, and the different "family" voices relate the story of their entangled lives.

While Erdrich narrates *The Beet Queen* in a more linear way than *Tracks* or *Love Medicine*, the storyline is picked up, dropped, and taken up again by the various narrators. Still, she makes it easier on readers who do not have to struggle to grasp the most significant stories in the lives of this oddly merged family. She accomplishes this by signaling to the reader that something crucial happens in the life of a character when the title of the chapter is their name and "night." This occurs on six different occasions, and the voice is always in the third person, as if to put the reader on notice that what is being told is important and that Erdrich as author will tell you directly what has happened to this character.

"Karl's Night" recounts his first homosexual encounter, just as "Wallace's Night" does his first. "Mary's Night" brings an unwanted reminder to Mary of her mother Adelaide who has sent her a sewing machine. Mary retreats to the occult to escape this painful memory, and she wills a sign that comes in the picture of Celestine's unborn baby, Mary's niece Dot. "Russell's Night" depicts a great Indian warrior and United States Veteran as he succumbs to wounds from two different wars with a stroke that paralyzes his broken body. "Sita's Night" finds her in a state mental hospital where she has been placed because of her insistence that she is no longer able to speak. Sita has always needed to live as the center of attention, and whenever she is thwarted, as happened when Mary came into the Kozka family, she resorts to cruel or unusual behavior. Her muteness is another in a long line of attention getters, but this time her patient and long suffering second husband Louis Tappe commits her to a place where attendants do not tolerate any of Sita's vapid attempts at muteness. Sita finds her voice and rekindles her fragile hold on reality.

"Celestine's Night" conveys her deep and abiding love for her baby Dot, when one night after Dot finishes nursing and is sleeping heavily in her mother's arms, a tiny white spider spins its nest in Dot's hair. "A web was forming, a complicated house, that Celestine could not bring herself to destroy" (BQ 176). Erdrich discloses that this image is the heart of the book,[7] and the inviolable maternal bond, along with the strong ties Mary and Wallace form to Dot and the love Karl finds with Wallace, acknowledges the enduring human need and capacity to care for another.

Love Medicine, the first published novel in the series, began as a collection of short stories about reservation families which Dorris helped Erdrich shape into a novel. This volume offers the clearest sense of community in the reservation novels, since it contains the largest cast of characters. Three characters from *Tracks*, Lulu, Marie, and Nector, are adults and are now raising their own children. Nanapush is dead, and Fleur and Sister Leopolda are now the old ones. The lives of the Kashpaws, Lamartines, Morrisseys, Lazarres, Puyats, and Pillager/Nanapush have become so entwined and interrelated that they are truly one big tribal family bound, not only by tradition, but also by blood connections. Therefore, the touchstone family stories in *Love Medicine* thread through and impact the lives of the novel's major characters.

Obliquely referring to the alarmingly high mortality rate for Indians, Erdrich shows death affecting the lives of everyone in this related community. Erdrich emphasizes death as an occasion to remember loved ones and to reflect upon their impact in one's own life, and the majority of the touchstone family stories in *Love Medicine* revolve around death or a near death. These are the stories that cannot be put to rest as long as the dead drift through the talk, the thoughts, and the dreams of the family. June never had much of a chance in life, and by the time she dies in the Easter blizzard, she has been near death on two other occasions. Left to fend for herself when her alcoholic mother Lucille dies in a remote part of the reservation, June survives on pine sap. She learns to live in the woods, and a part of her never loses this wild and untamed spirit. When she comes to Marie, she is a scared, scrawny, starved, and stubborn survivor. So when Marie's children Gordie, Aurelia, and Zelda pretend to hang June in a childhood game, June chooses to use the occasion to end her short and pitiful life and becomes enraged at Marie who saves her. June walks into the Easter blizzard with the same sense of defiance of life and fearlessness of death, demonstrating that she is willing to accept the force that prevails, just as she has done on previous occasions. Death claims her, but her life lives in the memory of her niece Albertine, Marie, her husband Gordie, her lover Gerry, and especially her son Lipsha. In fact,

June has such an impact on all their lives that the stories of these other characters can only be told in relationship to June.

June's brushes with death cause her to be careless of its power, and she flings her newborn love child into a slough in a sack filled with rocks to assure its certain death. This incident is narrated by so many different people and from so many different points of view in *Love Medicine* and in *The Bingo Palace* that the reader is never quite sure of the details. Lipsha has his own truth, since he was the child sent to die in the cold muddy waters, as does Zelda who says she rescued him, Marie who takes him in, and Lulu whose son is Lipsha's father.[8] June never denies or confirms the story, repeating Erdrich's narrative strategy throughout the novels regarding most matters of utmost importance. It is left once again to the reader to move through the maze of events and come to a sense of the truth. As always, though, Erdrich tips the scales in one direction. June makes the dangerous trip back to the living immediately after Zelda has emphatically declared Lipsha was deliberately meant to die at his mother's hands. June's action suggests that Lulu's theory that June was just upset and didn't know what to do with this baby is nearer to the truth. In any event, Lipsha satisfies himself that June abandoned him instead of trying to murder him, and what actually happened that day becomes relative to each narrator's stake in the matter.

Lipsha, according to Zelda, was under the water for twenty to thirty minutes and still did not drown. There are at least two explanations of this incident—either the story is not true or Lipsha was safeguarded by the water monster Misshepeshu, who protected his great grandmother Fleur when she tried unsuccessfully to kill herself in the lake. The Pillagers are said to have brought the water monster with them when they left the Leech Lake area to move on to the Plains, and their special relationship with this powerful Manitou prevents death by drowning, a death especially feared by the Chippewa, since the spirit of a drowned person can never be at peace.[9] Lipsha's near drowning and Fleur's near drownings are family, cultural, tribal, and mythic stories that continue to assert themselves throughout the North Dakota novels.

Not protected by the water Manitous, Henry Lamartine, Jr., meets a tragic death. Not as lucky as his brother Lyman, he is called to duty during the Vietnam war. Tom Holm insists that during

Vietnam, Native Americans tended to draw the worst battle assignments, which led to a high proportion of Indians being killed or wounded (3). Henry becomes a wartime casualty, but not until he returns home. He sees nine months of combat before the Viet Cong capture and imprison him for six months. Afterward, the war never stops for him, and when he is released, he has lost his interest in life. He ends his life by allowing himself to be sucked into the current of the Red River while his shocked brother Lyman helplessly watches. Henry's horrifying death has a great impact on Lyman and Lulu especially, and because of its terrible implications, it is a story that resounds throughout *Love Medicine* and *The Bingo Palace*, just as the death/suicide of Henry Sr. is a Lamartine family story that continues to assert itself throughout the years.

Lulu is a major character in three of the novels, *Tracks*, *Love Medicine*, and *The Bingo Palace*, and several key events in her life stand as touchstone stories. In *Love Medicine* she remembers back to when she was a little girl and found the body of a dead man in the woods. This echoes a story from *Tracks* when Pauline strangles Napoleon Morrissey with her rosary beads, deluded with the idea that she is killing the water monster. She then flings beads into the brush (which June finds) and drags the body into the woods (which Lulu finds). Another memorable event in Lulu's life occurs when Nector burns down her house. His chronic indecision renders him incapable of deciding whether to stay with Marie and his family or go to Lulu, for whom he has had a passionate attachment for years. He decides in favor of Lulu and writes both a note. While waiting for Lulu to return home, he drops a half lit cigarette onto Lulu's crumpled up note and watches impassively as her house begins to burn after the fire reaches nearby gasoline cans. This incident is typical of Nector, and it is only when Zelda rescues him and brings him home that he is saved from the fire.

Nector, Lulu, Marie, and Lipsha are the major characters in the last important family story in *Love Medicine*. Nector in his old age reverts back to a second childhood. Since he never fought for anything in his life and always took what he wanted and left the consequences to others, it is not surprising that in his old age his mind simply slips away into a nether world in which he does not have to think or to account for himself. When he sees Lulu in the Senior Citizens' home, he characteristically rekindles his hankering for her, much to Marie's distress and embarrassment. Lipsha, who has the touch, takes a short cut to providing a love medicine for Marie and Nector that ends up causing Nector's death. Lipsha's failed medicine, his indirect responsibility for his grandfather's death, and his lack of patience to use his gifts wisely are noted and discussed by the community.

The Bingo Palace resumes Lipsha's story and the community's disgust with his wasted potential. This novel recounts many of the touchstone stories with "one story hinging into the next" (BP 48): June's death, Lipsha being found in the slough, Lulu finding Napoleon's body in the woods, Nector burning down Lulu's house, Lipsha's failed medicine, Henry's drowning, Fleur's three drownings and her being brought back to life when others take her place on the death road. The novel offers its own significant stories to be added to the composite story of the Plains Chippewa people. Lulu's story as the traditional elder who fights for treaty rights and promotes cultural values begins in *Love Medicine* with her role in returning the buffalo to the reservation and in helping to bring down the BIA factory erected on Lamartine property which produce tourists' trinkets. In *The Bingo Palace*, she fights to return the reservation to its original size; she consistently wins at bingo; and she defies federal marshals who haul her to prison for allegedly helping her son Gerry escape from prison. Previously she has not utilized her Pillager powers except to win at bingo and to glare the dreaded witch's glare at those who displease her. Now, she carries on Pillager powers in a different way by being a political activist and promoter of traditional values. The medicine powers pass through her to her grandson Lipsha who inherits the Pillager gifts from his doubly blessed father Gerry, who has Pillager blood from both his mother and his father's side. This story in *The Bingo Palace* is of primary importance to the tribe, which is why the community narrates that part of it which concerns the identity of Fleur's successor.

Essentially, *The Bingo Palace* is Lipsha's story, since he is the one who will carry on the sacred powers, but in different ways. Because Fleur has not trained him, or anyone else, his gifts have to be honed in his own style. For this reason, Lipsha's coming into his powers and sense of tribal responsibilities provide the touchstone stories of the novel. He comes home to the reservation, leaving his job working in a Fargo beet factory. Lulu has called him back, and Lipsha returns to try and find his place in the tribe. His mother June's spirit appears to give him winning bingo tickets. He goes on a vision quest and is visited by a skunk who reminds him of the sacredness of the Pillager property that Lyman has scheduled to be the site of the new tribal bingo hall. Finally, Lipsha goes to Fargo to pick up his dad who is evading federal officers. He steals a car with a baby in it (Jack Mauser's son) and drives Gerry to freedom and to a rendezvous with June, while Fleur saves Lipsha for a future that promises to have Shawnee Ray with him.

Even though *The Bingo Palace* is primarily Lipsha's story, it is nevertheless the story of the community and its respective families, and Erdrich again helps out the reader as she did in *The Beet Queen* by using chapter titles to signal events of grave importance to particular characters. In *The Beet Queen* she uses the word "night" and the character's name. Apparently pleased with the technique, she develops a variation of it. In keeping with the theme of gambling in *The Bingo Palace*, readers need to pay close attention to the word "luck" in a title merged with a character's name. These stories, like the comparable ones in *The Beet Queen*, are all narrated in the third person and relate deciding moments in the lives of major characters in the North Dakota novels. Most of the stories emphasize not good luck at all but rather luck's absence, an indirect commenting upon the whole gambling situation on reservations, a luck/luckless phenomenon for tribes. It is only for Shawnee, whose goodness and sincere respect for the Manitous protects her, and Fleur, a gifted Pillager gambler, that any true luck emerges.

Lipsha loses possession of Nector's pipe at the Canadian border when guards suspect him of possessing a drug pipe. "Lipsha's Luck" is to see the Kashpaw sacred pipe handled carelessly by the first non-Indian to touch it. For Lipsha, this is a moment of intense awareness of how much his cultural traditions mean to him. "So many things would happen in the next months, soon after, that Lipsha wouldn't have time to take in or understand. But always, he could think back to that action, which seemed to happen slowly and to last for timeless moments" (BP 34).

A comparably awful moment in June's dismal childhood is recounted "June's Luck." Her mother Lucille, who has few sober moments, saves her affection for June's brother Geezhig and her boyfriend Leonard. Geezhig, feeling some responsibility towards

June, urges her to slip away once Leonard and Lucille begin their lovemaking. However, Lucille in a lucid moment notices June's departure and is enraged. Lucille finds the luckless June, physically abuses her and ties her up, leaving her an easy victim for Leonard's sexual abuse. June, seven or eight at the time, vows to herself that no one will ever hold her again, and, as an adult, is unable to ever trust or completely love anyone.

Lyman, now in possession of the Kashpaw sacred pipe, loses it when he pawns it for money in a night of frenzied gambling delusions about his inherent "luck." The lure of easy money seduces even Lyman, who has an entrepreneur's gift of making money. Dejected and beaten, Lyman considers ending his life by jumping into a river, as his brother Henry did. However, the Truckee River near Las Vegas is so shallow that the attempted drowning only results in a pitiful attempt at solving his problems, and Lyman remains alive to ponder the implications of his luckless night.

In contrast, Shawnee Ray is a woman on the verge of taking over control of her life. Her luck is that she has the strength to sever her stifling ties with Zelda Kashpaw, to visit her no-account sisters whom Zelda loathes, to try for prize money in the women's division in a large Montana memorial powwow, and to admit her love for Lipsha. The community knows that she is one of the bright hopes of the tribe's future, and Shawnee's Ray "luck" is to begin moving onto the path that will see her realize her full potential.

Her inherited Pillager gifts account for Fleur's luck. She returns to the reservation for the fourth time to once again reclaim Pillager land. Each time she leaves the reservation, it is to earn money so that she can regain the sacred lands of her Pillager ancestors; and she always gets what she wants. She "had studied the situation and kept track of time, calculated justice, assessed possibilities" (BP 143). Her lands are now in the possession of the former Indian agent Jewett Parker Tatro, and she lures him into a game of cards by baiting him with the promise of her Pierce Arrow car and by bringing a spirit child who serves as the dealer. One of the distinctive characteristics of the Pillagers is that their hands "are strong and knotted, big, spidery and rough, with sensitive fingertips good at dealing cards" (T 31), and the child who sits down to play cards with Nanapush, Fleur, and Agent Tatro has long fingers "strong, spidery, and rough" (BP 144). He is a manifestation of a Pillager with all the family's power, and she regains her lands and more, for "Fleur was never one to take an uncalculated piece of revenge. She was never one to answer injustice with a fair exchange. She gave back twofold" (BP 145). The agent never has a chance, and Fleur's premeditated plan constitutes not as much luck as intentional use of her powers. "Fleur's Luck" consists of her gambling gifts and powerful medicine that combine to return Pillager lands back to the rightful owners.

Redford has inherited some of the Pillagers' intuitive powers through his grandmother Lulu, for he senses that his visit with Mary Fred, his mother's sister, is about to come to a disastrous conclusion. His "luck" is to correctly portend the chain of events set in motion by Zelda and Lyman, who enlist the tribal policeman Leo Pukwan and a social worker Vicki Koob to legally dislodge Redford from his Toose relatives. Redford is the victim of adult interference in his life and in his mother's life, and as a child he cannot resist the stronger adult forces but only let out "a great rattling scream" (BP 179).

On returning home for a visit, Albertine finds Zelda lavishing her attention and affection on Redford and exerting her strangling hold on Redford's mother Shawnee. Albertine as an adult realizes her mother's inability to trust herself to love those closest to her, for Zelda never wanted to give in to the uncertainties of love after witnessing her father Nector's vacillating passion for Lulu and dutiful love for her mother Marie. Still, Albertine as an adult has great need for her mother's love, but Zelda keeps her at a "careful and mutually calibrated distance" (BP 208). Albertine's "luck" is the double-edged sword that is her relationship with her mother. Albertine may not ever feel the comfort she wants from her mother's love (that is left for her to derive through her work as a medical healer), but she is able to jolt her mother into a recognition that Zelda has once loved deeply and that the flames of that love are not completely extinguished. "Albertine's Luck" thus ushers in "Zelda's Luck," for Zelda's brush with death due to her heart attack propels her into an ability to finally accept her love for Xavier Toose and to go to him with no object in mind other than to give in to her feelings. Zelda has never allowed herself to let her heart rule her head, and her "luck" of a near fatal heart problem allows her to thaw one icy portion in her heart.

The Power of Love as Medicine

Gerry's Pillager blood allows him continually to escape harm's way. He may not be able to stay out of prison, but unquestionably he is capable of escaping from any man-made facility. Lulu's machinations have resulted in his transfer to a prison in Minnesota, and when the plane on which he is riding crashes and kills the pilot and the guard, Gerry the trickster once again escapes to freedom. His Pillager intuition has told him "his luck is coming back, floating down on him like a nylon net to drag him to the top" (BP 225). His luck prevents his death in the airplane crash and affords him some time of freedom with his family. Thus, Erdrich signals stories which constitute pivotal moments in her characters' lives through the word "luck." These and other family stories are the events most profoundly affecting the tribe and its future.

Tales of Burning Love is significant for the large number of characters Erdrich brings together from the other novels. While the story revolves around the descendants of European immigrants who live in towns in proximity to the reservation, it is primarily the story of two mixed-blood Chippewas, Jack and Dot. Jack is a descendent of "the old strain" (28), and Dot is a Kashpaw married to a Nanapush. The novel is the tale of Jack's wives, and the foremost narrative voice in the group of wives is that of Dot. Jack and Dot's connections to the reservation families and their stories is what establishes the novel as a part of the North Dakota series, and the connecting threads of narratives weave from *Love Medicine* all the way through to *Tales of Burning Love*.

The novel opens with June's story of being lost in an Easter Chinook, a touchstone story that continues its haunting presence throughout the series.[10] The lives of Dot and June intertwine not only as Jack's first and fifth wives but also as the lover/wife to Gerry and the mother of his child. Jack leaves his son in an idling car outside the train station. Lipsha, June's son, steals this vehicle in order to spirit away his father Gerry who has miraculously escaped dying in a plane which crashed transporting him from one prison to another, Lulu's doings (BP). Gerry fights his way through a blizzard (aided by June) in order to be reunited with his wife Dot and daughter Shawn, characters in *The Beet Queen* and *Love Medicine*.

Other characters from the previous novels emerge from the background to play leading roles in the lives of Jack and his five wives, reinforcing the idea of complementary novels revolving around a group of people, Native American and Anglo, who occupy a special geographical region. Father Jude, Mary and Karl Adare's abandoned baby brother from *The Beet Queen*, is now a visiting priest at Our Lady of the Wheat Convent in Argus where Sister Leopolda at 108 years of age is ending her days. Eleanor is consumed with her research project on Leopolda's major life events, which include Marie's story of the stigmata in *Love Medicine* and Mary's story of the Manifestation at Argus in *The Beet Queen*.[11] And Lyman, the entrepreneurial Kashpaw from *Love Medicine* and *The Bingo Palace* comes to Jack's funeral to pay his respects, to see if Jack is really dead, and to tell his sister-in-law Dot that Gerry has escaped. Lyman ultimately emerges as Jack's savior, for in rescuing Jack from bankruptcy and jail by giving him the contract to build the casino on the reservation, Lyman secures a lucrative deal for himself and ensures that the project, which required an enrolled Chippewa as general contractor, will be started. Additionally, the novel is still very much about the land, and Jack's work as a contractor exemplifies how this particular area in North Dakota is being transformed from croplands and fields of sunflowers to mobile home parks, housing developments, fast food strips, and farm implement and grain stores.

While fragments from the other novels weave in and out of *Tales of Burning Love*, the special touchstone stories of Jack and his "family" of wives exemplify the awesome and formidable power of love, the major theme of all the novels. Erdrich plays with the symbolism of love—love as passion, fire, flames, candles, a red slip and then contrasts this "tale of burning love" to its antithesis, lack of fire, coldness, blizzard. It is as if in this novel she is answering Robert Frost's implied question of whether or not the world will end in fire or in ice, for "For what I have tasted of desire/I hold with those who favor fire" ("Fire and Ice"). It is passion which inflames her characters, and the novel weaves one tale of burning love to the next. "Love—which the young expect, the middle-aged fear or wrestle with or find unbearable or clutch to death—those content in their age, finally, cherish with pained gratitude" (448).[12]

Eleanor grows up with love's power to cherish and to banish through blinding jealousy. As she says, "All of our love stories begin with our mothers" (209). When Eleanor is six years old, her mother defies death by affecting a daring leap from an adjacent tree to Eleanor's second story bedroom window, an acrobatic act of faith honed by her years on the trapeze with the Flying Kuklenskis. Anna Schlick rescues Eleanor from a burning home, an event that leaves her daughter in awe of love's power and which leaves her searching to replicate this passion in her life. Even so, Eleanor also feels love's shadow, jealousy born out of passion, for in a furious rage, her father temporarily banishes both her and her mother from their home. It is finally in her love for Jack that she is able to replicate a passion that controls and ultimately fulfills her life. "This love for Jack [which] was still alive, disguised as everything. It ached pulled from the ground, it drew the air from her chest, sat on her head like bricks, closed across her lips like the wings of a moth" (83). She learns this power to love from her mother and from her father, who at his wife's death, lovingly prepares her for cremation and then at the last moment, joins her in the consuming fire. His passion for his wife is his life, and to die with her is preferable to living without her. Eleanor inherits both the passion and the rage, but, like her father, it is the love that triumphs in the end.

Jack's third and fourth wives, Candy and Marlis, enter adulthood unceremoniously, without passion, without love. Candice is committed to her dental practice, and Marlis has learned to get by however she can, which includes living off of accident payments and living under her sister-in-law's trailer. "Candice Pantamounty, D.D.S., kept herself in hard focus no matter what the circumstances" (121), an unlikely candidate for consuming passion, yet passion takes hold of her with a fury in an unlikely object of her love, the manic-depressive blackjack dealer Marlis, mother of Jack's only child, Jack Joseph Mauser. Candice's perforated uterus, which rendered her sterile, has closed the door of motherhood to her. Even so, the maternal instinct remains strong, is transferred to her animals, and eventually finds a resting place in Jack Jr. and Marlis. Candice cares for Marlis during the pregnancy, supports the baby, moves them in with her to care for them, and is soon swept away by the power of her love for Marlis. Marlis in turn, always flexible to arrangements which provide for her, grows to return Candice's affection and to want to share not only her life with her but also her son. Erdrich in all her novels explores the many facets of love, and the satisfaction and joy Candice and Marlis find with each other reveals another dimension to the mysterious and the inexplicable power of love.

Dot Adare Nanapush Mauser is Jack's fifth wife and his most formidable opponent. He is fond of her rather than loving her, and she in turn has not divorced her first husband Gerry when she marries Jack. Dot's love is reserved for Gerry. "Love is what I feel for Gerry Nanapush. A lost cause. Burnt hope. But it's something. It's all I've got" (416). Her marriage to Jack is convenience, not passion, affection, not love. She loves Gerry, their daughter Shawn, and her mother Celestine, to whom she is finally able to express her love after her mother's vigil when Dot lay locked in a deep sleep in the hospital after her rescue from the blizzard. It is Celestine's steadfast and abiding love for her daughter that gives Dot her strength of character and her power for enduring passion for a husband whom she sees only when he breaks out of jail and finds his way home.

Jack, the erstwhile husband of five, is sentimental, tender, wayward, and unfaithful. The impact of his brief marriage to June leaves him emotionally unstable and riddled with guilt for not trying to follow her into the blizzard and rescue her. In atonement for this lapse in action and integrity, he bounces from one relationship to the next, always seeking to fill the hole made by June's death and his indirect role in it. With Eleanor he finds passion, with Candice he is content, with Marlis he is able to live his dream and express himself, and with Dot he is able to experience practicality and toughness, and he regards her more as a business partner than a wife. Even so, he can never be faithful to any of the women he loves. It is only when he earns his manhood that Jack finally experiences the joy made possible through selfless and devoted love. Fatherhood awakens these nascent qualities, and when the stone virgin falls on him in the convent garden, he recognizes in her face the face of all of the women who have loved him. It is the strength of their combined love which fills him with wonder and allows him to float into the soft ground beneath him in a state of awe and gratitude and to escape death. This profound awareness of the power of love leads him back to Eleanor, for each new relationship after her frightened him with its newness and its potential for failure. It was only with Eleanor that he felt truly comfortable, "For him, Eleanor was all history, all knowledge" (40). Finally, he is able to acknowledge "the depth of what he felt about Eleanor [as it] broke in upon Jack with such heat that he shuddered, and then melted right through" (452). Sister Leopolda, whose life story is being written by Eleanor, has spoken of love as pure salvation, of her prayer as "a tale of burning love" (53). Her words resonate for Eleanor and Jack who finally accept themselves, each other, and the mysterious power of love that ultimately brings them together.

The Antelope Wife is distinguished from Erdrich's other novels not only by its predominantly urban setting in Minneapolis but also by lack of connection to the families and events chronicled in the five North Dakota novels. *The Antelope Wife* relates the stories of the Roys, Shawnos, and Whiteheart Beads and the ways in which their lives are interwoven and connected as in a vast and intricate beaded design. "Pull one string of this family and the whole web will tremble" (239). Therefore, the touchstone stories for one family influence and shape the stories of all families.

The story of the Roys provides the framework for the book, and they are not only the descendants of the Antelope People but also the family most closely connected to the dog helpers. It is this family's stories that link together all the characters in the novel as a connecting thread binds together individual beads. What happens to Augustus Roy and who is Cally's grandmother are major refrains played throughout the novel. Additional narrative threads include how the Roy women possess and pass down traditional powers and how Cally becomes both the rightful heir of the power and the one who finally uncovers the fate of her grandfather and the identity of her grandmother.

The touchstone stories of the Shawnos and Whiteheart Beads all connect through Cally, whose mother Rozin is a Shawno-Roy and whose father Richard is a Whiteheart Beads. Rozin is the first Roy storyteller in the novel, and her journey through pain and her transformation by Frank's love is one of the important stories in the novel. Death is her ubiquitous attendant. Only her mothers Zosie and Mary survive a flu epidemic that wipes out their entire family, and her twin sister Aurora dies of diphtheria at five years of age. Her own daughter, Cally's twin sister Deanna, dies a tragic death by asphyxiation at eleven as she attempts to prevent her father from leaving home. It is this death that totally debilitates Rozin and sends her "shrinking into the wall of grief" (85). When Richard, her ex-husband, attempts suicide at her wedding and finally succeeds in killing himself in Rozin and Frank's honeymoon suite, Rozin's retreat from the world makes her a vulnerable victim for the Original Shawno, a Windigo. However, it is love that saves her and love that transforms her, the foremost narrative thread in all of Erdrich's novels. Her love for her daughter Cally and the security she is able to accept in Frank's caregiving restores Rozin to a place of power, reconfigured in contemporary times as she studies for her law degree.

Richard is the scion of the Whiteheart Beads who have the power to change the weather. All he can transform, however, is a good job, devoted wife and daughters, and a respectable place in the community to ruin. He takes bribes and destroys his future in the Native American Disposal Service, he inadvertently kills his daughter Deanna through his bungled attempt to die from gas fumes in a closed garage, he loses his wife's love and respect, and he becomes an inebriated, self-pitying, pathetic man. As someone who was once a tribal hopeful, his fall from grace is absolute and impacts all the families. One of the major narrative threads is the chronicling of his tragic downfall.

The Antelope Wife, the story of three urban Anishinaabe families, is an intricate and closely connected design being beaded by mythic twins. Pull out any of their stories, and the whole design falls apart. Certain beads (stories) comprise the heart of the pattern, and it is only through the exact bead being placed in its designated site that the larger design emerges. The touchstone stories in this novel are the beads that compose the design of their interwoven lives. The North Dakota novels and *The Antelope Wife* are ultimately an intricately beaded Ojibwa design of family stories whose individual parts assembled together construct a colorful, enigmatic, and interconnected floral pattern symbolizing the history of twentieth-century Plains Ojibwa people.

Family Characteristics

Since families are at the heart of the novels, the manner in which they arrange themselves and inherit and carry on particular traits and characteristics is of interest, especially since these family features become the defining aspect of a person's identity. As Lipsha comments, "The blood tells" (LM 349), and by reviewing characteristics of reservation and urban families, one derives a composite tribal picture consisting of the mixed-breeds, the assimilationists, the bureaucrats, and the traditionalists. In her novels, Erdrich traces the lives of their families in the last century.

The Métis families of mixed Indian and French ancestry represent the majority of families on the Turtle Mountain Reservation today, and the Lazarres, Morrisseys, Lamartines, and Puyats all favor their French ancestry. James Howard explains that the designation full-blood is given to those who choose to retain an Indian way of life, even though they may carry European surnames and blood (a definition close to the one Patrick Gourneau gives). They differ from the Métis, who distinguish themselves through their French customs—food, dances, dress, and religion—and who tend to look down upon those tribal members adopting a more traditionally Indian lifestyle and outlook. It is often the case, too, that in any given family there will be individuals who identify themselves as Indians while others label themselves Métis or French (8–9).

The Lazarres and Morrisseys are related families who favor their French ancestry. In fact, the Lazarres' Indian blood has become so weak, and they have led such a marginal existence that they are considered poor white trash by other reservation families. The Lazarres and Morrisseys, on their Indian side, are clan members and too closely related to marry, but both Sophie and Clarence Morrissey marry Lazarres, causing the downfall of the once prominent Morrissey family. The Morrisseys are known in the beginning of the century as some of the best farmers on the reservation, and as allotments of the traditional Chippewas become available because taxes are not paid or titles are not filed, the Morrisseys increase their sizable land holdings. Their 640 acre farm prospers, as does their livestock, and Bernadette, the head of the Morrissey family, becomes a powerful force on the reservation. She speaks and writes French and assumes French ways. All of this culture and power dies with her, for the Lazarre blood stains and dishonors the once respected Morrissey name. In *Tracks*, the Morrisseys begin their downfall, and within a short period of time, their name is as besmeared as the no-account Lazarres. By the end of the century, Lipsha categorizes them thus, "The Morrissey are no-goods, a family that for bad give the Lazarres a run" (BP). King is the contemporary Morrissey prototype, a cruel, shiftless, lying, alcoholic, cowardly, quick-tempered disgrace, the product of inbreeding and mixing of the lowest common human denominators.

Though coming out of this Lazarre/Morrissey environment, Marie is really a Puyat/Morrissey. The Puyats are another Métis family with French Canadian ancestry mixed with Indian blood. Pauline says of her family, "We were mixed-bloods, skinners in the clan for which the name was lost" (T 14). Pauline is one of the last of this less than illustrious family whose members are dying out or dispersing to the point of vanishing. They too assume French ways, and Pauline's father's sister, Regina, speaks French and teaches it to her daughter Celestine. Pauline, on the other hand, speaks Indian and has to learn her French from Bernadette Morrissey. The Puyats are a family respected by neither the Métis nor the traditionals, and when Pauline returns to Argus after the devastating sickness on the reservation, nobody has any real knowledge of what has happened to her family. They either died or left, and nobody seems to know or to really care which.

Marie, the driving force behind Nector Kashpaw's tribal prominence, the compassionate and nurturing woman who takes in the unwanteds—abandoned children and her fierce mother-in-law Margaret—is presumably the last Puyat child born on the reservation. Sophie Morrissey/Lazarre raises her when Bernadette takes Marie, her niece, from Pauline who doesn't want her and has tried to prevent her birth. With Bernadette's death from consumption, Marie is taken in by Sophie who raises her as her own. None of the Morrissey/Lazarre children come to any good, as exemplified by Lucille, Sophie's daughter and June's mother, who becomes an alcoholic who never marries June Morrissey's father. Sophie too becomes an alcoholic, and her offspring become the scourge of the reservation.

Despite living in such a dismal environment, Marie inherits her mother's strength. Sophie is not very bright and malleable, while Pauline is strong, driven, and tenacious. Unfortunately, Pauline's ferocious persistence is funneled into religious martyrdom, because she aspires to sainthood. She stops at nothing to achieve her goal, and her acts of renunciation are masochistically bizarre: she wears her shoes on the wrong feet to remind her of Christ's last painful journey walking in his bare feet on rough cobbles; she only relieves herself twice a day; she wears a short rope around her neck to remind her not to betray Christ as Judas had done; she leaves the pins in her head-dress; she puts burrs in her armpits, screwgrass in her stockings, and nettles in her neckband. Pauline is determined to be a perfect martyr, and there is no act too extreme or painful for her to endure in order to achieve her desired end, sainthood. She is a deluded, deranged fanatic, but she gains the begrudging respect of her fellow sisters. While inheriting this tenacity, Marie's energy is channeled into nurturing her family, strengthening her husband, caring for the unloved, and in her old age, strengthening tribal cultural values.

The Lamartines are another Métis family who choose to assimilate into the dominant culture. They are a prosperous group who in the beginning of the century are considered, along with the Morrisseys, to be the best farmers on the reservation. They look down upon those who choose more traditional lifestyles, and like Bev who moves to Minneapolis under the Indian Relocation Act in the 1950s and marries an Anglo, they consider themselves French or Black Irish. Lulu's only true Lamartine child is Henry Jr., and Bev, not Henry Sr., fathers him. It is interesting, if difficult, to speculate concerning how Henry Jr. might have lived his life had Vietnam not intervened and made him into a soldier. He definitely is influenced by Lulu and her ties to a cultural past, for Henry Jr. is the best grass dancer on the reservation, and his skill and pride in performing the traditional dances makes him a respected powwow figure. His familial bonds, especially with Lyman, keep him near home, and he is one Lamartine who chooses to identify with his Indian heritage.

Jack Mauser, like the Lamartines, comes from a Métis family, and, like Bev, Jack chooses assimilation in the city and negation of his Indian blood. His mother, Mary Stamper, is an enrolled fullblood from the old strain with Métis ancestors somewhere in her background. She is the amalgamated full-blood on the Turtle Mountain Reservation coming from "some wandering people who joined right in with the Ojibwas but might have been created out of a lot of different other tribes—Crees, Menominees, even some secretive Winnebago knowledge may have been hers. Who knew?" (TBL 184). She marries an Anglo of German descent, and Jack is raised off reservation with no cultural ties. In fact, most people do not identify him as Native American. Like Lyman, he is entrepreneurial, ambitious, proud, and driven by misplaced energies. Lyman, however, as he ages consolidates into a harder version of himself, while Jack softens under love's formidable powers.

The Pukwans and the Kashpaws are government Indians, those who serve the BIA and the Anglo policies often at the expense of their tribe. The Pukwans are the tribal policemen, and Edgar, Edgar Jr., and his son Leo all act as agents of the United States Government. They carry out rules and regulations imposed on the tribe by the BIA, and their ultimate loyalty is to their position.

The Kashpaws are hereditary tribal leaders whose shrewd minds and business acumen propel them to the top of tribal politics and keep them there. Resounding Sky, the original Kashpaw, smoked his pipe with the United States Government in order to confer a blessing upon the treaty establishing the Turtle Mountain Chippewa Reservation. Nector, like his father, is a born politician, who was spoiled by his mother Margaret as a child and raised to believe he is somebody special. Even as a young boy, he and Margaret connive together to use the money Eli, Fleur, and Nanapush entrust to them to pay off the Kashpaw allotments and to allow Nanapush and Pillager fees to go unpaid, and characteristically they lack the nerve to confront these latter families with the reality that they have lost their land. Nector always takes the easy way out, and for him, no decision becomes a decision. He goes along in life's currents, propelled by the strongest force and maintained by his hereditary tribal position. He cannot say no; he just floats through life and takes what is most convenient and pleasing to him at the moment. Because she seeks respect for herself and her family, Marie pushes Nector into tribal politics, and she is the strength of that family, not Nector. As he ages, his selfishness increases, and even his mother Margaret becomes ashamed and disgusted with her once beloved son.

Recalling his father Nector, Lyman becomes the BIA kingpin on the reservation working for economic development in the form of the tomahawk factory and the bingo palace. While he has his minions who support him, for the most part the tribe has little respect for him. The communal voice in *The Bingo Palace* characterizes him this way:

> Here was a man everybody knew and yet did not know, a dark-minded schemer, a bitter and yet shaman-pleasant entrepreneur who skipped money from behind the ears of Uncle Sam, who joked to pull the wool down, who carved up the reservation the way his blood father Nector Kashpaw did, who had his own interest so mingled with his people's that

he couldn't tell his personal ambition from the pride of the Kashpaws. (5)

If Eli is Lulu's father, then Lyman is a Kashpaw on both sides of his family, and as such can be understood as the inheritor of the worst of the Kashpaw traits, doubled.

Erdrich defines Lyman in opposition to the never do well Lipsha, because they share Nector's blood and Shawnee Ray Toose. Lipsha explains this when he positions himself to ask Lyman a favor by calling upon their entwined familial connections, "Your mother is my grandmother, you're my half uncle and half brother and my boss" (BP 158). Lipsha is lazy and immature, but he is nevertheless appealing and innocent in his lack of understanding of himself and in his devoted loyalty to those he loves, Albertine, Marie, Nector, and Shawnee Ray. He inspires love, while Lyman, on the other hand, inspires fear and disgust. Lyman represents the end of the Kashpaw line of males on this reservation.[13] Eli, Nector's brother, favors the old traditional ways, but he has no son. If Lulu is indeed his daughter, then she does continue the Kashpaw penchant for running tribal business, yet her goals are to try and undo all the damage the Kashpaw government males wrought on the tribe. Russell has no children, and Gordie has killed himself with alcohol. Gordie's son King inherits the worst traits of his Kashpaw and Morrissey heritage.

The Kashpaw hope for the future resides not in Lyman but in Zelda Kashpaw's daughter Albertine and in Lyman's son Redford. Albertine's lifelong frustrated struggle for her mother's love results in her determination to devote her life to helping others. She may not be able to heal her soul, but she knows she can heal bodies. She believes "that the only answer to her need would be realized in healing others the exact way she herself needed to be helped" (BP 209). First attending nursing school and then medical school, Albertine considers herself a part of the Indian community, even though her father is white. *The Bingo Palace* opens with a winter powwow that Albertine has come home to attend, the object of communal concern for how hard she works and of respect at the way in which she always leads with her heart. Lyman's son Redford is a Toose on his mother's side, thus a descendent of medicine people and traditionalists. Shawnee Ray, Redford's mother, is a bright, energetic young woman who seeks to advance herself through education, while still respecting and following the old cultural ways. She and Albertine embody the hope of the Chippewa future; and Redford, Shawnee Ray's son, is sure to have his Kashpaw entrepreneurial blood attenuated by the more culturally sensitive Toose side of his heritage.

Shawnee Ray's uncle Xavier Toose is a medicine man who supervises sweat lodges and vision quests. Russell Kashpaw, the bemedaled veteran, assists him in helping the people acquire spiritual guidance in this most traditional Indian way. Xavier provides people the means to renew spiritual ties, and old lady Aintapi sells love medicines. The most powerful medicine people on the reservation, though, are the Pillagers, true healers and mythic survivors. Theirs is a family tradition extending back to the Woodland days, where even there they were "filled with a daring and independent spirit" (Warren 256). They are staunchly individualistic and adept in medicine powers, both for good and for evil. Lyman says of them, "The Pillagers had been the holdouts, the ones who wouldn't sign the treaties, the keepers of the birch bark scroll and practitioners of medicine so dark and helpful that the more devout Catholic Indians crossed their breasts when a Pillager happened to look straight at them" (LM 312).

Moses and Fleur, distant clan members, lose all their family members to the terrible consumption that sweeps through the reservation around the turn of the century, and the one Pillager child of the next generation is Lulu, who is not trained in Fleur's powerful medicine because she is sent off to boarding school and becomes estranged from her mother. Still, Lulu is the one who ensures the survival of the name and the medicine, since her child with Moses, Gerry, inherits the Pillager gifts from both sides of his heritage. Gerry is the manifestation of the Ojibwa culture hero Nanabozho, for he receives all the magical powers of the people and thus serves as the cultural manifestation of the trickster hero of old. When Fleur loses her family, old man Nanapush adopts her as his daughter and gives Lulu his name, so that Gerry even carries Trickster's name. This legal and familial joining of the Pillagers and Nanapushes creates the most powerful medicine family on the reservation. The most obvious Pillager gift is their extraordinary ability to always win at cards, and this legacy is manifested from Fleur, through Lulu, and on down to Gerry and Lipsha. With the power surfacing in Gerry and then in his son Lipsha, there is assurance that the mighty Pillager magic will not die.

The off reservation family of the North Dakota novels, the Adares, are notable for their ability to survive without their immediate family group intact. When a distraught and post-partum depressed Adelaide flies off leaving a son of fourteen, a daughter of eleven, and a young infant son, the children must learn to rely on themselves then and for the rest of their lives. The more effeminate Karl can never establish his true identity, for as a lover of both men and women and wandering traveling salesman, he doesn't really know who or what he is. Wallace gives him a definition as a lover, and that appears to be the most binding relationship possible for Karl, who continues to be simultaneously drawn to and repulsed by Wallace's enduring love. Mary, on the other hand, immediately puts down her roots in Argus and ingratiates herself into her Aunt Fritzie and Uncle Pete's family by calculating "to be essential to them all, so depended upon that they could never send me [her] off" (BQ 19). Her personality and her appearance are both square, grounded, and practical, in contrast to her vain, feminine, and impractical cousin Sita, Fritzie and Pete's daughter. Mary's only break with the solid and practical world she creates for herself is her excursion into the occult with her tarot cards and fortune telling.

When Karl impregnates Celestine, the Adare and Puyat/James families join and produce the child Dot who, Wallace observes, inherits the worst traits of all her family members: her father's irresponsibility and adeptness at lying, Sita's vanity and selfishness, Celestine's ability to be cruel, and Mary's blunt and stubborn streak. Nevertheless, she is redeemed by her willingness to be different, and as noted earlier, she is the only child in an extended family created around her, and as such she receives the best that her adult family members are able to offer her. Mary, "Uncle" Wallace, and Celestine all devote their lives to making Dot happy, and even her absent father shows up at crucial times. In contrast, Sita, characteristically, has no time or patience for her. The Adare, Puyat/Jameses, and Pfef (through "adoption") are a peculiar family lot, but their ability to create and maintain bonds through Dot distinguishes and sustains them. Dot's family loves her, even though they all help create an angry, selfish bully through their inability to tell her "no."

Dot as an adult (LM, TBL) retains the toughness of her childhood, but she has softened into an adult version of her adolescent self. The qualities that made her a difficult child have evolved into adult strengths. She is still tough, but practical, pugnacious, but principled, confident and able to handle any situation, even thriving on emergencies. Her self-hate as a teenager has turned into maternal and wifely passion, and her mercurial disposition finds her able to forgive as easily as to explode. Her daughter Shawn inherits not only her mother's toughness and strength but also her father's wolf-like grin, the mark of the Pillagers.[14] Dot is a formidable human being, but the intensity of the love with which she was raised by so many family members marks her as one of Erdrich's most interesting and memorable characters. Dot's evolution as a character reflects how, even though she can annoy, she can also captivate. In an interview with Hertha Wong, Erdrich explains how Dot developed as a character. Erdrich found herself writing about a personality type, strong-willed, domineering, yet ultimately fascinating. Even though this character had different names, it was Dorris who finally realized that it was indeed the same person, Dot, who had taken hold as a fictional character and kept metamorphosizing in different forms. She was Wallacette in *The Beet Queen* and Dot in *Love Medicine*, and once she realized she was writing about the same person all along, Erdrich named her Dot and continued to use her as a main character throughout the North Dakota series.

The Minnesota Chippewa families in *The Antelope Wife* differ only in location, not in family characteristics. Resembling the Pillager clan, strong women and women with powers abound in the Shawno/Roy family. The twins born out of Blue Prairie Woman's desperate and immoderate love-making become the prototype for all Shawno/Roy women: they are linked by the powerful and mysterious bond of twinship, they are inheritors of Blue Prairie Woman's devotion and connection to her deer husband and the antelope people, and they possess the powers of transformation and naming. The grandmothers Zosie and Mary inherit the powers to name, to bless, and to seem to manifest themselves in several places simultaneously. When Rozin rejects Zosie and Mary, traditional names that bestow power to Shawno/Roy twins, she loses ancestral protection. Her daughter Deanna's death results from breaching this sanctioned naming tradition. From her grandmothers Zosie and Mary, Cally gains the gift of insight, and she inherits the power to survive from her great grandmother Blue Prairie Woman. The Shawno/Roy women are incarnations of the mythic twins Matchikwewis and Oshkikwe[15] and as such function to carry on traditional powers in the same way that Fleur and her descendants possess ancestral powers that since the forming of the human world by Nanabozho allow designated humans the ability to access the mythic world.

The Roy men are nonexistent. Augustus Roy, founder of the line, falls victim to his twin wives' powers. Deciding their bond of twinship supersedes their love for Augustus Roy, Zosie and Mary dispose of him. With no male descendants, the Roy line carries on exclusively through the women.[16] However, there are Shawno men. As descendants from the group of people who have left for the South, their family branches and survives, and the contemporary Shawno men represent a new generation of competent, caring tribal leaders and role models. Perhaps it is strength passed down to them by their mother Regina whose family carries the bear totem combined with power from the original Shawno who was a holy man, albeit a bad one, who was a bear walker and a Windigo. These powers to harm have dissipated through the years, and in the contemporary male Shawnos lies the promise of restored male Indian pride. Puffy Shawno is a tribal judge, and Frank is a caregiver who like Marie Lazarre Kashpaw takes in those in need of shelter and/or a job. His rooms above his bakery provide a refuge in the urban reservation for his sister Cecille, Cally when she returns from the reservation, and Antelope Wife when she leaves Klaus. He additionally nurtures people through his job baking the breads and sweets that nourish and delight his Indian people. His bakery as well as his home become a meeting place and a sanctuary for urban Indians. It is Frank's powerful love for his wife Rozin which gives her the strength to endure Deanna and Richard's death and to survive the original Shawno, the Windigo, who comes for her. Frank's love vanishes this ancestral evil, just as his love and caring have safeguarded those Indian people who become lost in an often hostile urban environment.

His brother Klaus Shawno falls victim to the beauty of the Antelope Women which wreaks havoc on his once peaceful life. He had learned to successfully navigate the hazards of Minneapolis, hold a job, and be a respectable citizen until he kidnaps Antelope Woman from her plains home and transports her to Minneapolis. In imprisoning Antelope Wife in the city, he destroys all vestiges of the good life he has known. He cannot live with her and he cannot let her go, and his weakness manifests in a decline into alcoholism. However, unlike Richard Whiteheart Beads, Klaus survives. He dreams of restoring himself to power by wearing the red stripe of the drum down the middle of his face. He earns the stripe, although in a most untraditional way. As he lies homeless and sleeping off a drunk in a park, Windigo dog, his advisor and protector, deflects a lawnmower headed for him leaving only a bloody streak down the middle of his startled face. This mythic intervention propels Klaus into doing what he has known he had to do all along, releasing his Calico Sweetheart. This accomplished, he restores the natural balance he violated and restores himself and his world to health. However, his selfish act of capturing Antelope Woman is part of the mythic design, for as destructive as it is to Klaus personally, it reconnects Cally with her Antelope People and brings her the coveted blue beads, her link to the stories and power of her grandmothers.

Richard Whiteheart Beads, once a tribal chairman hopeful like the Kashpaws and Klaus's drinking buddy, does not surface from his plunge into alcoholism. His family descends from the one who as a child loved the precious red beads with the white center adorning his cradle blanket. These are the very beads Midass, mother of Blue Prairie Woman, bought from Augustus Roy generations before, and his name symbolizes a link to tribal history. Even so, he does not possess either the protection of his ancestors or integrity, and his good looks, charm, and entrepreneurial skills lie wasted in the ruins of alcohol. He is Lyman Kashpaw gone bad, and the emptiness of his self leaves him powerless and weak. Unable to acknowledge the truth of his life, he prefers a dramatic suicide rather than reform. He becomes another statistic in the ledger of Indian alcoholics.

These tribal families are an eclectic mixture. The Roys are descended "of the three-fires people and an Ivory Coast slave" (AW 35), Henri Laventure a French adventurer, and the Antelope People. When Midass marries a Shawno, the people from the north, she brings in the blood of Shesheeb, the bad holy man who has been convicted of being a windigo. Their descendants are lightened by the Roy blood, given power through their connection to the Antelope People, and protected by their animal helpers. Living in the city away from the reservation, they redefine how to live

The Power of Love as Medicine

communally and hold on to traditional beliefs. Their success is symbolized by the community which gathers to participate in and to bless Frank and Rozin's wedding. This community of well wishers with their traditional and not so traditional foods who bring traditional and not so traditional blessings is the reality for urban Indians, for they remain a community which blesses, sustains, and forgives. *The Antelope Wife* ends on a hopeful note with tradition and culture still intact in this urban reservation.

Love Medicines

Norval Morriseau, Ruth Landes, and Sister Coleman all document various types of traditional Ojibwa love medicines,[17] and Erdrich distinguishes between two different types. There is the kind that can be bought and for which the Chippewa and Cree are well-known.[18]

Nanapush, Moses, Fleur, and old lady Aintapi have the ability to concoct a medicine from smoky powders, crushed roots, nails, and the pubic hairs of the beloved. This is a medicine one could buy, and Eli goes to Nanapush for a love medicine to help him with Fleur, Pauline buys a love medicine from Moses to entrap Sophie and Eli, and Lipsha goes to Fleur to ask for a love medicine to help him with Shawnee Ray. All these, though, are artificially produced love often inspired only by lust. A love that has the power to heal and to endure comes from the heart and needs no feigned stimulants to make it real. Lipsha proudly asserts his ability to produce the love medicines through his Pillager ancestry, but Shawnee Ray corrects him saying, "'You got the medicine, Lipsha. But you don't got the love'" (BP 112). The real love medicine comes from the heart, as with Nanapush, Marie, and Lulu's love for their families, Wallace's love for Karl, Gerry's love for Dot, Celestine, Mary and Wallace's love for Dot, Xavier's love for Zelda, Anna's love for Eleanor, Eleanor's love for Jack, Dot's love for Celestine, Shawn, and Gerry, Rozin's love for her children, and Frank's love for Rozin. Lipsha has to learn that there is no shortcut to love, as he tries to create for Marie and Nector, with disastrous results. Love is unconditional, accepting, and enduring. When Lipsha finally realizes this, his healing powers return. He then sees that true love is loving over time and distance and that love is "true feeling, not no magic" (LM 257).

Love as the most powerful of all medicines is the major theme of Erdrich's novels, and the families where love is strong are those families in which people survive and feel a part of the whole, of the community, because they have a place where they belong and are wanted. Lipsha notes, "Belonging was a matter of deciding to" (LM 348), and many of the family units are constructed not so much by biological ties but rather by ties of the heart: Nanapush adopts Fleur and Lulu, Sophie takes in Marie, Marie takes in and loves June and Lipsha, Eli raises June, Marie cares for Margaret in her old age, Fritzie raises Mary, Wallace adores Dot and gives her his name in a feminized form, Zelda takes in Shawnee Ray and Redford, Jack's living wives form a community, and Frank takes care of Cecille, Cally, and Sweetheart Calico. Moses dies of love for Lulu, and Lulu lives to love, "I was in love with the whole world and all that lived in its rainy arms" (LM 276).

True love has a staying power that endures and lasts through good and bad times. Lipsha, ever ready to take the easy way, even for love, finally realizes this when he sees his grandmother Marie's steadfast love for Nector even when he is old and foolish. Lipsha comments, "You see I thought love got easier over the years so it didn't hurt so bad when it hurt, or feel so good when it felt good. I thought it smoothed out and old people hardly noticed it" (LM 233–34). But that is not the case, for as Lipsha again notices, "People's hearts are constructed of unknowable elements" (BP 45). There is no accounting for the reasons people love, and there is no limit to the amount of time people will wait for true love to triumph. Zelda wastes a lifetime rejecting love, but in her later years rekindles the love she has always felt for Xavier Toose and goes to him. June, always too distrustful of love in her lifetime, loves her son Lipsha from the other world, Lawrence's passion for his wife Anna turns temporarily into jealousy and abandonment, and Frank survives cancer and rejection in his wait for Rozin. The communal voice in *The Bingo Palace* comments, "We do know that no one gets wise enough to really understand the heart of another, though it is the task of our life to try" (BP 6). The task of trying to understand and accept love in all its facets comprises the heart of Erdrich's novels. It is through her family stories that the power of love most clearly manifests itself, and it is through a family's love that a community, a tribe, and a nation endure.

Chapter 5

"Power Travels in the Bloodlines, Handed Out Before Birth": Louise Erdrich's Female Mythic Characters

THE ANTHROPOLOGIST A. IRVING HALLOWELL COINED THE TERM "ethnometaphysics" to suggest that cultures do not necessarily organize human experiences in the same way and that there are as many different ways of conceptualizing the world as there are different cultures. "Ethnometaphysics" concerns itself with philosophical inquiries into differing notions of reality and the degree to which people in various cultures organize their experiences based upon their perceptual notions of "reality" (Overholt and Callicott xi). When reading Native American texts, clashing cultural realities often present problems for Anglo readers steeped in western Civilization's rational philosophical and empirically based tradition. Women turning into bears, marriage between a deer and a woman, talking dogs, Antelope People—this cannot happen exclaims the western voice, yet Native Americans have traditionally accepted as "real" occurrences which have no rational explanation. To try to perceive and then adopt the Anishinaabe worldview, therefore, becomes of prime importance to readers of Erdrich's work where there exist animal transformations, animal-human marriages, and mythic power manifested in animal beings.

Readers who come to Erdrich's work with knowledge of Ojibwa traditional stories will already have placed themselves within her worldview, where relationships within the natural world are not limited to human as master and animal as object. In the many traditional tales anthropologists have collected and Ojibwa people have recorded, animal transformations are often signals of power.[1] This is especially evident in stories of Nanabozho, the Ojibwa trickster and central figure in traditional Ojibwa tales. Nanabozho, principal mediator between humans and the Manitos, is considered to be both human and divine. According to Sister Bernard Coleman et al., who collected tales of the northern Minnesota Ojibwa in the 1950s, "Almost unanimously Nanabozho was mentioned as a brother to the animals, the plants, the trees, and the many different aspects of nature. As the legends show, Nanabozho has all of these characteristics and still others" (56). His metamorphoses into the Great Rabbit, signal him as trickster, but he also can change himself into an inanimate object like a pine stump. Traditional tales of ordinary Ojibwa people reflect these same possibilities of metamorphosis: a woman marries a man who turns out to be a beaver, a man turns himself into a miniature and hides inside a ball for safety, and women become wolves.[2] What becomes apparent in reading traditional Ojibwa tales is that there is no separation between the human and the supernatural world, and beings can alternate between human and animal forms. Hallowell assuages our western need for absolutes with his notion that the Ojibwa have a more inclusive notion of "person" than evident in Euro-American thought. A "person" in Ojibwa metaphysics can be both a human and other-than-human (Overholt and Callicott 142–43). Therefore, animals speak and have emotions, and people can assume animal bodies and characteristics—this is the way Ojibwa perceive reality. Erdrich's fiction reflects Ojibwa metaphysics and resides in a transformational space where antelope people, spirit bears, Windigo dogs, and the present of the mythic still exist.

Secondary Heroes

The mythic presence in Erdrich's work is a distinguishing feature of her fiction, as it is of the work of most contemporary Indian writers. In her analysis of this subject, Patricia Riley, a mixed-blood Cherokee, draws upon the Lakota word for mixed-blood, *iyeska*, which means one who both interprets between the Indian and Anglo worlds and between the world of humans and spirits. She theorizes that mixed-blood writers like Silko and herself (also Erdrich, Allen, Momaday, Vizenor, Sarris, and Hogan) find themselves positioned as mediators between the Anglo and Indian worlds and feel obliged to explain the Indian viewpoint, which they do in their writing. For these writers, their work becomes a vehicle by which they can distinguish themselves as Indians, and creating a sacred space in their fiction signals that they have adopted a Native American worldview. Riley then makes an insightful connection and compares mixed-blood writers acting as interpreters and contemporary mythmakers to Joseph Campbell's notion of a "secondary hero" (240). This is the hero of myth who revitalizes the tradition by reinterpreting it and making it viable for the modern experience. Contemporary storytellers like Erdrich who function as traditional storytellers by keeping alive the myths and stories of their people are the "secondary heroes" in Native American culture.

In writings of contemporary Indian mythmakers, a distinctive feature of the fiction and poetry is the transformational power of women, and the "gynocratic" approach to Native American literature is the central metaphor in Paula Gunn Allen's critical work. Allen highlights the importance of the powerful female spirit pervasive in Indian life. This spirit has many names and comes forth in many different guises, and it is her presence that ensures proper balances within a tribal community. Hers is the power to create life and to destroy, and this central figure known as Corn Woman, Earth Woman, Old Spider Woman, and Serpent Woman embodies the essence of life for tribal people (*Sacred* 13–14). She is the mythic dimension living in ritual and song, and it is to her that a tribe owes its ceremonial life and traditional ways of viewing the world. She is indispensable in an Indian frame of reference, for as Allen relates, "The mythic narrative, as an articulation of human thought and experience not expressible in other forms, must be seen as a necessary dimension of human expression and experience" ("Mythopoetic" 3).

As noted in chapter 2, Hallowell classified Ojibwa narratives as either news and tidings or myths, and he observes that in the myths or sacred stories, "The characters in them are regarded as living entities who have existed from time immemorial ... [and they] behave like people, though many of their activities are depicted in a spatio-temporal framework of cosmic, rather than mundane, dimensions.... To the Ojibwa they are living persons of an other-than-human class" (27). Such a female figure in Erdrich's North Dakota novels is Fleur, the powerful medicine woman, whose presence serves to bind together the people and to embody traditional Ojibwa ways of living and of knowing. In the Minnesota novel, Antelope Wife's transspecies presence is a reminder to urban Indians of their sacred connection to the land and to the animals.

In Fleur and Antelope Woman live the female mythic dimension of Ojibwa belief, which, by the beginning of the twenty-first century, has come under siege by the forces of assimilation, Anglo churches and boarding schools.[3] Fleur is known variously as a witch to be feared and a healer to be respected, and it is her presence within the community that stands in opposition to all things threatening the traditional ways in which Chippewas view and move within the world. It is Fleur's story that is the story of the female mythic life of contemporary Chippewas, and her presence throughout the North Dakota novels signals that this spiritual/mythic element still survives among her people.

A study of Fleur underscores the degree to which Erdrich values and honors the scared dimension of Chippewa life; and, like the great essence of being Allen notes for various southwestern tribes, Fleur serves as the embodiment of a female mythic dimension in Chippewa life. Erdrich does not outrightly characterize Fleur as a spiritual being; in fact, her character is easily read as simply the tribal medicine woman. However, a close analysis of the symbols with which Erdrich associates Fleur reveals her as the powerful spirit woman of a mythic past. Through Fleur's association with the bear, Misshepeshu, and other animals, her role in the first four North Dakota novels assumes a deeper and more significant presence. The complexity of her character develops throughout four novels as she grows into her full strength as a medicine woman. No single book contains the breadth and depth of this otherworldly being, and Erdrich's story cycle allows for the truth of Fleur's complex character to emerge. This chapter examines the significance of animal beings in Erdrich's novels, and how for Fleur they signal her otherworldliness, her role as hereditary healer based on the powers of a traditional Midéwinin medicine person, her Pillager origin, and her importance as a character throughout the first four North Dakota novels. The Antelope Wife and other metamorphosed animal beings likewise signal a mythic presence still embedded in contemporary life, and this chapter concludes with assessment of how Erdrich with her transformational characters positions herself as the maker of myths, a "secondary hero."

Fleur's Bear Power

Fleur's association with the powerful bear is a signal not even the most casual of readers could miss. The outer cover of *Tracks*, Fleur's origin story, features an upright, otherworldly figure of a bear into which is subsumed a shadowy hint of a human figure. The novel's hard outer cover features two prints or "tracks" of bear paws, and so I will begin with a discussion of the bear in Ojibwa tradition and especially of the importance of Fleur's association with the bear.

Norval Morriseau, a contemporary Ojibwa artist and storyteller, maintains that legends tell of an early time when the bear was human or had a human form and clarifies that only later did it turn into an animal (39). David Rockwell in his book *Giving Voice to Bear: North American Indian Myths, Rituals, and Images of the Bear* corroborates this view, and he offers, "The Ojibwa often referred to bears as anijinabe, their word for Indian" (2). Rockwell attributes the association of the bear with humans to the fact that this animal is built not unlike a human. He further points out that since bears often walk upright and exhibit great skill in using their front paws for reaching and eating foods, their humanlike appearance is enhanced (2). Indians have traditionally honored and feared this awesome animal who embodies human traits in a more powerful form. The bear's way of walking and eating, similar gestation periods, and close bonding relationship between the mother and her child (cub) only serve to strengthen the humans' association with an animal seeming to possess such a strong resemblance to them.

Joni Clarke additionally suggests that the bear's hibernation and emergence in the spring "made him seem at once a symbol of both life and death" (33–34). The animal's connectedness to the natural cyclical rhythms of life through its winter retreat to a netherworld of death-like sleep and spring appearance fully rejuvenated as new life begins again positions the bear as an innate source of spiritual power. Clarke believes people attribute special powers to the bear precisely because it is "'betwixt and between'" the two worlds (34). Since humans can only attain connection and entrance to this other dimension in life through spiritual practices, it is a natural consequence of the bear's existence that people would attribute to it the power to mediate between the two worlds. Rockwell offers related insights as to how many tribes "incorporated bears into their healing and initiation rituals because those traditions, too, were fundamentally rites of renewal, or of death and rebirth" (7).

Animal Helpers and Totems

Native Americans traditionally considered bears, as well as other animals, integral parts of their world. Indian peoples adopt animals as spiritual guides and helpers because of their abundance, of their importance as a food and clothing source, of their enigmatic qualities, of their instinctual abilities to survive, and of their connectedness to the great natural order. This animal helper is chosen by clans for qualities the humans wish to emulate, and Basil Johnston points out that the Anishinaabe endeavored to take the animal's distinctive quality and make it their own. He explains, "Each animal symbolized an ideal to be sought, attained, and perpetuated" (53).[4] Therefore, animal beings not only distinguish a chosen group through their distinctive animal qualities, but in addition the animal becomes the human's vital link to the spiritual world.

Animals are identified both with individual people and with family groups. In tribal lore, a person seeking a vision was often visited by an animal helper who then became a personal spiritual helper throughout the person's lifetime.[5] This animal becomes their sacred guide, and its likeness is emblazoned on the individual's shield, tent, medicine bag, or other personal items. A totem, on the other hand, "refers to the mystical relationship between a kinship group and an animal" and are not to be confused with the guardian spirit of an individual (Rockwell 107). Groups of families form a separate exogamous unit, and through their animal totem determine their relationships with other peoples, for example, who is an eligible marriage partner. People with the same animal totem are considered too close in kinship to marry, and so one's animal totem serves additionally to regulate suitable marriages within the community.

The Historical Pillagers

It follows, then, that bear cults and bear rituals would proliferate among tribal peoples and that the bear would become an animal totem associated with only the most powerful tribal members. Thus, Erdrich foregrounds the Pillagers' association with prominent animals, especially the bear. Johnston reports, "Animals of fierce disposition, the bear, wolf, and lynx, were the totems of warriors" (67); and the Pillagers, a historical Ojibwa band from Leech Lake, are of the Ojibwa bear clan. Erdrich additionally connects them also to both the wolf (the Pillager wolf-like grin) and the lynx (another name for the underwater manito). As far back as history records them, the historical Pillagers were known as a belligerent, brave, and fiercely independent group. William Warren says they first received their name in 1781 after occupying Leech Lake where they became known as Pillagers, Muk-im-dua-win-in-e-wug, or "men who take by force" (256). They earned this name when, in the late 1700s during contact with a sick trader on the lower Mississippi, this group took advantage of the weakened white man's condition and carried off most of his merchandise. The trader fled for his life, as the clan, aroused by liquor and by the excitement of the impending Midéwinin ceremony, "pillaged" all of his trade goods. This rash and ill-advised act dissuaded other traders from attempting to trade with such a fierce and impetuous people, and the group ended up sending great quantities of beaver pelts to Fond du Lac in order to appease the traders.[6]

This act of foolishness with its tragic consequences (contracting smallpox) earned the clan their deprecating name; however, for the most part, they were respected throughout the villages for their brave and daring exploits, especially against their traditional enemies, the Lakotas. Once they had established their dominance over their Indian enemies, the Pillagers redirected their energies to trying to eradicate their new and even more powerful enemies, the Anglo missionaries and the United States Government. Christopher Vecsey reports that when Rev. Boutwell attempted to missionize the Leech Lake Pillagers in the 1830s, they rejected wholesale his school, his church, and his attempts to turn them into farmers. When Rev. Boutwell finally left after four years of proselytizing, he had not made a single convert (47–48). The Leech Lake Pillagers were also the Indians who "conducted the last Indian uprising in 1889 against the government polities" (Vecsey 18). With the Dawes Act of 1887 eliminating traditional tribal ownership in favor of individual allotments, this independent group initiated one last attempt to test their strength against an enemy now beginning to control all aspects of their life.

The traditional Pillagers were hunting in the Dakotas in the late 1700s, and a group from Leech Lake permanently moved onto the Plains in the 1800s. It is from this group that Fleur has her origins, for Old Man Pillager, her father, reportedly moved into this new area bringing with him Misshepeshu, the water monster. However, her clan almost dies with the death of her parents, two sisters, and a brother. Fleur and Moses remain the sole surviving Pillagers, and they are both rescued from death by Nanapush, who cures Moses (who thereafter retreats to his island home) and who adopts Fleur and her daughter Lulu as his own flesh and blood. This joining of the mighty Pillagers with the traditional trickster figure Nanabozho signals a merging of two of the most powerful figures in Ojibwa life. Trickster Nanabozho is humankind's patron and fool, healer, and bungler. His awesome powers are rivaled only by those of the Thunderbird, the Great Spirit Kitche Manito, the Great Bear Spirit, and Misshepeshu, and it is he who has created the present world, taught the people how to hunt and fish, shown them the gifts of medicines to insure good health, and given the people totems by which they can distinguish themselves. That the Pillagers with their brave and independent spirit merge with the culture hero Nanabozho through Nanapush's adoption of Fleur is a clear indication that Fleur is indeed no ordinary person.

Fleur's Immortality

Adding to Fleur's designation as a powerful and mythic figure is her uncertain origin. Where Fleur and her family reside is obviously a house of power, for when Edgar Pukwan of the tribal police attempts to burn down the family house according to the Indian agent's instructions, the Pillager house of spirits proves impervious to kerosene and fire. While Nanapush says he found her nearly dead in a house containing the bodies of her family, Nanapush is the trickster, and Trickster is known to lie. Fleur is clearly marked from the beginning as an otherworldly character, and Erdrich installs doubt in the reader's mind as to who and what Fleur really is—this doubt that lingers throughout the novels. Perhaps her origins lie far beyond the Pillagers to a mythic past, where the great spirits do not die but rather adopt different form. Nanapush fulfills his role as cultural carrier by rescuing Fleur and Moses and ensuring the continuity of a tribal healer.[7] Once he passes on, his "daughter" Fleur and her progeny remain to link the people to their mythic past.

Jay Cox and Catherine Catt note that one of the trickster's qualities is the ability to survive death (Catt 73), and Fleur's inability to be killed certainly raises the possibility that she is no ordinary mortal.[8] The ending of *The Bingo Palace* validates this interpretation. Fleur finally passes back to the spirit world when "annoyed" (BP 272). She takes the place of Lipsha, her successor, on the death road. She was the oldest person in the community, over one hundred years old, yet she has endured in order to ensure the spiritual survival of her people. When she leaves, she is believed to walk away to her island home where her guardianship of the people continues. The spirits greet Fleur as she returns to them, but she remains an ever-present figure for both the spirit world and the human one since the sense of her continuing presence in the lives of the Chippewas is the dominant image with which *The Bingo Palace* and Fleur's story ends. The Nanapush/Fleur "family" constitutes Erdrich's strong hint to readers that the mythic dimension of Chippewa life endures, albeit in continually different forms. It always remains a presence that aids and directs the people.

The Bear in Ojibwa Culture

Another method by which Erdrich signals Fleur's connection to myth is her repeated association with the bear. The importance of bears in Native American life has been previously noted, but the degree to which Fleur embodies some of the sacred dimensions of the bear warrants further discussion. Some of the best information in this area is found in Ruth Landes's book *Ojibwa Religion and the Midewinin* and the work of Selwyn Dewdney whose study of the sacred Midé birchbark scrolls (which describe origin myths, migration charts, song records, and ritual practices) of the

Southern Ojibway provides a wealth of information about the most sacred dimensions of Ojibwa life.[9] These scrolls were used as memory aids for the Midé practitioners, and their pictographic symbols represent the heart of Ojibwa spiritual tradition, the sacred Midé ceremonies.

There are many manitos or spirits inhabiting the Chippewa world,[10] but those of most importance are the ones Dewdney refers to as the "'super-manitos'—Misshepeshu, the Thunderbird, the Sacred Bear, the Great Turtle, and the Windigo—only the first three have a place in the Midewenin" (39). The bear's place in ritual is assured because this animal brought humans a new connection to an everlasting life after Misshepeshu flooded the earth in retaliation for Nanabozho shooting the underwater manito who had killed his brother wolf. Shell manito (Megis, or the Great Shell) wished to pass on its strength to the Indian people, and along with The Great Spirit and the Manito Council, they appoint Bear to carry manito power, "literally, 'doings' or 'midewiwin'" (Landes 98) beyond the waters, though this was a difficult task. Bear has to try four times to break through the four layers separating the spirits from the people. In some versions Bear uses his tongue to break through the four layers, and in others, it is done with a pole, now the central physical symbol of Midéwinin ritual gatherings. In most versions, Bear finally emerges, covered with megis shells, and this saltwater seashell remains at the heart of Midéwewin ceremonies.

After three unsuccessful attempts, when Bear does finally break through to the new world, she emerges into a Midé lodge. According to Dewdney, "The Bear has successfully carried the Pack of Life through the first obstacles and has been strengthened for the task ahead by passing through the Midewegun, that is, by himself undergoing initiation into the Midéwewin" (33). This pack of life is the pack of Midé rites which assures the Indian people of access to the powers of the manitos. Therefore, the bear earns the role of the guardian spirit for the Midéwewin and as its principal benefactor, "all Midewinin initiates were said to 'follow the bear path'" (Rockwell 18).

Thus, the bear is not only a spirit helper of the highest importance, but is as well associated with the Midéwewin, or Grand Medicine Society of the Ojibwa. These annual ceremonies induct initiates into one of the four degrees of increasing importance and power, and the society's primary purpose is to ensure the health of the participants. Powerful medicine is symbolically "shot" into the initiates by the Midé priests, who possess great powers of healing. Vecsey reports, "The Society devoted much of its instruction to the knowledge of medicinal herbs and other curing devices. Midewewin's major concern was the maintenance of health, the combating of disease" (179). These medicine men (and occasionally women) could absorb bear's power into themselves, and "[i]n various states of the Midéwewin both priest and candidate impersonated the Bear" (Dewdney 116). Because of its prominence in the origin myth and in Midéwinin ceremonies, the bear is associated with powerful medicine.

The association of the bear with curing also has its source in the way in which the animal digs up plants for its nourishment. Rockwell believes Indian peoples have always looked up to the bear for its ability to extract valuable plants from the earth. He cites Native people's belief that "The Bear knew the secrets of the plants. The bear appears again and again in native American myth and lore as a plant gatherer, as master forager, and as bestower of the secrets and mysteries of plants" (6).

Bears additionally served a role in Ojibwa female initiation rites, where their power was linked to the power associated with women's menstruation, especially the first one which was held to be a time of great potency for young women. Most tribes believed that during the time of menses a woman was particularly dangerous, and this came to be associated with the powerful and dangerous aspects of the bear in the ritual. The Ojibwa even termed the first menstruation *wemukowe* or "going to be a bear" (Rockwell 16), and the young woman's seclusion in den-like enclosure only serves to reinforce the likeness. Rockwell sums up the connection, "The bear in this case was not only a symbol of initiation but also a symbol of the maleficent powers of the menstruating woman" (17).

Not all of the bear's powers were associated with beneficial medicine, and the Ojibwa girl's first menses is only one instance of the power of the bear which is to be feared. Evil shamans were known to impersonate bears and to use their power for malevolent purposes, and the bearwalker is an especially feared misuse of a Midé priest's power. The Ojibwa believed that people who practiced bad medicine foraged in the woods for plants possessing the power to kill. They would then assume the form of the bear and leave these deadly plants at the home of their intended victim, who might never see the bearwalker but who would soon fall sick and die. James Howard reports that, although the Plains Ojibwa do not share the dread of witches that so terrorizes their Woodland ancestors, they do have great fear of the Bearwalks (120); and Dewdney reports that even into the mid-twentieth century on the Whitefish Reserve in Ontario, people believed a Bear-Walker was responsible for the deaths of many people on the Reserve (117–18).

Fleur's Bear Medicine

This dichotomy between a benevolent spirit bear and a deadly evil bear is an ambiguity Erdrich plays with in relation to Fleur's powers. Pauline relates how Fleur knew the secret ways to both cure and to kill, and she refers to Fleur as a "witch" because of her great powers. Pauline's reliability as a narrator is questionable, and her jealousy of Fleur's powers is indisputable; but in this specific case, Nanapush corroborates that Fleur possesses the power to harm her enemies, as seen when she puts her knowledge of dark potions to use on Boy Lazarre, who shamelessly protests that "Fleur was murdering him by use of bad medicine" (T 120). Fleur reduces him to a babbling idiot, which is only one instance of her use of bad medicine to revenge an enemy. Nancy Peterson maintains that Fleur causes the tornado in Argus immediately after her rape based on the fact that the destructive cyclone occurs immediately after Tor, Dutch, and Lily have violently assaulted her (987). As the threads of Fleur's story begin to become clearer and the pattern of Fleur's potential for violence and her proclivity to revenge all who wrong her emerges, Erdrich insinuates that Fleur uses her great powers to bring death/harm in the form of a tornado to her rapists.

Other people who cross Fleur also become her victims. Agents sent to survey Pillager land wander hopelessly in the dark woods. Even innocent people like Jean Hat and George Many Women have their kindness in helping Fleur repaid with death.[11] However, the most malevolent suspicion is that Fleur transforms herself into a bearwalker, in which form Clarke notes, she is suspected of practicing evil medicine like keeping the finger of a child in her pocket and placing the heart of an owl on her tongue so she can hunt at night (35). Even so, she apparently kills no one while in her bear guise. Fleur's sinister practices are reported by Pauline, whose fear and awe of Fleur's powers renders her incapable of distinguishing between fact and fancy. The novels describe Pauline's ambivalent feelings towards the potency of her Chippewa people's traditional medicines as they relate to the power of the Catholic church, which Pauline subscribes to as the only true spiritual power. What better way to discount the old ways than to subscribe the power of evil to them in contrast to a religion promising eternal salvation. However, once again to caution the reader that Pauline's statements can not be taken as pure fact, Erdrich positions this fanatical nun, who is responsible for the death of at least four people, as the sole reporter of Fleur's nefarious deeds.

To be sure, Fleur has the power to maim, to inflict harm, and to brutally punish her enemies, but Pauline's evidence of Fleur as a bearwalker is based on the fact that by night the people can hear "her chuffing cough, the bear cough" (T 12) and that if people try to follow her, her tracks turn into paws. Erdrich leaves no doubt of Fleur's ability to transform herself into a bear, but it is not because she is a bearwalker as Pauline and many critics suggest. Instead, Fleur is a human embodiment of the Great Spirit Bear, which the ending of her story in *The Bingo Palace* substantiates. Having already outlived all of her contemporaries, Fleur's only reason for continuing to live is as the bearer of traditional Chippewa medicine. She needs to be assured that the old ways will continue, even if they are practiced by the sometimes clueless, often bumbling, many times ill-advised, but always potentially powerful Lipsha Morrissey. Fleur returns to her spirit home on the island where she joins Moses and all of her earthly relatives only after taking Lipsha's place in death, an act that promises a continuation of the Pillager medicine. She leaves behind her tracks, and she signals her continuous presence in watching over the people through her low cough, "the bear laugh—the chuffing noise we hear ... unmistakable" (274), the sound of the Great Bear Spirit.

Fleur's bear medicine is that of the benevolent manito using her power to cure, not to destroy, and it is the power derived from the bear that strengthens and sustains Fleur. A spirit bear comes to assist Fleur at Lulu's birth. Fleur calls for help among the spirit manitos, and it is the bear who answers her and comes to her aid. The presence of the awesome creature fills Fleur with such power that she is finally able to deliver her child, who has been trapped between life and death. Fleur uses her medicine to mend Karl Adare's broken feet, and his memory of the night Fleur cures him is of a "bear [who] rose between the fire and the reeds" (BQ 51). When in *The Bingo Palace* Lipsha follows Fleur to the cabin to ask her for a love medicine, the spirits in her place envelop him, and he sees the medicine woman darken, broaden, and transform herself into a bear. These accounts of Fleur's bear powers serve to emphasize her role as a powerful healer of the Midéwewin where healing is directly associated with the Great Bear Spirit. The mighty medicine woman of her people owes her knowledge and power to her bear spirit.

Fleur's Wolf and Marten Characteristics

Fleur's association with powerful animals does not lie exclusively with the bear. Erdrich makes references as well to the wolf-like grin she turns on her victims and to her marten clan marker. Johnston catalogues various qualities assigned to different animal totems for the Anishinaabeg, and he reports that the bear embodies strength and courage, the wolf perseverance and guardianship, and the marten single-mindedness and judgment (53). These qualities coalesce and manifest themselves in Fleur's character. She is a big woman of enormous strength who can pull a cart, butcher any animal, walk tirelessly, and lift objects of great weight, all of which can be attributed to her bear-like qualities. Her role in the Chippewa community is that of healer and guardian spirit, and throughout the first four novels, she is the female mythic presence of the traditional Anishinaabe who sustains and strengthens her people. These are the qualities of the wolf that mark her. Clarke notes an added significance of the wolf—he is Nanabozho's adopted brother, and Nanapush's adopting Fleur parallels trickster's original joining with brother wolf (32-33). James Howard writes that the Plains Ojibwa hold that "*Wolf* is the younger brother of *Nanapus*. He was slain by the Underwater panthers, who were jealous of his brother's power. After his death, *Wolf* was made the master of the afterworld" (111), a fact that strengthens Fleur's identification as a spirit guardian for her people. Fleur's determination to exact revenge upon those who wrong her and her family and to wait patiently until she can bring them to judgment embodies her marten qualities. She appraises situations, "kept track of time, calculated justice, assessed possibilities" (BP 143), and when the time comes for revenge, she bestows it twofold and with a vengeance as seen when she returns to the reservation for the fourth time[12] in order to once again extract her lands from those (in this case former Indian Agent Jewett Parker Tatro) who wrongfully have taken them from her.

Fleur's Guardian, Misshepeshu

The bear, wolf, and marten are all animals whose powers and characteristics help fashion Fleur's character, strengthen her, and grant her the fortitude she needs to fulfill her mission among her Chippewa people. However, there is yet another very powerful animal Erdrich associates with Fleur, and that is Misshepeshu, the water monster, who along with the bear, is one of the five "supermanitos." Like the bear, Misshepeshu is neither wholly evil nor entirely good. Even Pauline with her mission to "transfix him [Misshepeshu] with the cross" (T 200) concedes he "was neither good nor bad but simply had an appetite" (T 139). He remains an ambivalent yet always mighty manito whom the people regard with respect and dread. As the spirit of the lakes, his power to calm the waters, to send the killing squalls, or to grant safe passage over the frozen waters in wintertime means the difference between life and death for Woodland people dependent upon the waters for food and transportation, and for this reason Dewdney maintains Misshepeshu is the "most powerful of all the Algonkian Manitos" (122). To this day, some Ojibwa people traveling on lakes throw tobacco offerings to appease this great underwater spirit.

This formidable manito is reported as having varying forms. James Howard writes that the Plains Ojibwa conceive of Misshepeshu as a panther with brassy scales and bison-like horns (113). Victor Barnouw gathered stories from the Ojibwa of an underwater lion, and in one account an intrepid girl cuts off the lion's tail with her paddle and takes it home, where it turns into precious copper. He attributes the association of the great cats with the underwater spirits to the fact that even until the beginning of the twentieth century, pumas and cougars were found in the Great Lakes area, with the latter possessing the ability to swim (133). Vecsey agrees that Misshepeshu combines the features of several animals: "The Underwater Manito was not a single manito but rather a composite. It consists of two main beings, the underwater lion and the horned serpent, whose identity and roles were interchangeable" (74). Dewdney adds that "The Lion" today designates the underwater creature variously called "Snake Monster, Underground Panther, Huge Cat, Great Lion" in earlier times (123).

The association of the powerful underwater manito with a feline is curious, since cats normally eschew water and are definitely land-based creatures. Dewdney conjectures that the association is allegorical since the Great Lynx was considered the "Source Being of the species" and therefore was imbued with remarkable powers. Add to this its natural ferocity and the fleeting glimpses the Indian people experience of this awesome creature in the woodlands, this same mighty elusive creature is possibly the one they believe they glimpse beneath the shadowy waters (124–25). It could be that Indians traveling in canoes, ever vulnerable to uncertain weather conditions, could associate the great carp or sturgeons (which grow up to ten feet) menacingly swimming beneath them in the dark waters with the ferocious great cats who lurk in the shadowy forests.

For whatever reason, the powerful underwater manito assumes a cat-like appearance and as such it occupies a place of prominence in the lives of the Ojibwa. This mighty feline whose tail could whip up the waters, whose breath stirs the winds, who controls the underwater animals, and who preys upon hapless people caught out in the open water could also be a protector of those with whom he was in right relationship. This relationship could be obtained through sacrifices, from tobacco, to guns, to liquor, to traps, to live dogs given as offerings around June to appease the manito during the period the Indian people would have most need of its protection (Dewdney 127). Morriseau notes that gifts such as tobacco help assure Indians of safe travel across the water ways, and he assures his Anglo readers that the powerful and wise water god, although very respected, is not to be feared if given the proper offerings.

Vecsey notes that in some traditions, the Underwater Manito gave the Indians copper and "offered medicinal powers to those who accepted it as [a] guardian (qtd. in Radin 1956, 74). Howard also associates the underwater manito with medicine powers. He offers, "They [the *Underwater panthers*] reside in the deepest parts of streams and lakes. They can also travel beneath the earth. They possess great knowledge of Indian medicine, since the herbs used spring from the depths of the earth. Sometimes they can be induced to impart some of their knowledge to humans"(113–14).

The medicine gifts and lake spirit as guardian directly tie Fleur and her family to this powerful manito. The North Dakota Chippewa of Erdrich's novels believe the Pillager family brought Misshepeshu from the Woodlands when they were driven west from Leech Lake; it was then they think that he "appeared because of the Old Man's connection" (T 175). Annette Van Dyke additionally notes that Warren "identifies the Pillagers as having the 'immense fish' as their family totem" (*Questions* 15). Because of Fleur's family's direct alliance with him, the people believe she owes her powers to him, and Nanapush makes this association clear. After Fleur loses her powers, thinking she owns them and forgetting they are a gift of the manitos, her "father" Nanapush urges her, "Go down to the shore.... Make your face black and cry out until your helpers listen" (177). Also, when Fleur is around, "she kept the lake thing controlled" (35), but when she leaves the reservation, harmful spirits linger among the people causing havoc and fear. Fleur honors spirit rocks from Lake Matchimanito among her most valued possessions. When she leaves the reservation for the first time in *Tracks* she carries with her only "weed-wrapped stones from the lake-bottom, bundles of roots, a coil of rags, and the umbrella that had shaded her baby. The grave markers [Nanapush] had scratched, four crosshatched gears and a marten, were fastened on the side of the cart" (T 224).

Fleur cannot drown. When she tries to kill herself after Margaret and Nector sell out Pillager land in order to retain their Kashpaw properties, Fleur is unable to do so. Misshepeshu's protection of Fleur is so great that as long as she properly respects him by acknowledging him as a source of her powers, he will recognize her as one of his beings and empower her with medicine gifts and deathless life. He also protects her family. Vecsey reports, "In some traditions it fed and sheltered those who fell through the winter ice" (74) as evidenced when her great-grandson Lipsha dreams back to the time his mother June threw him into the slough to drown. His recollection was not of a horrible death by drowning but rather of a peaceful cradling by a being who sustained him while he was under the water. Misshepeshu may have "hid himself and waited" (T 8) in the deepest waters for those who did not respect his powers or offer appropriate tobacco sacrifices, but he continues to protect the Pillagers and to give them powers. It is interesting to speculate whether Lipsha as he comes into his role as medicine man and healer for his contemporary Chippewa community will learn to avail himself of the gifts and protection Misshepeshu offers the Pillagers. When *The Bingo Palace* ends, Lipsha is still a self-taught healer, and with Fleur relinquishing her role to him, it would be interesting to know if Erdrich has Lipsha realizing and acknowledging this source of available power.

In addition to these elements in Misshepeshu's relationship to Fleur, Pauline plants the idea of a sexual relationship lying at the heart of their alliance. Pauline, an unattractive, sexually-repressed, self-deceiving, unreliable narrator, sublimates her unfulfilled sexual desires into the power and rituals of the Catholic church and, as Sister Leopolda, becomes Christ's bride, the only marriage offer available to her. Her jealousy of Fleur's sexual attractiveness in addition to her jealousy and fear of Fleur's powers cause her to fantasize that Misshepeshu's green eyes and coppery skin lure daring young girls like Fleur to him in order for him to satisfy his concupiscent desires. In her article exploring Fleur's relationship to Misshepeshu, Van Dyke points out that Barnouw reports a sexual connection tied to the snake or horned serpent (17). "The snake," Barnouw explains, "plays an erotic role in some Chippewa tales as a lover of girls" (137), not a surprising connection for a tribe that has been heavily missionized for three centuries. The lake monster thus seems to be a combination of the Genesis account of the temptation in the Garden of Eden and the Chippewa composite rendering of Misshepeshu as snake and great cat.

In light of her character, when Pauline piously warns unsuspecting girls not to be attracted to his beauty and sexual appeal, she seems to be protesting too much. Even so, as with most of Pauline's allegations and insinuations, there is a nugget of truth at the core of her embellished and perverted tale since Morriseau reports Misshepeshu as being a powerful demigod who had children by his female partner" (28). Pauline assumes Fleur is this partner, and the fanatical nun attributes Lulu's green eyes to her underwater father. Erdrich is provocatively obscure concerning the identity of Lulu's male parent, and even Eli wonders if perhaps Misshepeshu is the father of the baby he claims as his daughter. Readers know only that we will never receive the full explanation of why the enigmatic and mythical Fleur possesses all the secrets and that no one, not even Nanapush, comprehends the full workings of her mind.

Fleur, an Anishinaabe Medicine Woman

According to Clarke and Van Dyke ("Of Vision Quests"), Fleur is a transformational character since she assumes at various times the characteristics of the different animals just discussed: bear, wolf, and water-monster. Clarke suggests that "Indeed, she could be described as a visual pun who disorders the boundaries between human and animal" (28). Her approach is to suggest that transformational characters like Fleur depend on language for their power. Clarke's article explores the ways in which she believes Erdrich plays with the ambiguous aspects of language in Fleur's characterization, and Clarke applies concepts of theoretical discourse to position Fleur's character. Van Dyke posits that Erdrich signals to readers that symbolic transformations occur when humans like Fleur and her family take on animal form or characteristics. She concludes, "The descriptions of Fleur in *Tracks* are almost always animal-like; she is Erdrich's character who acts the most out of her own transformational power, or who, we might say, is most herself" (133–34).

Fleur's connection to mythic traditional Anishinaabe animals, bear, lion, wolf, and marten situates her as a being whose immense powers emanate from sources other than human ones. The bear and Misshepeshu associations additionally link her to the supermanitos whose power is rivaled only by that of the Great Spirit himself, Kitche Manito. She is the embodiment of the old-time sanctioned medicine person who seeks power from her animal manitos and who, in turn, is granted the gifts of healing. Fleur represents the old traditional ways in that she, along with the additionally mythical character Nanapush, calls on her animal helpers and exists as their manifestation. She knows the dark side of their powers, as represented by the dualism of good and evil found in Bear and Misshepeshu, but most of all she represents traditional ways of knowing and connecting to the world around her which are rapidly becoming relics of a distant past. She is the female mythic element continuing to assert itself in the lives of her people who are assimilating into Anglo lifestyles and religion at the expense of traditional beliefs, and nowhere is this demonstrated more dramatically than in Pauline's futile attempts to challenge Fleur's powers with her misguided Catholic fanaticism.[13]

Although Fleur's powers are foregrounded in *Tracks*, she is a significant presence as a healer and medicine woman throughout the other three North Dakota novels. In *The Beet Queen*, Fleur remains a shadowy background figure. Her healing powers save Karl who, as previously reported, sees her transform into a bear. Celestine reports Fleur to be her aunt who is now living again with Eli and taking care of the shattered Russell, and Mary regards her as the only person capable of disciplining the spoiled Dot.

In *Love Medicine*, Fleur is the community's healer called upon to deliver Marie's last baby. She is back living with Nanapush, and Marie refers to her as "the Pillager." Lipsha calls her "Old Lady Pillager," and he fears her so much he seeks an alternative to asking her for a love medicine for his grandparents Nector and Marie. He thinks Fleur "was serious business" (241), capable of placing terrible spells on people, and therefore avoids her.[14] Lulu gives an account of her mother Fleur in the novel, which is the only time in her adult life the reader hears Lulu speak of her mother with affection. In the newly added chapter, "The Island," Lulu tells how much she missed her mother when Fleur sent her off the reservation to a boarding school, and it was Fleur's voice coming "from all directions, [that was] mysteriously keeping me from inner harm" (LM 69). The main accounts of Fleur in *Love Medicine* are by her daughter and her great-grandson, both of whom regard her as a potent healer while having very little to do with her. It would have been fascinating to get Fleur's versions of these stories told by her family, but Erdrich, enigmatic as ever, silences Fleur's response, which lies somewhere outside the pages of the novel.

In *The Bingo Palace*, Fleur once again resumes the place of prominence she held in *Tracks*, but this is not surprising since *The Bingo Palace* is the story of Lipsha, her great-grandson and her successor. The community voice relates that Fleur is no longer feared, indeed her presence is regarded as a comfort. She is no longer called Fleur but rather *Mindemoya*, Old Lady. People are still in respectful awe of her powers calling her a "half spirit" (BP 6), and they wish she would confer her powers on someone, preferably not the confused Lipsha Morrissey, who knows he should connect with her but is too afraid of the risk contained in trying. He is finally driven to approach Fleur, because lust for Shawnee Ray has consumed him. He wants Fleur to help with a love potion, but he has no intention of asking her to teach him Pillager medicine. He is once again seeking a shortcut to love through powerful love medicines. Lipsha apparently did not learn his lesson when he previously took a shortcut and caused Nector's death.

Lipsha recounts the good Fleur has done as healer, in contrast to Pauline's accusations of her as witch. He recalls, "The old lady cures fevers, splints bones, has brought half the old-timers in the Senior's Lounge into this world" (BP 126). Like Karl, Lipsha sees Fleur transform herself into a bear, and these two young men, unlike Pauline, are reliable narrators. The community voice records Fleur's final transformation into the Great Bear Spirit. When she chooses to take Lipsha's place on the death road and to save him from freezing to death in the blizzard, Fleur goes to her spirit helpers for good. Her tracks remain behind as a permanent reminder of her presence along with her occasional chuffing noise, her bear laugh. She continues to watch over her people, although in a different form, and the people are comforted and reassured by the spirit of this powerful medicine woman.

Fleur does not speak for herself. All of her actions throughout the four novels are reported by others, who may or may not be speaking the truth. In *Tracks*, Nanapush and Pauline alternately relate Fleur's early years. Nanapush finds Fleur in a near-death state, when "All she had was raw power" (T 7), and he continues to strengthen and support her throughout her life. He acknowledges her awesome powers, and realizes how dangerous she can be. He relates how after Eli's seduction of Sophie, Fleur reproves Eli by going into the frigid lake at night, most likely to reunite with her guardian Misshepeshu; and Erdrich hints at the fact that this may involve a sexual union which Fleur deliberately initiates to punish Eli. In a very telling comment, Nanapush says that Fleur knew medicine songs even he has never heard before. This observation means that Fleur even transcends Nanapush or a traditional trickster possessing the gifts of medicine and healing, a position that could only exist if she has inherited gifts from one or several of the super-manitos whose powers were second only to the Great Spirit Kitche Manito himself. Nanapush as narrator of Fleur's story also has a vested interest in her future in that he has lost his beloved wives and children and has chosen Fleur to take their place. She is his family, and while he appears to be the more reliable of the two narrators, he is still trickster and he is still her family; thus, misdeeds may be glossed over and her healing powers exaggerated.

Throughout the North Dakota novels, various community members narrate Fleur's story, for her story is their story and there are as many versions of the truth of her being as there are people. By allowing Fleur to narrate her own story, Erdrich would demystify her presence and bring her into the ordinary human realm. Fleur remains outside this dimension, living between two worlds as a powerful spirit bringing the gifts of the manitos to her Chippewa people and as a human subject to life's hardships.[15] She represents powers inherited from a mythic past which continue to provide guardianship to her Chippewa people at a time when alcohol, the Anglo cities, and America's various wars claim the souls of many of her Indian people. Fleur comes as a reminder that the traditional ways of being in right relationship with the world still hold, even in a time when corrupting Anglo influences threaten to separate the Chippewa people from their traditional beliefs.

Fleur is the female mythic presence throughout four novels who serves as a counter to the rapid assimilation taking place among her people, and her story passes into the mythic repertoire of her people when she leaves the reservation for the final time to rejoin the spirit world. Her presence has bound the community together as no other mortal character could possibly have done, and it is the myth of Fleur and her link to the super-manitos that sustains the people's spiritual health. They may fear Fleur, and they may only half-believe her abilities to deliver manito power to them, but they still situate her among the beings of old whose presence is a gift to the community. Once the trickster Nanapush was Fleur's ally, but now that he is no longer around, Fleur stands as the sole symbol of transformational power.

The Antelope People

Erdrich shifts the location of *The Antelope Wife* from North Dakota to the urban reservation in *Gakahbekong*, Minneapolis, an area from which Turtle Mountain Chippewa migrated in the 1700s and 1800s and the area to which groups of Chippewa return a century later. Chippewa bands from Minnesota and Wisconsin were originally part of the group settling in the Red River Valley known collectively as the Pembina band.[16] When the land cessions made it impossible for all of the Chippewa to remain in North Dakota, the United States Government in 1863 established two western Minnesota reservations, Red Lake and White Earth, to which some of the Chippewa returned. However, when they returned, they were no longer exclusively a Woodlands Culture, as the mythology of the Plains Indians was indelibly imprinted upon their worldview. Thus, the antelope people of the western plains become integrated into Ojibwa mythology. Gregory Camp explains, "The salient feature of the Chippewa migration onto the plains was their ability to adapt to the new environment, incorporate it into their old way, and meld the two into a new lifestyle" (*Turtle Mountain* 36–37).

The antelope people are transformational beings who become a part of Chippewa mythology once the Ojibwa establish themselves on the plains. The American antelope, called a pronghorn, lives on the open grasslands and occupies a range extending from central Saskatchewan to Central Mexico. On the plains, one sees them at great distances, and as the antelope disappear into the horizon, they seem to be leaving this world for another. They, therefore, like the bear, appear to mediate between this world and the spirit world, and the mythology of the Plains Indians incorporates this ethereal creature into its traditional stories. Pretty-shield, a medicine woman of the Crow Tribe, speaking through an interpreter to Frank Linderman relates the following:

"The antelope are a strange people. They are beautiful to look at, and yet they are tricky. We do not trust them. They appear and disappear; they are like shadows on the plains. Because of their great beauty young men sometimes follow the antelope and are lost forever. Even if these foolish ones find themselves and return, they are never again right in their heads. This strangeness has always belonged to the antelope"(114–15). Readers will recognize this quote from the foreword to Erdrich's poem "The Strange People," where, as Van Dyke explains, "an antelope woman defies the hunter who thinks he has killed her, and yet she still waits for one with whom she could share the transformational power" ("Of Vision Quests" 132).

This is not the only tale of antelope people Pretty-shield relates to Linderman. There is also the story of Pretty-shield hearing an antelope sing to her threatened babies. This song remains with Pretty-shield and becomes the one she sings to comfort fretful children and grandchildren at night. The tale of four young girls playing kick ball and the two strangely beautiful girls befriending them is another Crow story of the strange antelope people. When the Crow girls see the hind ends of their new friends, they see antelope tails. Pretty-shield concludes the tale, "The Crow girls, glad to be rid of the strange beautiful ones, spat four time on the ground, over their left hands. Ahhh, the antelope are deceivers, not helpers" (117).

Tales of antelope people are not exclusive to Plains Indians. In the Southwest, the Hopi also have a tale "The Antelope Kids" from Oraibi mesa which relates the story of an older childless couple who travel to sacred shrines to ask to be granted children. The woman soon delivers twins, "or 'antelope kids' as the Hopi call them" (Malotki 393). The father soon realizes the children are endowed with special powers, and he cautions his wife not to scold them. However, the mother does scold and punish the children over time until the twins' antelope father comes for them. The antelope people had given the children to the couple, but when the twins were mistreated, the children were transformed back into their animal bodies and rejoined their animal people (Ekkehart Malotki, *Hopi Animal Tales*). The antelope are additionally important to the Hopi in the Snake Ceremony where the Antelope Priests and four small boys ceremonially prepare for the arrival of the Snake Priests (Jesse Walter Fewkes, *Tusayan Flute and Snake Ceremonies*).

The Apache also have a folktale of a young man from outside the village who woos and wins the heart of the most beautiful maiden in the community. When they marry and join his people, they become the antelope people, sent to humans to teach them respect for all living beings. The husband and wife divide their time between their two families, transforming themselves at will from human to antelope. Realizing they ultimately belong with the antelope people, the young couple jump through four hoops and remain permanently transformed as antelope. This tale ends with the lesson to the people that out among the antelope are Antelope Woman and her children who are a part of their village, and for this reason, they must always be respectful and honor all creatures, especially the antelope (Michael Lacapa, *Antelope Woman*).

Erdrich plays with these pan-tribal perceptions of the antelope people in *The Antelope Wife*: antelope as deceivers, the beauty of the antelope women, antelope people as guardians to humans, and the ability of the antelope people to transform themselves at will to human form. The motif of the mythological antelope people frames *The Antelope Wife* along with the story of the mythic twins and their often violent attempts to secure the perfect beads for their design, which turns out to be the stories of the three families—Shawnos, Whiteheart Beads, and Roys. Blue Prairie Woman, who takes a deer husband and whose animal family rescues her motherless seven-year-old daughter Matilda Roy and raises her, has a descendent who has been kidnapped and transported to the city of Minneapolis. She is Sweetheart Calico, with "her lean face, clear and smooth and pale milk-caramel, sweet as a hen's egg, her tea-brown eyes, her hair a powerful wing sweeping down her slim back. She has slender, jutting hips, long legs, on her feet black stiletto heels like shiny fork prongs. Perfect honed features " (AW 105). Klaus is the man so intoxicated by the beauty of Ninimshe, his Sweetheart Calico, that he foolishly binds her (with calico trade cloth) and carries her away to Minneapolis where she languishes from lack of the open plains and the companionship of her daughters. In doing so, Klaus violates the honored bond between the Antelope People and those they protect. They are sacred beings whose beauty lure the unsuspecting like Klaus and leave him changed forever, but they are not to be captured or held with risk of violating the order of the world, as evidenced when Jimmy Badger, medicine man of the Plains Ojibwa where Klaus was trading, calls Klaus begging him to return Antelope Wife to her plains home where she belongs. Without her, Jimmy's tribe experiences continual bad luck. Only when Klaus releases her from the city which has imprisoned her can he begin to set aright the order he had violated when he tried to possess her and carried her away from her plains home. Before Antelope Wife begins to run westward back to her home, she must enact her part of the story. This story began in the distant past when the original Blue Prairie Woman secures her daughter to a cradle board, hangs on the board a necklace of blue beads, and uses her faithful dog to carry her infant away from her ravaged village. Antelope Woman passes on these blue beads to the one who will carry their story and relationship to the Anishinaabe mythic story, Cally Roy. Once the mystical antelope woman has played her part in the human Anishinaabe drama, she can return to her people on the western plains.

Mythic Dogs

Not only are there deer-to-human transformation, but also there are dogs that speak and play a central role in the survival of the people. "Original dog walked alongside Wenebojo" (81), trickster creator of humankind, and continues to link canine survival to the survival of the Ojibwa people. According to Almost Soup, the fast thinking dog who becomes Cally's devoted companion, dogs "have walked down the prayer road clearing the way for humans since before time started" (80). The dogs' story begins with Sorrow, who as a puppy Blue Prairie Woman nursed in order to bring relief to her breasts throbbing because of her lost child, and this story parallels the mythic story of Oshkikwe nursing a pup.[17] Sorrow accompanies Blue Prairie Woman on her journey to retrieve her daughter and ends up being sacrificed in order that Matilda Roy might have food to survive once her mother dies of the fever. Almost Soup, a descendent of Sorrow, also saves a human from Blue Prairie Woman's lineage, Cally Roy, whose sickness is so life threatening that only by taking Cally's life into his body was she spared. Another dog touchstone story is that of Windigo Dog, mythic dog, who cracks jokes and saves Klaus from being run over by a lawnmower and brings Klaus to a full realization of how his kidnapping of Antelope Woman has imprisoned them both. This event is pivotal in forcing him to reassess his actions, give up drinking, and finally release his Antelope wife.

The Mythic World of *The Antelope Wife*

Just as the human stories are beaded together, so are the stories of the dogs and the antelope people sewn into the pattern which connects human and animal worlds. As Almost Soup relates, "Though I live the dog's life and take on human sins, I am connected in the beadwork. I live in the beadwork too" (91). The role of transspecies transformation and animal guides as helpmate to hapless humans abounds in Ojibwa mythology and traditional tales and evidences a manifestation of power released to humans through their animal brothers. According to Overholt and Callicott, most metamorphosis stories take place in the mythic world when the human world is not firmly established and where the definition of "human" is inclusive of both human and animal beings (142–43). *The Antelope Wife* is a contemporary rendering of the traditional Anishinaabe belief in the intimate interconnection between human and animal, mortal and divine.

Erdrich, the Maker of Myths

In fashioning Fleur, Antelope Wife, and Windigo Dog, Erdrich becomes a mythmaker like her characters who stand as symbols of the possibility that the unknown spirit world can still assert itself in the lives of her contemporary Chippewa people. When Fleur brings the great powers of the spirit bear and Misshepeshu into the lives of her people, she exemplifies the possibility of living in right relationship to the spirits. Chippewa people regularly used to seek access to manito powers through the Midéwewin ceremonies, and this relationship remains available, even in modern times, to those willing to seek it. The Antelope People and Windigo Dog easily move with the Anishinaabeg from the Woodlands, to the Plains, to the cities where they continue to exist alongside their human relations. It is this continual co-existence with powerful mythic beings from the past that will continue to be a vital part of contemporary Anishinaabe life, if only the people will seek their power. The possibility and probability of a continued relationship with the manitos exist through several community members by the end of the North Dakota novels: Shawnee Ray knows how to talk sweetly to the spirits, and her uncle Xavier Toose serves as an intermediary to the spirits by directing traditional sweat lodges. Lipsha bumbles along being granted visions he does not understand and powers he does not know how to use, but he is beginning to understand the role he is destined to fill in the community. The urban Indians, likewise, still have access to animal helpers if only they live in respect and right relation with them. In the character of Cally, descendent of Antelope Woman and one protected and nourished by the spirit of Original Dog, lies the possibility of a continual mythic presence being sustained and passed on to future generations. In her novels, Erdrich creates female characters who embody or are recipients of manito power still aiding her Indian people. Fleur's story and Cally's story are Erdrich's tribute to an enduring spiritual dimension in Chippewa life, and the myth Erdrich creates around Fleur and Antelope Wife positions Erdrich as a secondary hero, one who passes on traditional stories in contemporary form. Erdrich through her novels sustains the mythic tradition of a people who, having survived for at least a millennium, enter the twenty-first century attended by the presence of their ancestral spirits.

Chapter 6

Louise Erdrich, An American Storyteller

Native American literature has nudged its way into recognition as part of the American literary tradition with the garnering of prestigious literary awards such the Pulitzer Prize (N. Scott Momaday's *House Made of Dawn*), a National Endowment for the Humanities Creative Writing Fellowship (Paula Gunn Allen), a five-year MacArthur Foundation grant (Leslie Marmon Silko and Ofelia Zepeda), and the National Book Critics Circle Award (Louise Erdrich's *Love Medicine*). However, do these prizes represent the incorporation of Native American writers into the canon of American literature, or have these prize-winning authors merely been relegated to a separate class within the American tradition as successful minority writers who have managed to steal away the hegemony's prestigious awards? Related to this question is the issue of whether Native American writers are authentically "different" from their Anglo counterparts. These complex issues concerning multiculturalism and the canon are far from resolved today. Still, there has been tremendous progress, especially in the last thirty years of the twentieth century, in opening up the canon to all accomplished American writers regardless of their race, gender, or sexual preference. In order to situate Erdrich in what has conventionally been designated as the American literary mainstream, it is helpful to consider first how critics and academics position Native American writers like Erdrich and then to discuss her as a product of both the American literary as well as the Native American tradition.

The American Literary Canon and Multiculturalism

Houston Baker, Jr., in an introductory essay to the MLA's 1993 issue of *Profession* devoted to multiculturalism asserts that "During the past quarter century ... we who have been othered have awakened ... [and the academy] has witnessed the coming to fullness of such denominations as black studies, women's studies, Chicano and Chicana studies, gay and lesbian studies, Native American studies, and Asian American studies. Here, we might say—in these denominations—is the earth's plenty" (5). Henry Louis Gates, Jr., in the same issue asks for a definition of multiculturalism and comes to the conclusion that it is nothing more than an acknowledgment and recognition of difference and queries, "whose differences? which differences?" (6). These questions seem to cut immediately to the heart of the matter. The traditional Anglo-male dominated American canon has positioned as "other" those who are different from themselves, so that women and people of color could carry off literary awards, but would, nevertheless, be positioned within the separate categories to which the ascendant voice had assigned them. Thus the dominant voice maintains and perpetuates distance. Gates argues elsewhere that by assigning writers to a separate race-based category, Anglo critics are choosing to emphasize their difference from these "others." He concludes, "Race is the ultimate trope of difference because it is so very arbitrary in its application" ("'Race,' Writing, and Difference" 5).

It is thus worth reconsidering the practice and its consequences of assigning writers of color and women writers to separate and thinly veiled unequal categories. While grouping by categories is a common literary/analytical tool, it is important to reflect on whether the groupings are to identify differences and thus provide a framework for better appreciating women and writers of color or whether, in fact, the separate categories help maintain a distance of marginal "others" from a dominant white male hegemony. Critics and readers alike endorse the creative talents of many minority writers, and it thus becomes problematic to justify dispatching such acclaimed authors as Zora Neale Hurston, James Baldwin, Richard Wright, Ralph Ellison, Alice Walker, and Toni Morrison to the confining category of Black American writers just as it is equally limiting to position Louise Erdrich, N. Scott Momaday, Leslie Marmon Silko, James Welch, and Gerald Vizenor at the margins of the canon in a separate Native American literature category.

Even so, the relegation to categories of the "other" continues in reviews, critical work, and college courses.

Nancy Hartsock offers some interesting insights into the reasons for this continuing practice. Drawing upon Albert Memmi's *The Colonizer and the Colonized,* she offers a list of reasons for "this artificially created Other" (192). The first reason, she believes, is because the Other is seen as lacking those qualities prized by the dominant society; the second reason is that the dominant society, unable to understand those different from themselves, views the Other as mysterious and unfathomable; and third, the Others are assigned to a place outside the 'human community' where chaos governs the lives of this "anonymous collectivity" (192). Hartsock concludes that this way of looking at the world from a privileged white male "puts an omnipotent subject at the center and constructs marginal Others as sets of negative qualities" (192), which complements Gates's notion that the very acknowledgment of race is the acknowledgment of difference.

While these complicated issues of race and difference in America's literary tradition cannot be resolved here, it is important to place the question of the canon and the fate and role of Native American literature in a larger context. One must consider whether Indian writers will always be categorized by their difference from the dominant culture, a difference that infers and implies inferiority. Moreover, the issues of canonical placement can easily be raised in regard to an established Brahmin writer like Henry James in relation to a frontier satirist like Mark Twain and gifted minority writers with Ph.D.s like N. Scott Momaday, Paula Gunn Allen, and Greg Sarris. Relating Momaday, Allen, and Sarris to a separate and not quite equal category of Indian writers does not make sense if writing is the denominator, but it does, unfortunately, make painful sense if ethnicity and gender are the informing factors. Thus, when regarding the work of minority and women writers, a reader must be aware of subtle implications of categories. Considering a work's cultural context enhances a reading; yet the question remains as to whether categories help to appreciate or to promote differences.

In his book *The Voice in the Margin: Native American Literature and the Canon,* Arnold Krupat provides us with a working definition of "the canon" that is useful for this discussion. He asserts that

"The canon is taken simply as the name for that body of texts which best performs in the sphere of culture the work of legitimating the prevailing social order" (22). He makes the point that, through the years, traditional Indian narratives in order to elevate their legitimacy gradually have assumed western literary forms, so that the oral narratives, myths, legends, coup stories, songs, and chants gradually evolved into the novels, poems, and short stories of the dominant society. Allen does not find this transition problematic, for she asserts that, on the other hand, the Native American literary tradition is a dynamic one that continues to reassemble itself in order to adjust to an ever-changing world. It is the process, after all. Time cannot be arrested—though it can be enriched. She emphasizes that "Native cultures and consciousness include western cultural elements and structures. Assuming they do not seriously dislocate the tradition in which they are embedded, this inclusion makes them vital rather than impure or 'decadent'" (*Spider* 7). She concludes that, if western cultural elements are used to enhance the Native tradition, they become "as vital as the oral tradition which also informs and reflects contemporary Indian life" (*Spider* 7). Krupat reflects a similar view when he posits that a new category called *Indigenous literature* be named which embraces traditional Indian modes that have merged with literary genres of the dominant society. He offers, "Indigenous literatures is that type of writing produced when an author of subaltern cultural identification manages successfully to merge forms internal to his cultural formation with forms external to it, but pressing upon, even seeking to delegitimate it" (*Voice* 214).

Literary works by talented writers of Native American ancestry warrant an unqualified invitation to join the ongoing conversation about the American literary canon. It asks to be judged on its merits as a literary work with importance assigned to the cultural identification of its author to be used only as a means to enrich its reading. Readers can gain a deeper appreciation of Indian literature by understanding the frame out of which Native American authors write: they tell tribal stories that ensure cultural continuity, they affirm a communal identity, and they revere a sense of place. These are deserving reasons to consider the different cultural context out of which Indian literature arises.

For a people whose ancestors have resided on the American continent for over 10,000 years, the inclusion of acclaimed, educated, and gifted Native voices in the American literary canon does not seem an unreasonable request. Placement in the canon does matter, since it ensures a larger audience for a work when anthologized and taught in colleges and universities. Canonical acceptance thus becomes crucial to how widely a book is distributed. Additionally, into what category should the canon place mixed-blood writers like Silko and Erdrich? These prominent writers with fractional amounts of Indian blood choose to identify themselves as Native American writers, thus further complicating the issue of rigid categories.

Categories seem to be satisfying and useful for readers and critics alike when they endeavor to situate a particular author's work within a certain frame in order to clarify the context out of which the work arises. This seems to be a legitimate reason for emphasizing differences and one that is not based on the assumption of hierarchical categories of more legitimate and less legitimate literatures. To appreciate the Kiowa culture out of which Momaday writes, the mixed Laguna, Mexican, and Anglo heritage which informs Silko's writing, and Erdrich's Chippewa and German ancestry of survivors on the harsh North Dakota Plains is to appreciate these three writers' unique frames of reference, just as one notes with interest the ways in which Edith Wharton's aristocratic upbringing informs her stories and the manner in which Emily Dickinson's reclusive Amherst environment helped produce one of the world's great poets. Noting difference can and should be a stimulating exercise for intellectually open minds, and the more that differences in American writers are recognized for the distinctive voice with which they speak, the more the American literary tradition will cultivate a dynamic and deracinated center.

Writing out of the Dominant Culture

When one examines the degree to which prominent writers like Erdrich appropriate traditional Euro-American literary forms and even echo familiar characters and moments from past Euro-American writing in their work, their restriction to a Native American category becomes even more problematic. Erdrich is a writer who identifies herself with her Indian ancestry and who writes out of that specific tradition. However, by the beginning of the twenty-first century, the Native American literary tradition has become so influenced and shaped by the dominant Euro-American literary voice that it is impossible to speak of "pure" Indian writing since literary history by its very nature is a history of borrowing and appropriating. The American voice was shaped by the British, by the African Americans, and by the voices of ethnic people. Likewise, as Allen notes, the Native American literary voice has continued to evolve and redefine itself as influences from the dominant culture continue to assert themselves in Indian experiences.

However, not all Indian scholars view the process of literary adaptation as a natural or a desirable process. Jack Forbes, an Indian anthropologist, in his article "Colonialism and Native American Literature: Analysis" considers the current shape of Indian literature as a form not just influenced by but forced on Natives by a dominant culture. He maintains that *"since the sixteenth century Native American literature-making has existed largely within the confines of colonialism and imperialism"* (19). He believes that the powerful force called Colonialism "distorts, suppresses, oppresses, falsifies, changes, warps, and destroys" literature of the Natives (19), and he insists that the Indian literature of today has been radically altered because it was not allowed to evolve naturally. He calls for contemporary Indians to write for Indians, but this seems to be needlessly restrictive since Native Americans comprise only 1% of the population and, as such, are not a sizable enough market to make economic sense for Indian writers. Additionally, he is being as restrictive as the Anglos who seek to keep him out of the dominant literary frame.

Toni Morrison likewise considers the implication of domination on the production of literature in her book *Playing in the Dark: Whiteness and the Literary Imagination.* Since she regards the American literary canon as being written to and about white Americans, she examines the degree to which "literary whiteness" is an embedded, subconscious force shaping the ways Blacks have been portrayed in literature. She regards canonical authors as representatives of the dominant viewpoint and wonders about the implications of this situation for African Americans who remain outside as subjects and as audience. Her exploration of this question leads her to the conclusion that Blacks in literature subsequently have become stereotyped, dehumanized, and dehistoricized. While her concerns are for the representation of African Americans in literature, the issues she raises speak as well to the problems Native Americans face in their representation in literature, their acceptance into the literary mainstream as "Indian" writers, and their ability to get published.

One acceptable way for minority writers to produce texts is to write in a style and form acceptable to the dominant culture, that is, to write like its writers; and one can wonder if by a certain point in history, minority groups do genuinely write like the dominant group through a natural process of cultural assimilation. The early "successful" Indian voices were of this kind: William Apes (a Methodist minister), George Copeway (another Methodist minister), and William Warren (a Minnesota state representative). It was not until 1854 that the first novel by an Indian was published with John Rollin Ridge's *Life and Adventures of Joaquin Murieta*, and for the next 120 years, a sporadic production of texts by Indian authors appeared for a largely Anglo readership. Black American authors articulated a clear voice in the Harlem Renaissance of the 1920s, but Native Americans saw the nascence of the most productive literary period in their history only in the last quarter of the twentieth century. By this point in their history, as Forbes suggests, the Native American production of texts was largely generated on an Anglo model, since their traditional oral culture did not provide a written tradition from which authors could work. Thus, while a reader can read contemporary Indian works as coming out of a Native American cultural tradition, contemporary authors remain the product of four hundred years of assimilation and acculturation.

Erdrich and the American Literary Tradition

Erdrich is a prominent example of a successful Native American author who is clearly the product of two traditions. Most of this study is devoted to articulating the various creative ways in which she writes out of her Native American tradition generally and her Chippewa tradition specifically. Nevertheless, as a graduate of both Dartmouth College and the Johns Hopkins MA Creative Writing Program, it was in the Euro-American tradition that she received her literary training. A reader does not have to look very far to find the influence of the American literary tradition on her work. In *The Beet Queen* when Sita finds herself in a mental hospital because she refuses to speak, she becomes paralyzed by the terrible yellow walls, and "The light made the sick yellow of the walls blaze and throb" (BP 210). The debt to Charlotte Perkins Gilman's *The Yellow Wallpaper* is unmistakable. Additionally, the most engaging character in the first four of the North Dakota novels is the good-hearted but bumbling, self-conscious Lipsha Morrissey who, while trying to grow into himself, more often than not ends up subverting his own attempts at maturity. He is self-reflective, honest, funny, humble, well-intended, loving, and kind; but he is constantly in trouble because in his immaturity he too often leads with his heart and not his head. His soul searching, self-deprecating, humorous first-person narratives warm a reader's heart in the same ways that Huck Finn and Holden Caulfield struggle to come into themselves in a world that does not make much sense to intelligent and sensitive young men.

Erdrich not only echoes characters and scenes from American literature, but she also utilizes a format common to both traditional Native American storytellers and the western European literary tradition, story cycles as Helen Jaskoski ("From") notes about *Love Medicine*.[1] Erdrich's story cycles (described in chapters 2 and 3) are stories clustered around people and events, and her five North Dakota novels one long story cycle. Susan Garland Mann's *The Short Story Cycle: A Genre Companion and Reference Guide* becomes an invaluable guide to understanding the form of the traditional American story cycle that Erdrich mingles with her Native American story cycle. Mann's study extends the work of Forrest L. Ingram and Joanne V. Creighton, two of the first scholars to offer systematic descriptions of this distinct genre, lying somewhere between the short story and the novel, in which "the stories are both self sufficient and interrelated" (15). Although Mann sees the short story cycle as growing out of the framed stories in Boccaccio's *The Decameron* and Chaucer's *The Canterbury Tales*, it wasn't until the 1920s with Sherwood Anderson's *Winesburg, Ohio*, Jean Toomer's *Cane* and Ernest Hemingway's *In Our Time* that American authors began to appropriate this form. Its characteristic features include a series of different protagonists with less emphasis on plot or chronology than contained in a traditional novel.

Creighton writes that "The composite lends itself to an exploration of unique cultural identity shared by a group of people, whereas the novel is suited to an intensive study of an individual or a few individuals" (154). Creighton's work arises from her dissertation examining the short story composite found in James Joyce's *The Dubliners* and William Faulkner's *Go Down, Moses*, in which she positions the main characters as evolving Southern and Dubliner prototypes. Indeed, as Mann points out, many short-story cycles are character-dominated, but one also finds short story cycles unified by theme, especially the theme of loneliness, with *Winesburg, Ohio* clearly falling into this category. These short story cycles can also revolve around a community, especially those "devoted to a particular place which has mythic rather than historic importance" (Mann 13), and here we find an important confluence of Erdrich's native and American literary models. Quoting from Ingram, Mann suggests that "The writers of today often seem intent on building mythic kingdoms of some sort. Faulkner has his Yoknapatawpha County, Steinbeck his Pastures of Heaven, Camus his kingdom of solidarity, Joyce his city of paralysis, and Anderson his Winesburg. Heroes, usually diminished in stature, roam the imaginary streets and plains of these kingdoms"(25).

I would add Erdrich to this distinguished list because of the mythic reservation she creates on the Plains of North Dakota. Her story cycle concerns a community of Indians and Anglos living in an environment that finds only the heartiest souls surviving, and often this survival requires people to bridle emotions and sociability in order to save strength for the basic necessities needed for endurance. Erdrich's characters, though, do more than endure, and chapter 4 demonstrated the power of love as a salve to the demands of life in this physically challenging environment. Her Indian families are equipped with a strong sense of tradition and maternal love, and her Anglo family with a rebellious but lovable Dot at the core are the survivors in an environment that weeds out the weak and strengthens the tenacity of the strong.

The short story cycle utilized by both Native American storytellers like Erdrich and twentieth-century authors privileges shifting narrators in this multi-voiced, multifarious, and centerless narrative. Postmodern theorists like Jacques Derrida argue that to search for a center or governing structure in works is a fruitless exercise since the shifting nature of language necessitates that there is no center, there is only discourse (84). If language is unstable and signals different meanings to the people interpreting it, then unity becomes a construct no longer applicable to fiction. This is especially seen in the works of twentieth-century authors who deliberately set out to create a seamless yet centerless novel where different people relate their stories, stories that can contract, explain, or offer alternate points of view to the lives of the various characters. Faulkner's *The Unvanquished, As I Lay Dying, The Sound and the Fury,* and *Absalom! Absalom!* come to mind immediately.[2] What becomes apparent by juxtaposing Erdrich's storytelling techniques is that she writes out of two traditions. Although she grounds her work in the Chippewa storytelling tradition, she also utilizes the same modern literary forms used by some of America's best twentieth-century writers, like Faulkner. The language is western; some techniques like story cycles, shifting narrators and a centerless novel are both a twentieth-century western literary construct and common to native traditions. However, what distinguishes Erdrich as a writer is the degree to which she functions as a tribal storyteller, one who speaks for the community, and the degree to which her writing is grounded by a native way of organizing and perceiving the world.

From Myth to Rhetorics

Claude Lévi-Strauss in his important book *The Raw and the Cooked* asserts that myth is never stable and is always in process since "It is a phenomenon of the imagination, resulting from the attempt at interpretation; and its function is to endow the myth with synthetic form and to prevent its disintegration into a confusion of opposites" (5–6). Mythmaking is a human endeavor to shape meaning and to structure experience, and as Lévi-Strauss argues, myth is not a fixed and stable commodity to be handed down to succeeding generations but rather a body of narrative created from experience and always in flux as people continually reassess their place in the world. Myths are ever in process, for in this way they continue to have relevance for the people who consciously and subconsciously absorb their meaning. Philip Fisher's insightful article in *Redrawing the Boundaries*, noted in chapter 1, analyzes how for the American literary tradition, the myth has changed from the Puritan myth to Frederic Jackson Turner's frontier myth. These myths served to define the identity of a new people, European immigrants who since their landing at Plymouth Rock in 1607 have been engaged in an ongoing attempt to forge a new and distinctly American identity. In this way, the American myth has served to unify experience and to provide a base from which the culture can always interpret itself. As Fisher explains, "Myth is adopted as a fixed, satisfying, and stable story that is used again and again to normalize our account of social life" (232).

The American myth, however, is once again transformed as the Puritan and frontier stories become no longer inclusive enough to accommodate America's ever changing population. Again according to Fisher, "If the frontier myth was a myth of the West, the Puritan myth was a myth of a New England culture, asserting its right to a permanent steering function in national life" (234). As America's population burgeoned with the influx of new immigrants beginning in the late 1900s, the need became apparent for a new, more encompassing myth since the American populace no longer could endorse the myths developed when a national identity was assuming its initial shape. As the old myths failed and no longer explained a people's experiences, a void evolved that demanded to be filled, but this void was not to be replaced with another myth. Fisher posits that a singular myth no longer is adequate to include the variety of American experiences, and he argues that rhetoric or cultural studies currently operate to define our experiences. Cultural studies replaces a singular hegemonic ideology with a plurality that is open to redefinition and reformulation.

Fisher's work concerns itself with how first myth, then rhetorics, shaped the literary traditions arising from shared assumptions about the American experience. Allen in a similar way considers the Native American literary tradition and the degree to which it has changed and reformulated itself as it continues to encompass the dominant Anglo culture. Since so much of Native American life and culture has been infused and shaped by the dominant Anglo ideology, one must question just how deep that influence extends. American life has certainly imprinted itself on Indian religion, systems of government, education, language, clothing, and housing, and, conversely, Indian ways have influenced the dominant culture. From the League of the Iroquois adopted by the American forefathers while writing the Constitution to contemporary Anglos wearing moccasins, living in tipis, and participating in sweat lodge ceremonies, Indian lifestyles continue to assert themselves on the American mainstream.[3]

Continuance of the Mythic for Native Americans

The crucial question to consider is has this Anglo influence seeped into the mythic dimension of the Indian peoples as well? Allen reflects on this issue when she considers the degree to which western cultural elements and structures have shaped the Native culture of today. She acknowledges the influence as fact, but she believes it is only an influence and not an ideology changing basic Indian assumptions about themselves. She believes, as Fisher does, that literature is the likely vehicle by which the underlying myths and assumptions of a people find expression, and she acknowledges that as Native ways have become infused with Anglo ways, Indian literature reflects these outside influences. "The Native literary tradition is dynamic; it changes as our circumstances change. It pertains to the daily life of the people..." (*Spider* 7).

This influence does not extend itself into the mythic dimension of the Indian people, however. Myth for Native Americans is a more enduring and stable narrative than for the American population in general. The enduring Indian myths and basic assumptions about themselves and their place in the world continue even today in the wake of the dominant culture's prolonged attempts to eradicate Indian culture and even Indians themselves through the sanctioned, if unwritten, policy of cultural genocide Anglo Americans waged against Native Americans for centuries.[4] It's no wonder that contemporary Indian authors like Erdrich feel committed to pass on cultural values and traditions since she and her people against overwhelming odds have managed to survive into the twenty-first century.

The Importance of Stories and of Storytelling

For many Native people, culture and tradition still inform their lives, and contemporary literature is one area where the old traditions and myths still live. Chapter 2 deals extensively with the extent to which contemporary Native American writers, especially Erdrich, are storytellers whose function has always been to preserve, pass on, and reformulate the Indian experience. For Erdrich, the mythic dimension of her Chippewa people finds continuous expression in the persons of Nanapush, Gerry Nanapush, Fleur and Antelope Woman, whose presence in the novels is a reminder of the extent to which the old myths still survive, somewhat transformed but always vital. Contemporary Native American authors feel the need to articulate myths as culturally unifying expressions, and the novels of Welch, Momaday, and Silko hinge upon the degree to which the mythic dimension in tribal life continues to inform and renew the people. This study examines the ways in which Erdrich not only uses the mythic dimension of her Chippewa people, but also how she positions herself as tribal storyteller and the creator of a new myth that merges with traditional ones to tell the ongoing story of a tribal people.

Erdrich's novels serve as her offering of the significance of the lives of the contemporary Plains Ojibwa living in North Dakota and Minneapolis. Stories are people's search for meaning, and Allen suggests, "For all of us, Indian or not, stories are a major way we make communal, transcendent meaning out of human experience" (*Spider* 8). Erdrich's novels reflect the degree to which stories and storytellers change over time, all the while retaining a basic tribal integrity.

Wlad Godzich examines what follows in a society when the storyteller no longer serves as the repository of shared wisdom, reflecting Walter Benjamin's premise that the storytellers have lost their authority. The implications of this premise reflect the degree to which American culture has changed. When people no longer learn from the experiences related by a storyteller and instead acquire disconnected information about people, objects, and places that allow them to formulate their own conclusions, their society has become so individualistic that shared experiences no longer constitute knowledge.

Working with Ross Chambers's ideas from *Story and Situation* as well as Benjamin's theory that the storyteller no longer functions as the shared repository of communal wisdom, Godzich argues that stories today must stand on their own, divorced from their teller and recognizable as a separate commodity available in the open market of art. He asserts that with the demise of a respected storyteller guaranteeing the story's authenticity, "the story, commodified as it has become, will take on the guise of an object rather than being a process between human beings" (103). This development, though, is not all bad, for according to Chambers, the stories now begin to "exert powers of their own" (Godzich 104). A society valuing its individualism, one of the lingering effects of the frontier myth, would embrace this new concept of the story in which it is available on the common market to be individually digested and served up to benefit the person or to be discarded as one's needs demand.

In the Native American community, in contrast, individualism is not valorized as it is in the Anglo community. In fact, as chapter 4 points out, Native Americans define themselves by their family, tribe, and community. Belonging and knowing one's place in tribal life is the operative state; and when Indians position themselves outside this structure, the results are usually disastrous, as Momaday in *House Made of Dawn*, Silko in *Ceremony*, and Welch in *Winter in the Blood* so poignantly narrate. In these works, identity is belonging to the community in much the same way that community functions in contemporary African-American writing. Elizabeth Schultz writes of the importance of community in the contemporary African-American novel. She explains, "With its insistence upon the community as the source of life, the contemporary Afro-American novel stands in antithesis to those novels by white and black Americans which have made the alienated American a fixture in our American literature curricula and in our imaginations"(183).

The role of the Indian storyteller takes on new urgency as succeeding generations attempt to define themselves anew in an ongoing struggle to survive as tribal people. The role of Indian storytellers is as vital as ever, and today some of the storytellers are products of America's finest educational institutions like Allen, Vizenor, Erdrich, and Momaday. They use features from the oral tradition in their work while writing their stories in a manner not only acceptable to the Anglo audience but also to their Indian people. Unlike Anglo stories functioning as separate entities available for use by anyone who chooses to connect with them, the Native American story, as Jarold Ramsey argues, can never be divorced from the tribal identity from which it emerges; and the best Indian writers today all write out of their tribal traditions.

Allen analyzes the role of storytellers in the Native American community in her introduction to *Spider Woman's Granddaughters*: "In the old ways practiced by many tribes, a person who is so inclined and capable on occasion sits and tells stories. The stories are woven of elements that illuminate the ritual tradition of the storyteller's people, make pertinent points to some listener who is about to make a mistake or who has some difficulty to resolve, and hold the listeners' attention so that they can experience a sense of belonging to a sturdy and strong tradition" (*Spider* 1). This role of Indian storytellers has not changed. Whether the medium is the novel, poem, short story or oral story told to tribal members, this legacy emanates out of a tradition that continues to adapt itself and to evolve; and contemporary fiction by Native American authors stands as a conflation of both oral and written traditions. The distinctive voice of contemporary Native American writers emerges from these tribal and communal experiences.

Chambers points out that a story is not only talking about experience but also is "experience itself" (Godzich 103). Erdrich's unique contribution to her tribal community and to literature is the way in which she creates a story of her people constituted from tribal epistemology, and she engages readers in a process of making meaning from her stories in much the same way traditional storytellers present their art. In the traditional tribal world, stories were not a commodity to be consumed, but rather they stood as a perspective on tribal experiences, often opaque, but always discernible to a community willing to share in the experience and make meaning from the parts. Erdrich writes out of her Indian heritage and positions herself as a tribal storyteller through her presentation and her shared cultural knowledge, while at the same time making use of the American literary tradition learned in her schooling and through her Anglo heritage. She narrates the story of Indian communities struggling to survive the forces of nature, the forces of the United States government, the forces of a dominant culture continuing to assert itself in the lives of the Indian community, and the pull of assimilation upon urban and reservation Indians alike. Her novels are not an elegy for a people who have been swallowed up or eliminated by Anglos; rather, they are a testimony to the strength and endurance of a people whose will to survive remains unchecked by agents seeking its demise. In her novels, Erdrich heralds the triumphant voice of a people whose survival is nothing less than miraculous. Erdrich's mythic rendering of the story of her Indian people is her literary tribute to their abiding endurance.

NOTES

PREFACE

1 Which name, Chippewa, Ojibwa or Anishinaabe, tribal members use is a personal choice. A bit of history serves to explain the various names. The Ojibwa tribe, Algonkian people, split into different groups when they settled in the Lake Superior area. The southern tribes came to be known as Chippewa and the northern tribes were known as the Northern Ojibwe. Gerald Vizenor in *The People Named the Chippewa* further explains: "In the language of the tribal past, the families of the woodland spoke of themselves as the Anishinaabeg until the colonists named them the Ojibway and Chippewa. The word Anishinaabeg (the singular is Anishinaabe) is a phonetic transcription from the oral tradition. Tribal people used the word Anishinaabeg to refer to the people of the woodland who spoke the same language" (13). Frances Densmore further explains that the government used the name Chippewa in the treaties but that older tribal members still prefer Ojibway or Anishinaabe (qtd. in Vizenor, *The People Named the Chippewa* 16). All terms can be used interchangeably when referring to Erdrich's tribe, The Turtle Mountain Band of Chippewa Indians who migrated from the Lake Superior region onto the Plains. Erdrich refers to herself as Chippewa. See chapter 3 for a more detailed account of her tribe.

2 The areas of critical work on Erdrich include:

Oral tradition and storytelling foundation of her work: dissertations by Jennifer Sergi, Kathy Whitson, Pauline Woodward, and articles by Joni Clarke, James Flavin, Karl Kroeber, Nancy Peterson, John Purdy, Kathleen Sands, Anna Secco, and Michael Wilson.

Chippewa culture and history: Victoria Brehm, Tom Berninghausen, Kathleen Brogan, Catherine Catt, Susan Friedman, Michelle Hessler, Julie Maristuen-Rodakowski, James McKenzie, P. Jane Hafen, Catherine Rainwater, and Annette Van Dyke.

Narrative style: Daniel Cornell, Ursula Le Guin, Louis Owens, Barbara Pittman, James Ruppert, Karla Sanders, Lissa Schneider, Lydia Schultz, Robert Silberman, James Stripes, and Victoria Walker.

The Function of Humor: Julie Giese, William Gleason, Nancy Peterson, and Katrina Schimmoeller.

Feminist approaches: Sarah Aguilar, Susan Castillo, Jeannette Cooperman, Kathleen Donovan, Louise Flavin, Alison Gallant, Susan Meisenhelder, Marya Ryan, Lydia Schultz, and Lee Schweninger, and Jennifer Shaddock.

Erdrich's collaboration with Dorris: Kay Bonetti, Gail Caldwell, Laura Coltelli, Dan Cryer, Shelby Grantham, Michael Huey, Michael Schumacher, and Charles Trueheart.

Gambling: Paul Pasquaretta, John Purdy, and Kristan Sarve-Gorham.

Chapter 1
Continuing the Tradition: Louise Erdrich and the Native American Literary Renaissance

1 The term *squaw* is not an acceptable word today. Although commonly used in the nineteenth and first half of the twentieth century by writers and in Hollywood films, *squaw* is a term of derision and insult to Native women.

2 Mary Rowlandson's "The Sovereignty and Goodness of God"; James Fenimore Cooper's *The Deerslayer* (Chingachgook), *The Last of the Mohicans* (Chingachgook and Magua), *The Pathfinder* (Dew of June); Henry Wadsworth Longfellow's *The Song of Hiawatha*; Herman Melville's *Moby Dick*; Mark Twain's *Tom Sawyer*; Helen Hunt Jackson's *Ramona*; Evan S. Connell's *Son of the Rising Star: Custer and the Little Bighorn*; Walt Whitman's *Leaves of Grass*; Oliver La Farge's *Laughing Boy*; Ernest Hemingway's "Ten

Indians"; William Faulkner's "The Bear."

3 See *Hollywood's Indian: The Portrayal of the Native American in Film*, edited by Peter C. Rollins and John E. O'Connor.

4 Samson Occom *A Sermon Preached at the Execution of Moses Paul, an Indian Who was Executed at New Haven, on the 2d of September, 1772* (1772); Elias Boudinot *Poor Sarah, or Religion Exemplified in the Life and Death of an Indian Woman* (1823); William Apes *The Experience of Five Christian Indians of the Pequod Tribe or, An Indian's Looking-Glass for the White Man* (1833); George Copway *The Life, History, and Travels of Kah-ge-ga-gah-bowh* (George Copway) (1847); John Rollin Ridge *Life and Adventures of Joaquin Murieta* (1854); Sarah Winnemucca Hopkins *Life Among the Piutes* [sic]: *Their Wrongs and Claims* (1883); Simon Pokagon *Queen of the Woods* (1899); Charles Eastman *Old Indian Days* (1907); Alexander Lawrence Posey *The Poems of Alexander Lawrence Posey* (1910); and Zitkala-Sa (Gertrude Bonnin) *American Indian Stories* (1921).

For a complete listing of early Indian authors, see A. LaVonne Brown Ruoff's *American Indian Literatures*, Andrew Wiget's *Native American Literature*, and Helen Jaskowski's *Early Native American Writing*.

5 The irony is, of course, that the "new" voices being heard, those of Native American writers and poets, were part of an oral/literary tradition that preceded by centuries the dominant body of American writing.

6 Frank Waters writes about Hopi, Navajo, and Pueblo life in *The Man Who Killed the Deer, Book of the Hopi, Pumpkin Seed Point, The Woman at Owoti Crossing* and *Masked Gods: Navajo and Pueblo Ceremonialism*; Oliver La Farge won a Pulitzer Prize for *Laughing Boy*, whose book jacket declares it "The first authentic novel of the Navajo Indians"; Hal Borland portrays Thomas Black Bull's life as a young Ute Indian living in the wilderness in *When Legends Die*; and Forrest Carter, the former Klansman, writes a sympathetic portrait of a young Cherokee boy in *The Education of Little Tree*.

7 In addition, there are Native American scholars and writers who claim Indian blood who are not always recognized by the

Indian community. Elizabeth Cook-Lynn (Crow-Creek Sioux), for instance, bitterly denounces several well known people in the field: Dr. Rayna Green who claims Cherokee blood; Jamake Highwater (a.k.a. J. Marks), a New York Jew who reinvented himself as an Indian; David Seals, writer of *Powwow Highway* who represents himself as an American Indian; and Hertha Dawn Wong who "found" an Indian great-grandmother in the course of her work on Indian autobiographies. Cook-Lynn asserts that these people are not found on any tribal rolls ("Literary" 47–48).

8 Figures differ and, of course, cannot be scientifically verified, but Henry Dobyns, a noted demographer, estimates that "By A.D. 1500, between seven and fifteen million people inhabited the present-day United States" (190).

9 The power of language and how sounds become meaningful developed as an area of serious scholarly work at the end of the nineteenth century with the work of Charles Sanders Peirce, an American philosopher. Together with the work of Ferdinand de Saussure, a Swiss linguist, they opened up this topic in the academy where it formed the basis for a new field of study, semiotics or the study of "the arbitrary nature of the sign" (Saussure). Because of their work and that of others, academics no longer make assumptions about the permanency of language that scholars did only decades previously. The work of the great twentieth-century French philosopher, Michel Foucault, is particularly noteworthy as he forces us to consider the very point that Momaday makes about the potential uses and abuses of language as well as the inherent nature of language which makes it both unstable and controlling at the same time.

10 The range for membership in particular tribes is varied, since each tribe sets its own tribal requirements after the Indian Reorganization Act of June 1934. In the Lakota Nation alone, there are differing requirements for tribal membership: the Lower Brule Sioux accept one-fourth blood, as well as all persons of Indian blood whose names appear on the census rolls of April 1935 and September 1958; the Cheyenne River Sioux Tribe accept as members anyone on the official roll as of June 1934, people of the River Sioux who are admitted upon a two-

thirds council vote, and all children born to any member of the tribe who resides on the reservation at the time of the birth; the Oglala Sioux accept anyone on the official roll as of June 1934 and all children born to members of the tribe who reside on the reservation at the time of the children's birth; and the Rosebud Sioux accept children with one-fourth blood, those on the official census as of April 1935, and children born after 1935 to any member of the tribe regardless of the parents' residence.

The Caddo Indians now residing in Oklahoma have particularly interesting membership requirements. They have the standard clause of accepting all persons of the tribe who are on the official census as of January 1937. In addition, they accept any children born after 1937 to members on the official census; children born to any Caddo member and to a member of another tribe who wishes to affiliate; children born to a Caddo member and anyone else, if the child is enrolled on the tribal rolls before the age of five; and any illegitimate child whose mother is Caddo.

The Cheyenne Tribe of the Northern Cheyenne Indian Reservation shows another variance in tribal membership. They accept any tribal member whose name is on the census roll as of January 1935; any person with one-half Northern Cheyenne blood, regardless of residency; and any children born to any member of the 1935 roll.

The Turtle Mountain Band of Chippewas accepts any member who is on the roll before May 1940 and approved by the Secretary of the Interior in March 1943 and all descendants of parents of the official census, providing they possess one-fourth or more Indian blood and do not reside in Canada (Fay, *Charters, Constitutions, and By-Laws of Indian Tribes of North America*, parts 1, 3, and 6).

11 Critics use both *mixed-blood* and *mixed blood* to refer to popular Indian authors who identify with a particular tribe but who are a product of Indian and Anglo marriages. These authors include: Michael Dorris, Louise Erdrich, Gerald Vizenor, Paula Gunn Allen, Greg Sarris, Wendy Rose, and Linda Hogan.

12 Other Indian authors publishing fiction and autobiographies in the 1970s include: Janet Campbell Hale, Nasnaga, Chief George

Pierre, Ted Williams, Dallas Chief Eagle, Hyemeyohsts Storm, Denton R. Bedford, Virginia Driving Hawks Sneve, Charles Penoi, Joseph Bruchac, Maria Chona, Lame Deer, Simon Ortiz, Carol Lee Sanchez, Anna Moore Shaw, Martin Cruz Smith, John Stands in Timber, Don C. Talayesva, and Albert Yava.

13 *Love Medicine's* awards: National Book Critics Circle Award for Best Work of Fiction, Sue Kaufman Prize for Best First Fiction from The American Academy and Institute of Arts and Letters, and the Virginia McCormick Scully Award for the Best Book of 1984 Dealing with western Indians (Chavkin and Chavkin xxii).

Dorris's awards: Indian Achievement Award 1985, National Book Critics Circle Award for Best Nonfiction Book 1989, Christopher Award, and Heartland Prize for *The Broken Cord* (Chavkin and Chavkin xxiv).

14 Erdrich plays with this opposition, particularly in *Tracks* in the character of Pauline, the would-be Christian martyr, whose proselytizing voice is in direct contrast to the voice of Nanapush, the respected tribal elder. Her mission is to "save" the Chippewa people, of whom she does not consider herself a member, so that Christ can replace their traditional powerful gods, especially Misshepeshu, ruler of the lakes. Pauline represents the assimilated Christian voice still prominent in Indian communities, and the very fact that Erdrich gives her a voice throughout the North Dakota novels indicates the degree to which the conflict between fully Christianized Indians and Indian retaining traditional outlooks persists even today.

15 The Division of American Indian Literature was officially organized by the MLA on 15 May, 1992. Previous to this time, it had been a discussion group.

16 Ruoff's *American Indian Literatures: An Introduction, Bibliographic Review, and Selected Bibliography* gives background information on the field as well as crucial bibliographic materials. Owens's *Other Destinies: Understanding the American Indian Novel* also presents an overview of the Indian novel and stresses how Indian authors are caught between two discourse communities. Andrew Wiget's *Native American Literature* reviews the field from oral narrative through modern fiction and contemporary

poetry, and his *Critical Essays on Native American Literature* concentrates on describing the contributions of folklorists and anthropologists working with traditional Native texts.

17 Allen's *The Sacred Hoop: Recovering the Feminine in American Indian Traditions* not only describes the importance of feminine traditions in Native life, but is as well an important source for understanding the differences between the Indian worldview and Anglo concepts.

18 Krupat is a prominent scholar who devotes his energies in several important articles and books to Native American autobiographies. Brian Swann joins Krupat as editor for *I Tell You Now: Autobiographical Essays by Native American Writers*, and Gretchen Bataille and Kathleen Sands edit a collection of Indian women's autobiographies in *American Indian Women: Telling Their Lives*. H. David Brumble III also concentrates his work in the field of autobiographies in several articles and with his book *An Annotated Bibliography of American Indian and Eskimo Autobiographies*. The latest offering in this area is Hertha Dawn Wong's *Sending My Heart Back Across the Years: Tradition and Innovation in Native American Autobiography*.

Indian narrative is currently dominated by scholars and critics who concentrate on analyzing oral narratives and especially on studying how orality influences contemporary fiction. Karl Kroeber, son of the famous anthropologists Alfred and Theodora Kroeber, compiled and edited *Traditional Literatures of the American Indian: Texts and Interpretations* which seeks to make traditional oral narratives more accessible to non-specialists. He asks the crucial question, one with which I will deal in chapter 2, of how oral materials can be translated into a written text and still retain the flavor of an oral recitation. Swann edits *Smoothing the Ground: Essays on Native American Oral Literature*, a valuable critical collection of essays which deals with the issue of translation of Native text. *On the Translations of Native American Literatures* is another work Swann edits that deals with the formidable issue of translating texts from an oral tradition. He again collaborates with Krupat as editors in *Recovering the Word: Essays on Native American Literature* that also concentrates on the theory and practice of interpreting oral and written texts, and this work is particularly important because of its interdisciplinary approach to the topic. Dennis Tedlock is another important scholar in this area. His work on the relation between translations and literary criticism as well as his important work with Zuni materials, *Finding the Center: Narrative Poetry of the Zuni Indians* is a distinguished contribution to the field.

19 The work of the early anthropologists who collected Indian narratives while doing their fieldwork provides the basis for this branch of Native American literary studies. The list of contributors reads like a "who's who" of anthropology, as different pioneers in the field concentrated their efforts on particular regions of the country. The list includes one of the pioneers in anthropology, Franz Boas, who worked primarily with Kwakiutl tales, and he was followed by many Boasian anthropologists who continued with his investigation of Native texts. In the same region as Boas, Melville Jacobs analyzed Clackamas Chinook myths and tales, while in the southwest, Ruth Benedict worked in the area of Cochiti tales. Also in this region were Ruth Underhill with her studies of Papago works, Ruth Bunzel with her important rendering of Zuni texts, and Elsie Parsons with her studies of Tewa and Keresan tales. George Grinnell collected tales and legends from the High Plains, and his work with the Cheyenne, Blackfeet, and Pawnee is particularly noteworthy. Victor Barnouw concentrated on Wisconsin Chippewa myths and tales while Frances Denmore translated Chippewa music, a repository of mythic narratives of the people. Paul Radin made a significant contribution with his work on the Winnebago trickster cycle, and his book, *The Trickster: A Study in American Indian Mythology*, stands to this day as a seminal work on this fascinating aspect of Indian narratives.

This is in no way meant to represent a complete listing of all of the work done in the first half of this century. That inventory is extensive and not the focus of this book; besides, one need only be aware of some of the excellent bibliographic reviews of the field, such as Ruoff's *American Indian Literatures*, which offers a more complete listing. The studies cited above represent some of the best and most important work done in the area by scholars who were shaping the new field of anthropology as well as transforming, while translating, what had heretofore been primarily oral narratives.

20 Hymes authored *In Vain I Tried to Tell You: Essays in Native American Ethnopoetics* in which he concentrates his scholarly efforts on ethnopoetical and structural approaches to oral literatures. The structuralist principles of Claude Lévi-Strauss and Vladimir Propp foreground a great deal of the work done in this specialized field to the point that Vizenor complains that "Native American Indian literatures have been overburdened with critical interpretations based on structuralism and other social science theories... [which] never seem to enter stories as a language game without an institutional advantage" (*Narrative* x-xi). Jerome Rothenberg, a poet and translator, wrote several books on the problems of translations, one of which is *Shaking the Pumpkin: Traditional Poetry of the Indian North Americas*. In this work he seeks to indicate the range of interpretations possible within a given text, because he feels there is no prescribed and passive formula for transcribing materials into another's language.

21 Radin's study was the first to suggest the importance of the trickster in Indian tales, and his book contains a distinguished commentary "On the Psychology of the Trickster Figure" by the distinguished C. G. Jung. Other scholars with this particular focus are Jarold Ramsey and his coyote trickster in *Reading the Fire: Essays in the Traditional Indian Literatures of the Far West*, Alan Velie with his article on "The Trickster Novel," Kroeber's deconstructive approach to the Trickster-Transformer, Bright's history of the coyote, Wiget's article in Ruoff and Ward's *Redefining American Literary History* "His Life in His Tail: The Native American Trickster and the Literature of Possibility," and Vizenor with his stalwart dedication to elucidating the role of trickster in "Trickster Discourse: Comic Holotropes and Language Games" in his collection of critical essays *Narrative Chance: Postmodern Discourse on Native American Indian Literatures*. Also, Jay Cox examines the idea of female tricksters, Jeanne Rosier Smith's *Writing Tricksters: Mythic Gambols in American Ethnic Literature* includes a useful chapter on Erdrich's trickster characters, and John Slack examines the comic aspects

of trickster in "The Comic Savior: The Dominance of the Trickster in Louise Erdrich's *Love Medicine*."

In addition to writing about tricksters in his novels (*Darkness in Saint Louis Bearheart*, *Griever: An American Monkey King in China*, and *The Trickster of Liberty*) and amplifying their importance in contemporary fiction, Vizenor examines Indian texts from a postmodernist stance. His decidedly radical approach characterizes most of his work. He believes, "The postmodern opened in tribal imagination; oral cultures have never been without a postmodern condition that enlivens stories and ceremonies, or without trickster signatures and discourse on narrative chance —a comic utterance and adventure to be heard or read" (*Narrative* x).

There are several other good theorists in the field whose work brings Native American literature into the academic arena of critical theory. Elaine Jahner's article on "Metalanguages," Kroeber's deconstructive approach to the trickster, Gretchen Ronnow's Lacanian Reading of *Ceremony*, and James Stripes's revisionist historical approach to Erdrich's first three novels suggest the varied applications of theory to contemporary Indian texts.

Allen stands as the leading feminine theorist, and in *The Sacred Hoop* she argues for a gynocritical approach to Native American texts from a gynocratic approach, which she demonstrates is much more in keeping with traditional lifestyles and communal structures. Bataille and Sands offer the female point of view in their book *American Indian Women Telling Their Lives*, as does Rayna Green's (Cherokee) *That's What She Said: Contemporary Poetry and Fiction by Native American Women*. Helen Jaskoski and Judith Antell have also contributed articles that incorporate feminine principles in Native American literature.

22 See Ramsey pages 25–26 for a "Trickster gazetteer."

23 Mourning Dove *Cogewa, the Half-Blood* (1927); John Joseph Mathews *Sundown* (1934); and D'Arcy McNickle *The Surrounded* (1936).

CHAPTER 2
TRADITIONAL STORYTELLERS

1 See chapter one of Andrew Wiget's *Native American Literature* for a more comprehensive list.

2 The structuralists dominated the field for over a century examining the varying internal components of a work in relation to how they revealed themselves to be a product of a particular society. The oral narratives were examined as a part of the total system of the tribal worldview, and it was up to the folklorist to analyze the internal parts in order to fully comprehend the whole (the culture). Claude Lévi-Strauss and Vladimir Propp represent two of the best-known practitioners of this approach, and their work has been very influential in the field. The functionalists, on the other hand, examined the function of customs as they related to particular texts. Bronislaw Malinowski, one of the most prominent practitioners of this approach, connected the conditions of life to social organization and studied stories from this viewpoint.

R. Radcliffe-Brown, a British anthropologist, combined features of both approaches with his structural functionalism, which analyzed "the role that customs play in the maintenance of an organization" (Bronner 79). William Bascom, who established the master's degree program at Berkeley in folklore, espoused the psychological aspects of the functionalists' approach. He felt folklore was a result of people's anxieties, and in order to maintain an ordered society, they created stories. Functionalism began to lose favor in the mid 1940s; Simon Bronner offers his explanation of why functionalism no longer seemed an appropriate methodology:

Functionalism underscored the exclusiveness and authority of the profession who was studying other people and arriving at generalizations. Functionalism faltered, however, when it went beyond describing the relation of culture of a specific time and place in a closed society. (86)

3 Boas was also interested in the diffusion of story types, and he examined the role of stories in the history and society of a cul-

ture as well as how stories were constructed and spread. His approach emphasized the importance of living within the culture one was studying, which became a standard in anthropological practice, and during his career he collected and edited folktales of the Bella Bella, Salishan, Sahaptin, Kutenai, and Kwakiutl tribes.

4 Ben-Amos in his foreword to Orlick's *Principles for Oral Narrative Research* defines epic laws as "diagnostic tools with which a trained person can recognize the oral qualities of a text that is currently available in script or print" (ix).

5 Parry and Lord traveled to Yugoslavia in 1933 where they recorded illiterate singers (*guslari*) who composed their oral epics in the same manner as Homer had composed his 2,500 years ago. Parry wrote in his field notes, "The aim of the study was to fix with exactness the *form* of oral story poetry, to see wherein it differs from the *form* of written story poetry" (Lord 3). He sought to record singers working in a living tradition and to observe "How the form of their songs hangs upon their having to learn and practice their art without reading or writing" (Lord 3). The similarities between what he found in Yugoslavia and what he knew from his Homeric work allowed Parry to draw up a method for defining the characteristics of an oral style that proved to be a new theory of interpretation for oral narratives.

6 Lord continued Parry's work with Serbo-Croatian epic singers, recording their work and interviewing them about their compositional processes. His major work with Avdo, one of the traditional non-literate singers, revealed that this singer had a repertoire of nearly fifty-eight epics, and several of these songs approximated the length of the *Odyssey* (Foley, *Theory* 39). Lord wrote up his fieldwork in what became a groundbreaking work *The Singer of the Tales*.

7 Georges believes performance theory is the only way to appropriately approach an oral text. The work of Tedlock, Hymes, and Toelken also concentrates on this essential aspect of stories. As Swann asks in his introduction to *Smoothing the Ground: Essays on Native American Oral Literature* in relation to the per-

formance aspect of oral texts heretofore being ignored, "Why have we had to wait so long for attention to be paid? Milman Parry discovered the oral-formulaic structure of Homer about forty years ago. Why has it taken so long for his lead to be followed in America?" (xiii).

8 Alan Dundes, a folklore scholar who works with Native American stories, insists that "myth and folktale are not structurally distinct genres.... The distinction between them is wholly dependent upon content criteria or totally external factors such as belief or function" (qtd. in Wiget, *Native American Literature* 3). See Dundes's article "Structural Typology in North American Indian Folktales."

9 The work of Walter Ong offers insightful theories about orality. He, along with the anthropologist Jack Goody, examines how orality functions in a chirographic culture as the oral interfaces with the written, and Ong cogently argues that writing restructures human consciousness. In *The Presence of the Word*, he contrasts the preliterate way of viewing the world as a dynamic and active place to literate societies which see the universe as a static entity. In "Literacy and Orality in our Times," he examines how writing performs "the central noetic operation which a high technology culture takes for granted" (3) His best known book *Orality and Literacy: The Technologizing of the Word* explores the idea of "oral residues" and offers an important list that helps establish characteristics of oral-based expression. Ong's assessment of the nature of verbal memory in *Orality and Literacy* stands as one of the major contributions to the field.

10 Erdrich powerfully uses this concept in *Love Medicine*. Moses has been saved from the consumption that has decimated his entire family, because his mother gave him a different name to confuse death and make it pass over him (note the similarities to the biblical account). When Moses tells Lulu his real name, it is a moment for him of ultimate being. Lulu "whispered it, once. Not the name that fooled death, but the word that harbored his life.... I hold his name close as my own blood and I will never let it out. I only spoke it that once so he would know he was alive" (82).

11 This notion is also stressed by Ong, Havelock, and Goody who maintain there is a distinction between the thought processes in a written and an oral culture.

12 Exceptions to this include: Gloria Bird's (Spokane Tribe) master's thesis at the University of Arizona (1992) entitled "Bringing the Story Back Home: A Reading of *Ceremony* by Leslie Marmon Silko and *Tracks* by Louise Erdrich," Susan Perez Castillo's "The Construction of Gender and Ethnicity in the Poetry of Leslie Silko and Louise Erdrich," Alison Gallant's 1993 dissertation from Ohio State University entitled *'The Story Comes Up Different Every Time': Louise Erdrich and the Emerging Aesthetic of the Minority Woman Writer* (the other minority writers she examines are Silko, Maxine Hong Kingston, and Toni Morrison), Lee Schweninger's "A Skin of Lakeweed: An Ecofeminist Approach to Erdrich and Silko," and Jennifer Shaddock's "Mixed Blood Women: The Dynamic of Women's Relations in the Novels of Louise Erdrich and Leslie Silko."

13 Different terms for *Storyteller's* form range to an autobiography, a feminist rendering of Laguna history, a communal history, a polyphonic text, a scrapbook, and a collection of her poetry and short stories.

14 See Krupat's *Voice in the Margin* 177–82 and Kenneth Roemer's article "Native American Oral Narratives: Context and Continuity" 51.

15 The mythic dimension in Erdrich's work is the focus of chapter five.

16 This would account for the presence of legendary figures in the novels. Gerry Nanapush is the traditional trickster figure, Fleur is the sacred medicine woman, Antelope Wife comes from transformational stories, and Zosie and Mary are trickster grandmothers.

17 See Whitson, Peterson, Sergi, Flavin, Schneider, and Silberman.

18 Owens uses a similar expression in his article "Erdrich and Dorris's Mixedbloods and Multiple Narratives," in *Other Destinies: Understanding the American Indian Novel*. He calls the community centering on Dot "the 'Dot'-matrix of the text [*The Beet Queen*]" (207).

19 Dot gives birth to baby Shawn during the time of *Love Medicine*. With Gerry Nanapush as the father, Shawn is a wonderful receptacle for all the stories. However, Dot assumes a divorced status from Gerry when he gets sent away to prison for a long term. She moves away and remarries (or something like that since she is still legally married to Gerry). Shawn reemerges as an awkward adolescent in *Tales of Burning Love*, but Erdrich never has her telling her story. Her mother Dot's voice always subsumes hers.

CHAPTER 3
LOUISE ERDRICH,
A CONTEMPORARY TRADITIONAL STORYTELLER

1 In an oft quoted comment in "Where I Ought to Be: A Writer's Sense of Place," Erdrich relates, "Contemporary Native American writers have therefore a task quite different from that of other writers I've mentioned. In the light of enormous loss, they must tell the stories of contemporary survivors while protecting and celebrating the cores of cultures left in the wake of the catastrophe" (23).

2 In her 1991 interview with Michael Schumacher, Erdrich maintains:

> I think each of the books is political in its own way. I hope so. But *Tracks*, by virtue of its setting, was bound to be more political. There's no way to speak about Indian history without it being a political statement. You can't describe a people's suffering without implying that somebody's at fault. There's no way around it. You can't write a book about South Africa without it being political, and you really can't write a book about Native Americans without being political. Even writing about common, ordinary life is going to strike some people as a political statement. (Chavkin and Chavkin 174)

3 See Sidner Larson, McKenzie, Maristuen-Rodawokski, Peterson, Lydia Schultz, Stripes, Van Dyke, and Willard.

4 Some critics (especially Native American ones) don't think she

has "enough" Indian blood to call her herself a Native American writer. By contrast, even minimal African American ancestry has automatically identified one as black, which only points out the degree to which political agendas reside at the heart of issues of identity.

5 She was born Karen Louise Erdrich 7 June, 1954.

6 She also agrees with Dorris's definition of a reservation, "It's a place where culture has been kept alive" (Jones, *Conversations with Louise Erdrich & Michael Dorris* 8).

7 In her interview with Coltelli, Erdrich relates, "I began as a poet, writing poetry, I began to tell stories in the poems and then realized that there was not enough room in a poem unless you are a John Milton and write enormous volumes of poetry. There was not enough room to really tell the story. I just began to realize that I wanted to be a fiction writer; that's a bigger medium, you know" (45).

8 See *Studies in American Indian Literatures*, SAIL 3.4 (1991): 47–55 for differing opinions as to the merits of the book.

9 Erdrich's economic success has been a phenomenon in Native American literature. According to Stripes, "Each book has made the *New York Times* bestseller list shortly after initial publication. In fact, in fewer than ten years she has achieved a level of recognition nearly equal to that of longer established writers" (31).

10 Of particular importance is Sergi researching the degree to which Erdrich tells the story of the Chippewa people the Indian way and Peterson examining the oral markers in the novel. Additionally, Flavin illustrates how in the Nanapush section Erdrich utilizes oral tradition to ensure tribal culture. In *Love Medicine*, Schneider demonstrates the degree to which *Love Medicine* is a novel about the act of storytelling in theme and style and Ruppert maintains that Erdrich's multiple narrators are an attempt to create a traditional story telling situation ("Mediation"). Sands concurs with this approach by stressing that *Love Medicine* is as much about storytelling as it is about telling a particular story, and Silberman sees Erdrich as trying

to achieve "pure" story-telling in the novel.

11 Brumble specifies six different types of preliterate autobiography: coup tales, hunting and warfare stories, self-examinations, self-vindications, educational narratives, and tales of the acquisition of powers (qtd. in Brown Ruoff and Ward, *Redefining* 251).

12 Lipsha hasn't yet found his powers and assumed the role of tradition healer, and Lyman is thoroughly acculturated. Gordie and King are ravaged by alcohol.

13 See Sarah Bennett 83.

14 Today there are seven Anishinaabe (Chippewa) reservations in Minnesota: Red Lake, White Earth, Leech Lake, Mille Lacs, Nett Lake, Fond du Lac, and Grand Portage. There are five Anishinaabe (Chippewa) reservations in Wisconsin: Bad River, Red Cliff, Lac du Lambeau, Lac Courte Oreille, and Skokaogon—Mole Lake (Vizenor, *The People Named the Chippewa* preface).

15 There are various names for the traditional Chippewa trickster hero: Wenebozo (Barnouw), Nanapush (Johnston), Nehnehbush (Landes, *Ojibwa Religion*), Nanabozho (Coleman, Vecsey), Naanabozho (Vizenor, *The People Named the Chippewa*), Nanapus (Howard), and Man-abo-sho (Warren).

16 Gourneau offers important information on full-bloods and the Métis:

> The term 'full-blood' can be applied sociologically and does not imply that the group is made up entirely of people of pure Indian descent. It merely means that these individuals prefer and adhere to the Indian way of life instead of the Metis, or 'half-breed' way of life.... This 'full-blood' group definitely forms a distinct minority of the Turtle Mountain Band. The minority percentage of the Band population could be as small as a fraction of one percent by today's statistics. (9)

17 Gourneau relates, "The Ojibway began to enter into treaties with United States (sic) as early as 1815, and by the time the treaty making period between the Indians and the United States ended they were record breaking treaty makers, having been involved in a total number of 42. The Potowatomis, an

ally, shared this record with them" (8).

18 Owens positions Karl as the traditional trickster, while Rainwater argues he is the Fool from the Tarot deck. Both interpretations suggest an added depth and significance to Karl's character and, as such, offer added insights into his nature.

19 This is, of course, assuming that Eli is Lulu's father, a question Erdrich leaves open. If Lulu's father is one of the men who raped Fleur in Argus, then even Gerry is not a full-blood. However, given the alleged details of Lulu's conception, meaningful hints about her parentage like Lulu having the unmistakable Kashpaw nose, and Gerry's role as the traditional Chippewa hero, it is a safe assumption that Eli fathered Lulu.

20 Peltier remains in jail steadfastly maintaining his innocence, and many people believe the government chose him to pay for the deaths of two FBI agents on the Lakota Pine Ridge Reservation in South Dakota on 26 June 1975. His cause has been promoted by Indian activists as well as Indian people who are traditionally non-activists. Erdrich is one such supporter. See Peter Matthiessen's *In the Spirit of Crazy Horse* (New York: Viking, 1983) and Jim Messerschmidt's *The Trail of Leonard Peltier* (Boston: South End Press, 1983).

CHAPTER 4
THE POWER OF LOVE AS MEDICINE:
LOUISE ERDRICH'S FAMILY STORIES

1 See Silberman, Ainsworth, and Magalaner.

2 Jane Howard finds, "Only 16.3 percent of this country's 56 million families are conventionally nuclear" (15).

3 Erdrich's non-fiction book, *The Bluejay's Dance*, celebrates pregnancy and motherhood and all of the awe and reverence the state of motherhood inspires.

4 After her death, June attempts to call Gerry over to the otherworld to be with her in the hereafter so she won't be alone (BP). However, Gerry chooses to remain with the living and his wife Dot.

5 "Gahkahbekong" means Minneapolis. Erdrich uses numerous Cree words throughout *The Antelope Wife*, as well as *The Birchbark House*. At the time she was writing these two books, Erdrich was delving deeper into her Cree-Ojibwa past, as *The Birchbark House* reflects. She was studying the language and was learning some of the traditional arts of her Indian people, and her later books reflect this increased immersion in traditional Ojibwa culture.

6 Erdrich has offered a summary of the central concept behind the novels. In her interview with Kay Bonetti she asserts:

> I think all Native Americans living today probably look back and think, 'How, out of the millions and millions of people who were here in the beginning, the very few who survived into the 1920s, and the people who are alive today with some sense of their own tradition, how it gets to be me, and why?' And I think that quest and that impossibility really drives us in a lot of ways. It's central to the work and so as we go about telling these traditions; there aren't a lot of people who are going to tell these stories, or who are going to look at the world this particular way. (98–99)

7 Owens notes, "Erdrich has called this scene 'the real heart of the book.'" Everything in the novel seems to relate to this particular incident (*Other* 211).

8 Lipsha LM (230, 242, 334–35), BP (49, 217–18); Zelda BP (50–51); Marie BP (27, 49, 52); Lulu LM (335–37).

9 Moses has explained to Lulu the implications of a Chippewa drowning, and she remarks, "By all accounts, the drowned weren't allowed into the next life but forced to wander forever, broken shoed, cold, sore, and ragged. There was no place for the drowned in heaven or anywhere on earth" (LM 295).

10 LM (1–7, 10), BP (5).

11 LM (57–60), BQ (37–41).

12 The allusion to Elvis Presley's hit song "Burning Love" is unmistakable in the title and theme of this novel: "Ah, ah, burning love, I'm just a hunk, a hunk of burning love."

13 With ten Kashpaw children living on the Rocky Boy Reser-

vation in Montana, there are certainly more Kashpaw bureaucrats; it is just that they no longer live in North Dakota.

14 Shawn remains one of Erdrich's characters readers long to see develop through other novels. With all of the Adare stubbornness, honesty, and strength of character combined with her Pillager cunning and potential powers, she will be a formidable adult.

15 See pages 115–16.

16 It is interesting to consider the French "royalty" implication in the family name—Roy ("roi" meaning king) and Regina, the feminine form of the verb meaning regal or to rule.

17 Ruth Landes states:

> Love medicine was considered the ugliest sorcery and the explanation of rape; romantic sex was prized, seen as a 'hunt' and a game, by the men especially. There were several love-medicines prescriptions, transferred with or without cost, depending on the relation of the parties.... Like any sorcery, including the herbal, love formulas were revealed anciently in visions and were subsequently transmitted verbally. (65)

> Norval Morriseau reports that red ornamental sand often was used for love medicines when mixed with hair from the desired person and dried ground frog or sparrow's head. This was put in a small hide bag and worn around the neck. Another love charm was to find two mating frogs, pierce them together, and dry them. If a person tired of his partner, they simply pried the two frogs apart and released the love medicine (53–56).

> Sister Bernard Coleman et al. find, "The most popular type of love charm consisted of wooden or cloth figurines, about an inch or two in height, representing a man and a woman" (110). These were usually made out of cedar and were joined together by pieces of clothing from the person who was desired. She points out that the love medicines of paint, powdered herbs, and sometimes tobacco were joined or put into the figurine dolls and worn in a leather pouch. Also, as Morriseau reports, a love medicine powder without the doll could be put into the bag (111).

18 Alice Kehoe mentions that it is the Cree who are famous for knowing love medicines (517).

Chapter 5
"Power Travels in the Bloodlines, Handed Out Before Birth": Louise Erdrich's Female Mythic Characters

1 See Victor Barnouw's Wisconsin *Chippewa Myths & Tales and Their Relation to Chippewa Life*, Sister Bernard Coleman et al.'s *Ojibwa Myths and Legends*, Selwyn Dewdney's *The Sacred Scrolls of the Southern Ojibway*, Basil Johnston's *Ojibway Heritage*, Norval Morriseau's *Legends of My People*, and Thomas Overholt and J. Baird Callicott's *Clothed-in Fur and Other Tales: An Introduction to an Ojibwa World View*.

2 These stories are all recounted in Overholt and Callicott's *Clothed-in Fur and Other Tales: An Introduction to an Ojibwa World View*.

3 There are, of course, male mythic figures in Erdrich's novels, and the extent to which Nanapush and Gerry Nanapush embody the traditional Ojibwa trickster figure Nanabozho has been the subject of many articles. See Catherine Catt's "Ancient Myth in Modern America: The Trickster in the Fiction of Louise Erdrich," James McKenzie's "Lipsha's Good Road Home: The Revival of Chippewa Culture in *Love Medicine*," Louis Owens's "Erdrich and Dorris's Mixedbooks and Multiple Narrators," in *Other Destinies: Understanding the American Indian Novel*, Jeanne Rosier Smith's "Comic Liberators and Word-Healers: The Interwoven Trickster Narratives of Louise Erdrich," in *Writing Trickster: Mythic Gambols in American Ethnic Literature*, James Stripes "The Problem(s) of (Anishinaabe) History in the Fiction of Louise Erdrich: Voices and Contexts," Alan Velie's "The Trickster Novel," in Gerald Vizenor's *Narrative Chance: Postmodern Discourse on Native American Literature*, Karen Wallace's dissertation *Myth and Metaphor, Archetype and Individuation: A Study in the Work of Louise Erdrich*, and Kari Winter's "Refusing the 'Sovereign Territory of Language: The Trickster Nanapush vs. a Storm of Government Papers." Because no such list as the the one cited above exists for Erdrich's female mythic figures, that is the focus of this chapter.

4 Basil Johnston provides a list of the animals serving as totemic

symbols of the Anishinaabe (53):

CRANE	eloquence for leadership
HAWK	deliberation, foresight
EAGLE	courage, preknowledge
SEAGULL	grace, peace
LOON	fidelity
EAGLE (White headed)	foresight
BLACK DUCK	depth
GOOSE	prudence
SPARROW HAWK	perseverance
BEAR	strength and courage
MARTEN	single mindedness; judgement (sic)
MOOSE	endurance, strength
CARIBOU	grace and watchfulness
WOLF	perseverance, guardianship
LYNX	resolution, fortitude
BEAVER	resourcefulness, mind own business
MUSKRAT	endurance
PIKE	swiftness, elegance
SUCKER	calmness, grace
STURGEON	depth, strength
WHITE FISH	abundance, fertility, beauty
MERMAID (MERMAN)	temptation
FROG	transformation
WATER SNAKE	willingness
TURTLE	communication, emissary
RATTLESNAKE	patience, slow to anger
CATFISH	breadth, scope

5 Lipsha's spiritual guide in *The Bingo Palace* is a skunk. While not immediately appreciated by the seeker who was hoping for a more stately animal like bear, eagle, or lynx, nevertheless, the skunk offers Lipsha the wisdom he needs to consider if he is to take on the role of medicine man for the community. Spiritual gifts often come in strange packages, and Erdrich's characteristic humor in assigning Lipsha's animal helper serves to accentuate Lipsha's apprenticeship and lack of seriousness in undertaking his vision. Otherwise, one of the traditional animals associated with the Pillagers (bear, wolf, marten, or even Misshepeshu in the form of a lynx) would have appeared to him.

6 The Native Americans, as so often happened, became the true

victims in this incident. William Warren reports that the Pillager chief sent as an emissary to the traders contracted smallpox, which then spread through the area villages. The high death toll was blamed on the Pillagers who had earned the white man's wrath, because the people believed the traders revenged themselves by sending their deadly disease as a punishment to the Indians (260).

7 With Moses and Fleur rescued from death, the powerful Pillager magic can continue. Fleur's daughter Lulu mates with Moses, and they produce Gerry, who in turn fathers Lipsha—all of the bearers of a medicine so powerful that it travels undiluted in their blood.

8 Fleur is said to take after her grandmother Four-Souls who also was able to survive death many times. Erdrich is doing some really intriguing manipulation of history with the Pillagers, who are a historical Chippewa clan. In the four North Dakota novels, Erdrich ascribes supernatural powers to them.

9 Authors use varying spellings for the Ojibwa Grand Medicine Society: Midewinin, Midéwinin, Midewewin, Midéwewin, and Midaywewin. The adjective form is Midé.

10 See Vecsey, page 5, on the role of manitos.

11 Perhaps the reason these people die is because Misshepeshu causes their death when Fleur is close to being reunited with him, and they innocently thwart the process. A discussion of Fleur's relationship to Misshepeshu follows in this chapter.

12 The similarity to Fleur's returning to the reservation four times with the Great Bear Spirit breaking through the four world to bring the Midéwinin to the people is striking. It is another strong indication that Fleur is indeed associated with the Great Bear Manito, to whom she owes her strength and powers.

13 Pauline is Erdrich's character you love to hate. She reminds me of Emma, whom Jane Austen loved as an artistic creation yet knew her readers would dislike. Erdrich suggests Pauline even dies a saint's death in TBL, but her death cannot mitigate a life of deceit and destruction. Pauline is Erdrich's assault on the Catholic Church of the twisted and perverted souls their theol-

ogy can produce. To wit, Pauline renounces her Indian heritage when she enters a convent that accepts no Indian girls. Even before this time she has identified most strongly with her Canadian grandfather, and throughout her life she positions herself as different from her Indian brethren whom she classifies as the "other," the heathens, the ones in need of her saving redemption. While Fleur's powers are real, Pauline spends a lifetime deluding herself that she too can transform herself, influence Misshepeshu, administer healing power to the sick and dying, and be in communion with great spiritual powers, which for her are God, Jesus, and the Virgin Mary. Pauline believes she enters Sophie's body after luring Eli to her with love medicines, and Pauline vicariously experiences their sexual relation through Sophie. She believes she can leave her body and variously imagines herself flying and walking the death road, and she believes her shadow moves when she does not. She believes Christ has personally asked her to bring him more Indian souls, and so she travels to the middle of Lake Matchimanito to test her powers against Misshepeshu thinking her triumph will win the Indian souls Christ desires her to deliver. From Bernadette Morrissey she learns the art of attending to the sick and dying, since Pauline sees a release in death that her tormented soul cannot attain in life. Her most outrageous delusions are that God has talked to her while sitting on the stove in the nunnery and told her she is wholly white, that she can position herself to be Christ's champion and savior, and that she alone is insightful enough to ascertain that the reason the statue of the Virgin Mary weeps is because she really did not want to be God's chosen woman. Additionally, she believes she can detect Satan lurking in the lives of the Indian people; and she resolves to transfix the powerful Misshepeshu with her cross and deludes herself into thinking she has succeeded: "I *believe* [italics mine] that the monster was tamed that night, sent to the bottom of the lake and chained there by my deed" (T 204).

When Pauline endeavors to use her "powers" in relationship to Fleur, she always fails, for the simple reason that the powers she assumes she has are fabricated. This is most clearly exemplified in the incident just cited when Pauline's ineptness at helping Fleur when her second baby comes too soon results in the baby's death and nearly in Fleur's death. Pauline is powerless to aid this traditional medicine woman. Also, after Nanapush brings a cure from Moses to help restore Fleur's powers, Pauline interrupts the ceremony. Nanapush has plunged his arm into a kettle of boiling stew in order to replicate pulling out the sickness infecting Fleur. When Pauline attempts "the dreadful proof" (T 190) of her powers, she scalds her arms and burns her flesh. In an interesting re-enactment of this painful humiliation, in *Love Medicine*, Pauline, now Sister Leopolda, scalds her daughter Marie's hands by pouring boiling water over them.

There are no instances in which Pauline's cures, transformations, or powers can be substantiated, and in the novels she stands as an insignificant yet frustrating example of a mortal's attempts to position insufficient power against the genuine traditional Chippewa powers exemplified in Fleur. As John Desmond points out, "Erdrich is sharply critical of institutional Catholicism as a force that warps her Chippewa men and women" (8), and nowhere is this more clearly exemplified than in Pauline's character.

Daniel Cornell finds Foucault's *Madnesses and Civilization* to be useful in explaining Pauline's insanity, which "is 'other' because it has been substituted for something absent, a lack that is unthinkable" (52). It is an interesting point that her lack of family and of friends alienates her further from an Indian community she outrightly rejects, even though wanting all the time to belong. Even in the community of the convent she is alone, a condition self-imposed by her religious fanaticism. She is homely and bony, and the only sexual attention she receives is from a drunken old man. No other man wants her, as hard as she tries to be available to them. She is outside femininity, outside the traditional life of her Indian community, and outside her religious community, and she progresses further and further into a deluded state throughout the novels. However, Erdrich maddeningly also leaves open the slim thread of possibility that, just perhaps, Pauline is a religious visionary who has been positioned as "other" because of her gender, her unattractiveness, and her attempts to bring the "truth" of Christ to her

Indian people. When Erdrich assigns Pauline the name Leopolda, she is either being supremely ironic or she is suggesting the aforementioned interpretation that Pauline has indeed subdued the mighty Misshepeshu and taken on his power in her name. Pauline lives to be 108, and her death and subsequent possible connection to the statue of the Virgin Mary at the Convent leaves, once again, unresolved questions surrounding her supposed powers. Pauline is an enigmatic, annoying, and outrageous character placed by Erdrich in opposition to Fleur, and the "truth" of her life is something readers must construct for themselves, since Erdrich gives no definitive answers.

14 It is supremely ironic that Lipsha is avoiding Fleur precisely at the time he should be apprenticing himself to her in order to learn the secret medicine ways. He is self-absorbed and directionless, and Fleur does not seek him out in order to train him. Her secrets will pass with her, and Lipsha will have to refashion the role of traditional medicine person all by himself. With his father Gerry possessing Pillager blood from both of his parents, Erdrich suggests it is indeed possible for Lipsha to emerge as a healer without the benefit of a teacher. Fleur had no teacher, only the "raw power" (T 7) she was born with, and Lipsha has access to that power. Erdrich hints he will emerge as a community healer but that he will be different from Fleur.

15 This is another link between Fleur and the Great Bear Spirit who brought the Midéwinin to the Chippewa people and who was once regarded by them as human.

16 Murray provides these details on the Pembina band, "the name Pembina was given to those who previously considered Red Lake, Leech Lake, Rainy Lake, Fon du Lac, Grand Portage, Sandy Lake, Mille Lac, or Gull Lake as their home village" (15). In addition, large numbers of Métis claiming rights to the Red River Valley were part of the Pembina group.

17 This story of Oshkikwe nursing a pup can be found in Paula Gunn Allen's *Spider Woman's Granddaughters: Traditional Tales and Contemporary Writing by Native American Women* 43–47.

Chapter 6
Louise Erdrich, An American Storyteller

1. Rocio Davis extends this point by arguing that the short story cycle is a format which allows American ethnic writers to privilege community. See her article "Identity of Community in Ethnic Short Story Cycles: Amy Tan's *The Joy Luck Club*, Louise Erdrich's *Love Medicine*, and Gloria Naylor's *The Women of Brewster Street*."

   Robert Lewis likens Erdrich's stories in *Love Medicine* to a mosaic with each independent piece being a finely-crafted work of art, but when assembled revealing a more complex dimension of the artist's talents. Lewis sees *Love Medicine* as a serial novel reminiscent of both coyote stories and the kind of novel like *Winesburg, Ohio*, which I previously refer to as a short-story cycle.

2. Numerous critics note the degree to which Faulkner's work has been an important influence on Erdrich's. Not only is there a similarity in narrative style, but there also are the mythic kingdoms they populate with assemblies of sometimes grotesque, often amusing, sometimes frightfully mean, but always incredibly human characters. Erdrich herself in many interviews acknowledges Faulkner as one of her favorite writers. See the following interviews in Chavkin and Chavkin: Jones (4), Wong (38), Passaro (162–63), and Chavkin and Chavkin (232). The similarities between Erdrich and Faulkner offer a fascinating study in the degree to which a contemporary author uses the forms of a predecessor, acknowledges her debt, and then continues with her craft to transform the very tradition she appropriates. This comparison study, while worthy of an in-depth analysis, is beyond the scope of this book and deserves detailed investigation in a separate study. Jadwiga Maszewska's 1993 "Functions of the Narrative Method in William Faulkner's *Absalom, Absalom!* and Louise Erdrich's *Tracks*" and Susan Carr's 1994 "The Turtle Mountain/Yoknapatawpha Connection" begin the discussion of the Erdrich/Faulkner connection.

3. See Jack Weatherford's *Indian Givers: How the Indians of the*

Americas Transformed the World as well as his *Native Roots: How the Indians Enriched America* for comprehensive studies of Indian influences on American life.

4 In an interview with Bill Moyers, Erdrich argues, "Blankets were traded that were deliberately infected with smallpox because it was obvious that this was a way of clearing the path" (Chavkin and Chavkin 141).

Appendix

Important Dates in the History of the Turtle Mountain Band of Chippewa Indians

1780–82   A smallpox epidemic decimates the Ojibwa.

1780–1890   Chippewas from Leech Lake and Red Lake and Northern Ojibwe from the Rainy River country begin moving into the North Dakota area and successfully adapt to Plains life.

1797   The Northwest Company of Montreal builds a large trading post near Pembina in the Red River Valley.

1800   The Chippewa are hunting Buffalo with the Cree.

1848   Father Anthony Belcourt reestablishes a mission at Pembina.

1850   The Métis population stands at around 5,000 people, making them the largest group on the northern plains. Cree becomes the lingua franca on the northern plains.

1861   The Territory of North Dakota is created.

1863   The Plains Ojibwa surrender the Red River Valley.

1870   The Métis merge with the Pembina Chippewas and the Chippewa-Cree in the Turtle Mountain area.

1871   The Northern Pacific Railroad and the Pacific Railroad from the East reach the Red River Valley, accelerating the flow of settlers into the area.

1876   The Turtle Mountain Band petitions Congress for

3,000 square miles of reservation land.

1880s The great buffalo herds roaming the plains, once numbering 60 million, have been nearly exterminated by white buffalo hunters.

St. Ann's Catholic Church erected in Belcourt where today it remains the center of most religious life for tribal members.

1882 President Arthur creates the first reservation for 300 full-bloods; the land includes excellent farmland. The Métis settle on public lands next to the reserve.

Little Shell, Chief of the Turtle Mountain Band, posts a warning to whites not to encroach on Indian lands.

1884 The reservation is reduced from twenty-two townships to two, based on an erroneous assumption that only the 300 or so full-bloods were entitled to land. The best land is returned to the public domain.

The Sisters of Mercy and Father John Malo open a school; the children enrolled are Métis, not Chippewa. The beginning of children being sent off the reservation to boarding schools.

1886–87 150 people on the reservation starve to death during a harsh winter.

1887 The Dawes Act or General Allotment Act allowed reservation lands to be parceled into individual allotments.

1890 Little Shell and his group of Chippewa-Métis move to Montana seeking a reservation area where they could live a traditional lifestyle.

1891 The Band petitions the Secretary of the Interior asking for 446,670 acres be removed from adjoining public lands and annexed to the reservation.

1892 The McCumber Agreement restores 9,000,000 acres to the public domain without the consent of the tribe, who are paid $1,000,000 earning the name the "ten cent treaty," the effect being the United States Government now owns all of the Plains-Ojibwa land in North Dakota with the exception of the thirty-two by twenty-four reservation tract unsuitable for dry farming. This land is divided into allotments, and those not receiving land are allowed to settle on available public lands to which they believed they had legal title and consequently did not file for titles.

Many mixed-bloods are unfairly dropped from tribal rolls.

1893–96 A national depression.

1895 Game, fish, and fur-bearing animals nearly depleted on the overcrowded reservation. Many full-bloods move off the reservation and squat on public lands near Dunseith; they refuse to file on their land.

1890–1910 Smallpox and tuberculosis epidemics.

1900 Little Shell dies; he has been the leading spokesman against the McCumber Agreement. Kakenowash succeeds him as tribal leader.

1904 The "ten cent treaty" is ratified by Congress. The tribe continues to disperse as land is allotted to them in surrounding areas in North Dakota and in Montana.

1911 Tribal members issued off-reservation allotment land still have not received trust patents for their land. When they do, most of the mixed-bloods sell them within a year.

1920 Nearly 90% of tribal members receiving a patent have lost their land, increasing their government dependence.

1930 Many tribal businesses operating in Belcourt.

1932 The establishment of an eight-person tribal council.

1941	The government purchases 33,000 acres for landless tribal members.
1950	The termination policy enacted by the government who no longer feel obligated to help support reservation tribes.
1952	Indian Relocation Act seeks to move Indians into the cities.
1960s–1970s	The Vietnam War and the passage of the Civil Rights Act.
1966	American Indian Movement (AIM) formed by Dennis Banks, a mixed-blood Chippewa from the Leech Lake Reservation, and Clyde Bellecourt, a mixed-blood Lakota from the Pine Ridge Reservation. They seek to force the government to recognize Indian rights.
1971	Turtle Mountain Community College opens.
1979	The Indian Claims Commission awards $52,527,338 to the tribe in recognition of the unfairness of the McCumber Agreement.
1980s	Tribe establishes a shopping mall, a heritage center, a buffalo park, and a bingo palace.
1982	The government establishes "Chippewayan Authentics" to mass-produce Native crafts. The venture fails because there is no market for the machine-made goods.
1988	President Reagan signs legislation establishing a commission to regulate gambling on reservation lands.
1995	24,993 tribal members on the census roll, with 13,000 of them living off the reservation.
2000	28,021 tribal members on the census roll, with 15,000 of them living on or near the reservation.

WORKS CITED

Aguilar, Sarah. *Peripheral Visions: Postmodern Community in Contemporary Feminist Writing.* Diss. U of Connecticut, 1995. Ann Arbor: UMI, 1995.

Ainsworth, Linda. Rev. of *Love Medicine*, by Louise Erdrich. *SAIL* 9.1 (1985): 24–29.

Allen, Paula Gunn. "The Mythopoetic Vision in Native American Literature: The Problem of Myth." *American Indian Culture and Research Journal* 1.1 (1974): 3–13.

———, ed. *The Sacred Hoop: Recovering the Feminine in American Indian Traditions.* Boston: Beacon Press, 1986, 1992.

———, ed. *Spider Woman's Granddaughters: Traditional Tales and Contemporary Writing by Native American Women.* New York: Fawcett Columbine, 1989.

———, ed. *Studies in American Indian Literature: Critical Essays and Course Designs.* New York: MLA, 1983.

———. *The Woman Who Owned the Shadows.* San Francisco: Spinster's Ink, 1983.

Amiotte, Arthur. "The Call to Remember." *Parabola* 17.3 (1992): 29–34.

Antell, Judith. "Momaday, Welch, and Silko: Expressing the Feminine Principle through Male Alienation." *American Indian Quarterly* 12.3 (1988): 213–20.

Apes, William. *The Experience of Five Christian Indians of the Pequod Tribe or An Indian's Looking-Glass for the White Man.* 1833. Repub. as *Experience of Five Christian Indians, of the Pequod Tribe.* 2nd ed. Boston: Printed for the Publisher, 1837.

———. *Son of the Forest: The Experience of William Apes, a Native of the Forest, Comprising a Notice of the Pequod Tribe of Indians.* New

York: Author, 1829. Repub. as *A Son of the Forest: The Experience of William Apes, A Native of the Forest.* 2nd ed., rev. and cor. New York: Author, 1831.

Baker, Houston A., PRESIDENTIAL FORUM "Multiculturalism: The Task and Literary Representation in the Twenty-First Century." *Profession* 93 MLA (1993): 5.

———, ed. *Three American Literatures: Essays in Chicano, Native American, and Asian-American Literature for Teachers of American Literature.* New York: MLA, 1982.

Banks, Russell. "Border Country." Rev. of *The Beet Queen*, by Louise Erdrich. *The Nation* 243 (1986): 460–63.

Barnouw, Victor. *Wisconsin Chippewa Myths & Tales and Their Relation to Chippewa Life.* Madison: U of Wisconsin P, 1977.

Bascom, William. "Folklore and Anthropology." *Journal of American Folklore* 66 (1953):283–90.

Bataille, Gretchen M., and Kathleen Mullen Sands. *American Indian Women Telling Their Lives.* Lincoln: U of Nebraska P, 1984.

Beidler, Peter, and Gay Barton. *A Reader's Guide to the Novels of Louise Erdrich.* Columbia, MO: U of Missouri P, 1999.

Ben-Amos, Dan, ed. *Folklore Genres.* Austin: U of Texas P, 1976.

———. Foreword. *Principles for Oral Narrative Research.* By Alex Orlick. Trans. Kristen Wolf and Jody Jensen. Bloomington: U of Indiana P, 1992. vi-xi.

———, and Kenneth S. Goldstein, eds. *Folklore: Performance & Communication.* The Hague: Mouton, 1975.

Benjamin, Walter. *Illuminations.* New York: Harcourt, Brace, and World, Inc., 1968.

Bennett, Adrian. "Discourses of Power, the Dialectics of Understanding the Power of Literacy." *Rewriting Literacy: Culture and the Discourse of the Other.* Ed. Candace Mitchell and Kathleen Weiler. New York: Bergen and Garvey, 1991. 13–33.

Bennett, Sarah. Rev. of *The Bingo Palace*, by Louise Erdrich. *SAIL* 6.3 (1994): 83–88.

Berninghausen, Tom. "'This Ain't Real Estate': Land and Culture in Louise Erdrich's Chippewa Tetralogy." *Women, America, and Movement: Narratives of Relocation.* Ed. Susan Roberson. Columbia, MO: U of Missouri P, 1998. 190–255.

Bevis, William. "Native American Novels: Homing In." *Recovering the Word: Essays on Native American Literature.* Ed. Brian Swann and Arnold Krupat. Berkeley: U of California P, 1987.

Bird, Gloria. "Bringing the Story Back Home: A Reading of *Ceremony* by Leslie Marmon Silko and *Tracks* by Louise Erdrich." Thesis. U of Arizona, 1992.

———. "Searching for Evidence of Colonialism at Work: A Reading of Louise Erdrich's *Tracks*" *Wicazo Sa Review* 8.2 (1992): 40–47.

Black Elk. *Black Elk Speaks, Being the Life Story of a Holy Man of the Oglala Sioux,* as told through John G. Neihardt. Transcribed by John G. Neihardt. 1932. New York: Washington Square Press, 1959.

Bleeker, Sonia. *The Chippewa Indians: Rice Gatherers of the Great Lakes.* New York: William Morrow and Company, 1955.

Blowsnake, Sam. *The Autobiography of a Winnebago Indian.* Transcribed by Paul Radin. 1926. Lincoln: U of Nebraska P, 1983.

Boas, Franz. *Kwakiutl Ethnography.* Chicago: U of Chicago P, 1966.

———. *Race, Language and Culture.* 1932. New York: Macmillan, 1940.

Bonetti, Kay. "An Interview with Louise Erdrich and Michael Dorris." *The Missouri Review* 11 (1988): 79–99.

Borland, Hal. *When Legends Die.* Toronto: Bantam Books, 1963.

Boudinot, Elias. *Poor Sarah, or Religion Exemplified in the Life and Death of an Indian Woman.* Mount Pleasant, Ohio: Elisah Bates, 1823.

Brehm, Victoria. "The Metamorphoses of an Ojibwa Manido." *American Literature* 68.4 (1996): 677–706.

Bridenthal, Renate. "The Family: The View from the Room of Her Own." *Rethinking the Family: Some Feminist Questions.* Ed. Barre Thorne with Marilyn Yalom. New York: Longman, 1982. 225–35.

Bright, William. "The Natural History of Old Man Coyote." *Recovering The Word: Essays in Native American Literature.* Ed. Brian Swann and Arnold Krupat. Berkeley: U of California P, 1987. 339–87.

Brogan, Kathleen. "Haunted by History: Louise Erdrich's *Tracks.*" *Prospects: An Annual Journal of American Cultural Studies* (21): 169–92.

Bronner, Simon J. *American Folklore Studies: An Intellectual History.* Lawrence: U of Kansas P, 1986.

Brown, Dee. Rev. of *Love Medicine,* by Louise Erdrich. *SAIL* 9.1 (1985): 4–5.

Bruchac, Joseph."Whatever Is Really Yours: An Interview with Louise Erdrich." *Conversations with Louise Erdrich & Michael Dorris.* Ed. Allan Chavkin and Nancy Feyl Chavkin. Jackson: UP of Mississippi, 1994. 94–104.

Brumble, H. David III. *An Annotated Bibliography of American Indian and Eskimo Autobiographies.* Lincoln: U of Nebraska P, 1981.

Bynum, David E. *The Daemon in the Wood: A Study of Oral Narrative Patterns.* Cambridge, MA: Center for the Study of Oral Literature, 1978.

Caldwell, Gail. "Writers and Partners." *Conversations with Louise Erdrich & Michael Dorris.* Ed. Allan Chavkin and Nancy Feyl Chavkin. Jackson: UP of Mississippi, 1994. 64–69.

Camp, Gregory S. "The Turtle Mountain Plains-Chippewas and Metis." Diss. U of New Mexico, 1986.

———. "Working Out Their Salvation: The Allotment of Land in Severalty and the Turtle Mountain Chippewa Band 1897–1920." *American Indian Culture and Research Journal* 14.2 (1990): 19–38.

Carr, Susan. "The Turtle Mountain/Yoknapatawpha Connection. *The Bulletin of the West Virginia Association of College English Teachers* 16 (1994): 18–25.

Castillo, Susan Perez. "Postmodernism, Native American Literature and the Real: The Silko-Erdrich Controversy."

Massachusetts Review 32.2 (1991): 285–94.

Catt, Catherine M. "Ancient Myth in Modern America: The Trickster in the Fiction of Louise Erdrich. *The Platte Valley Review* 19.1 (1991): 71–81.

Chambers, Ross. *Story and Situation: Narrative Seduction and the Power of Fiction.* Minneapolis: U of Minnesota P, 1984.

Chapman, Abraham, ed. *Literature of the American Indians: Views and Interpretations.* New York: New American Library, 1975.

Chavkin, Allan, and Nancy Feyl Chavkin, eds. *Conversations with Louise Erdrich & Michael Dorris.* Jackson: UP of Mississippi, 1994.

Chona, Maria. *The Autobiography of a Papago Woman.* Transcribed by Ruth Underhill. *Memoirs of the American Anthropological Association,* no. 64; rpt. as part 2 of Underhill, *Papago Woman.* New York: Holt, Rinehart and Winston, 1936.

Clarke, Joni Adamson. "Why Bears are Good to Think and Theory Doesn't Have to be Murder: Transformation and Oral Tradition in Louise Erdrich's *Tracks.*" *SAIL* 4.1 (1992) 28–48.

Clifford, James. *The Predicament of Culture: Twentieth Century Ethnography, Literature, and Art.* Cambridge, MA: Harvard UP, 1988.

Cloud, Edna Martin. *North American Indian Cree Dictionary.* N.p: n.p., 1983.

Coleman, Sister Bernard, Ellen Frogner, and Estelle Eich. *Ojibwa Myths and Legends.* Minneapolis: Ross and Haines, Inc., 1961.

Coltelli, Laura. *Winged Words: American Indian Writers Speak.* Lincoln: U of Nebraska P, 1990.

Connell, Evan S. *Son of the Morning Star: Custer and the Little Bighorn.* San Francisco: North Point Press, 1984.

Cook-Lynn, Elizabeth. "Literary and Political Questions of Transformation: American Indian Fiction Writers." *Wicazo Sa Review* 11.1 (1995): 46–51.

———. "Who Gets to Tell the Stories?" (speech) *Wicazo Sa Review* 9.1 (1993): 60–64.

Cooper, James Fenimore. *The Deerslayer*. New York: Penguin, 1988.

———. *The Last of the Mohicans*. Des Plaines, IL: Bantam, 1982.

———. *The Pathfinders*. New York: New American Library, 1993.

Cooperman, Jeannette Anne. *Out of the Broom Closet: The Deep Hidden Meaning of Domesticity in Postfeminist Novels by Louise Erdrich, Mary Gordon, Toni Morrison, Marge Piercy, Jane Smiley, and Amy Tan*. Diss. St. Louis U, 1996. Ann Arbor: UMI, 1997.

Copway, George. *The Life, History, and Travels of Kah-ge-ga-gah-bowh. (George Copeway)*. Albany, NY: Weed and Parson, 1847.

Cornell, Daniel. "Turning the Story Over: The Narrative Perspectives in Louise Erdrich's *Tracks*. *Associacao Portuguesa de Estudos Anglo Americanos*. Aveiro: U of Aveiro, 1989. 33–42.

———. "Woman Looking: Revis(ion)ing Pauline's Subject Position in Louise Erdrich's *Tracks*." *SAIL* 4.1 (1992): 49–64.

Cornell, Stephen. "American Indians, American Dreams, and the Meaning of Success." *American Indian Culture and Research Journal* 11.4 (1987): 59–70.

Cox, Jay. "Dangerous Definitions: Female Tricksters in Contemporary Native American Literature." *Wicazo Sa Review* 5.2 (1989): 17–21.

Crawford, John. *Michif Dictionary: Turtle Mountain Cree*. Winnipeg, Manitoba: Pemmican Publication, Inc. 1983.

Creighton, Joanne V. *Dubliners and Go Down Moses: The Short Story Composite*. Diss. U of Michigan, 1969. Ann Arbor: UMI, 1970.

Cryer, Dan. "A Novel Arrangement." *Conversations with Louise Erdrich & Michael Dorris*. Ed. Allan Chavkin and Nancy Feyl Chavkin. Jackson: UP of Mississippi, 1994. 80–85.

Culler, Jonathan. *Ferdinand de Saussure*. Rev. ed. Ithaca: Cornell UP, 1986.

Dances with Wolves. Dir. Kevin Costner. Orion, 1990.

Davis, Rocio. "Identity in Community in Ethnic Short Story Cycles: Amy Tan's *The Joy Luck Club*, Louise Erdrich's *Love Medicine*, Gloria Naylor's *The Women of Brewster Street*." *Ethnicity and the*

American Short Story. Ed. William Cain and Julia Brown. New York: Garland, 1997.

Dawes Act (General Allotment Act). 1887.

Delorme, David P. "History of the Turtle Mountain Band of Chippewa Indians." *North Dakota History* 22 (1955):121–34.

DePriest, Marie. *Necessary Fictions: The Re-visioned Subjects of Louise Erdrich and Alice Walker.* Diss. U of Oregon, 1991. Ann Arbor: UMI, 1992.

Derrida, Jacques. "Structure, Sign, and Play." *Critical Theory Since 1965.* Ed. Hazard Adams & Leroy Searle. Tallahassee: Florida State UP, 1986. 83–93.

Desmond, John F. "Catholicism in Contemporary American Fiction." *America* 14 May 1994: 7–11.

Dewdney, Selwyn. *The Sacred Scrolls of the Southern Ojibway.* Toronto: U of Toronto P, 1975.

Dobyns, Henry. *Native Demography Before 1700. The Native North American Almanac: A Reference Work on Native North Americans in the United States and Canada.* Ed. Duane Champagne. Detroit: Gale Research, Inc., 1994. 189–98.

Donovan, Kathleen. *Feminine Approaches to Native American Literature: Coming to Voice.* Tucson: U of Arizona P, 1998.

Dorris, Michael. "Native American Literature in an Ethnohistorical Context." *College English* 41.2 (1979): 147–61.

———. *A Yellow Raft in Blue Water.* New York: Warner Books, 1987.

Dorson, Richard M. "Current Folklore Theories." *Current Anthropology* 4 (1963): 93–112.

Dundes, Alan. "Structural Typology in North American Indian Folktales." *Southwestern Journal of Anthropology* 19.1 (1963): 121–30.

———, ed. *The Study of Folklore.* Englewood Cliffs, NJ: Prentice Hall, 1965.

———. Preface. *The Theory of Oral Composition: History and*

Methodology. By John Miles Foley. Bloomington: U of Indiana P, 1988. ix–xii.

Eastman, Charles Alexander. *From the Deep Woods to Civilization: Chapters in the Autobiography of an Indian*. 1916. Lincoln: U of Nebraska P, 1977.

Erdrich, Louise. *Baptism of Desire*. New York: Harper & Row, 1989.

———. *The Beet Queen*. New York: Henry Holt and Company, 1986.

———. *The Bingo Palace*. New York: HarperCollins, 1994.

———. *The Birchbark House*. New York: Hyperion Books for Children, 1999.

———. *The Blue Jay's Dance: A Birth Year*. New York: HarperCollins, 1995.

———. *Jacklight*. New York: Henry Holt and Company, 1984.

———. *Love Medicine*. Toronto: Bantam Books, 1984, 1993.

———. *Tales of Burning Love*. New York: HarperCollins, 1996.

———. *Tracks*. New York: Henry Holt and Company, 1988.

———. "Where I Ought to Be: A Writer's Sense of Place." *New York Times Book Review* 28 July, 1985, sec. 7: 1+.

Erdrich, Louise, and Michael Dorris. *The Crown of Columbus*. New York: HarperCollins, 1991.

———. *Route 2*. Northridge, CA: Lord John Press, 1991.

Faulkner, William. "The Bear." *Go Down Moses*. New York: Vintage, 1990. 181–315.

Fay, George E., comp. and ed. *Charters, Constitutions, and By-Laws of the Indian Tribes of North America*. 18 vols. Greeley, CO: Colorado State College Museum of Anthropology, 1967. Vols. 1, 3, 6.

Fewkes, Jesse Walter. *Tusayan Flute and Snake Ceremonies*. Washington D.C.: Gov't Printing Office, 1901.

Fisher, Philip. "American Literary and Cultural Studies since the Civil War." *Redrawing the Boundaries: The Transformation of English and American Literary Studies*. Ed. Stephen Greenblatt and Giles Gunn. New York: MLA, 1992. 232–50.

Flavin, James. "The Novel as Performance: Communication in Louise Erdrich's *Tracks*." *SAIL* 3.4 (1991): 1–12.

Flavin, Louise. "Gender Construction amid Family Dissolution in Louise Erdrich's *The Beet Queen*." *SAIL* 7.2 (1995): 17–24.

Foley, John Miles. *Oral-Formulaic Theory and Research: An Introduction and Annotated Bibliography*. New York: Garland, 1985.

———, ed. *Oral Tradition in Literature: Interpretation in Context*. Columbia: U of Missouri P, 1986.

———. *The Theory of Oral Composition: History and Methodology*. Bloomington: U of Indiana P, 1988.

Forbes, Jack. "Colonialism and Native American Literature: Analysis." *Wicazo Sa Review* 3 (1987): 17–23.

Foucault, Michel. "What Is an Author?" *Critical Theory since 1965*. Ed. Hazard Adams and Leroy Searle. Tallahassee: Florida State UP, 1986. 138–47.

Friedman, Susan. "Identity Politics, Syncretism, Catholicism, and Anishinaabe Religion in Louise Erdrich's *Tracks*." *Religion and Literature* 26.1 (1994): 107–33.

Gallant, Alison. '*The Story Comes Up Different Every Time*': *Louise Erdrich and the Emerging Aesthetic of the Minority Woman Writer*. Diss. The Ohio State U, 1993. Ann Arbor: UMI, 1993.

Gates, Henry Louis, Jr. "Beyond the Culture Wars: Identities in Dialogue." *Profession* 93 MLA (1993): 6–11.

———, ed. *"Race," Writing, and Difference*. Chicago: U of Chicago P, 1985.

Georges, Robert A. "Toward an Understanding of Storytelling Events." *Journal of American Folklore* 82 (1969): 313–28.

Giese, Julie. *Comic Recourse: Feminism and Comedy in Contemporary American Fiction*. Diss. U of California, Los Angeles, 1995. Ann Arbor, UMI, 1996.

Gleason, William. "'Her Laugh an Ace': The Function of Humor in Louise Erdrich's *Love Medicine*. *American Indian Culture and Research Journal* 11.3 (1987): 51–73.

Godzich, Wlad. *The Culture of Literacy*. Cambridge, MA: Harvard UP, 1994.

Goody, Jack. *The Interface Between the Written and the Oral*. Cambridge, MA: Harvard UP, 1987.

Gourneau, Patrick. *History of the Turtle Mountain Band of Chippewa Indians*. 9th ed. N. p. n.p., 1993.

Grantham, Shelby. "Intimate Collaboration or 'A Novel Partnership.'" *Conversations with Louise Erdrich & Michael Dorris*. Ed. Allan Chavkin and Nancy Feyl Chavkin. Jackson: UP of Mississippi, 1994. 10–18.

Green, Rayna, ed. *That What She Said: Contemporary Poetry and Fiction by Native American Women*. Bloomington: U of Indiana P, 1984.

Hafen, P. Jane. *The Complicated Web: Mediating Cultures in the Works of Louise Erdrich*. Diss. U of Nevada, 1993. Ann Arbor: UMI, 1994.

Hallowell, A. I. "Ojibway Ontology, Behavior, and World View." *Culture in History, Essays in Honor of Paul Radin*. Ed. Stanley Diamond. New York: Octagon Books, 1981. 19–52.

Hargreaves, Mary Wilma M. *Dry Farming in the Northern Great Plains*. Cambridge, MA: Harvard UP, 1957.

Harkins, Arthur, and Richard Woods. *Attitudes of Minneapolis Agency Personnel Toward Urban Indians*. Minneapolis: U of Minnesota P, 1968.

Hartsock, Nancy. "Rethinking Modernism: Minority vs. Majority Theories." *Cultural Critique* 7 (1987): 187–206.

Havelock, Eric A. *Preface to Plato*. 1963. Cambridge, MA: Harvard UP, 1982.

Hemingway, Ernest. "Ten Indians." The Short Stories of Ernest Hemingway. New York: Charles Scribner's Sons, 1953. 331–36.

Hessler, Michelle R. "Catholic Nuns and Ojibwa Shamans: Pauline and Fleur in Louise Erdrich's *Tracks*." *Wicazo Sa Review* 11.1 (1995): 40–45.

Highwater, Jamake, ed. *Words in the Blood: Contemporary Indian*

Writers of North and South America. New York: New American Library, 1984.

Hirsch, Bernard A. "'The Telling Which Continues': Oral Tradition and the Written Word in Leslie Marmon Silko's *Storyteller.*" *American Indian Quarterly* 12.1 (1988): 1–26.

Holm, Tom. "Strong Hearts, Wounded Souls: Native American Veterans of the Vietnam War." *Wicazo Sa Review* 11.2 (1995): 1–15.

Hopkins, Sarah Winnemucca. *Life Among the Paiutes: Their Wrongs and Claims.* Ed. Mrs. Horace Mann. 1883. Bishop: Chalfant, 1969.

Horr, David A. comp. and ed. *Chippewa Indians VII: Commission Findings on the Chippewa Indians.* New York: Garland Publishing, Inc., 1974.

House Concurrent Resolution (HCR) 108. 1953.

Howard, James H. *The Plains-Ojibwa or Bungi. Hunters and Warriors of the Northern Prairies with Special Reference to the Turtle Mountain Band.* Lincoln, NE: J & L Reprint Company, 1977.

Howard, Jane. *Families*. New York: Simon and Schuster, 1978.

Huey, Michael. "Two Native American Voices." *Conversations with Louise Erdrich & Michael Dorris.* Ed. Allan Chavkin and Nancy Feyl Chavkin. UP of Mississippi, 1994. 122–27.

Hymes, Dell. *In Vain I Tried to Tell You: Essays in Native American Ethnopoetics.* Philadelphia: U of Pennsylvania P, 1981.

Indian Citizenship Act. 1924.

Indian Relocation Act. 1952.

Indian Reorganization Act. 1934.

Ingram, Forrest L. *Representative Short Story Cycles of the Twentieth Century: Studies in a Literary Genre.* The Hague: Mouton, 1971.

Iser, Wolfgang. *The Act of Reading: A Theory of Aesthetic Response.* Baltimore: The Johns Hopkins UP, 1978.

Jackson, Helen Hunt. *Ramona*. Dresden, TN: Avon, 1984.

Jahner, Elaine. "A Critical Approach to American Indian Literature."

Studies in American Indian Literature: Critical Essays and Course Designs. Ed. Paula Gunn Allen. New York: MLA, 1983. 211–24.

———. "Intermediate Forms between Oral and Written Literature." Studies in American Indian Literature: Critical Essays and Course Designs. Ed. Paula Gunn Allen. New York: MLA, 1983. 66–74.

———. "Metalanguages." Narrative Chance: Postmodern Discourse on Native American Literatures. Ed. Gerald Vizenor. 1989. Norman: U of Oklahoma P, 1993.

Jaskoski, Helen, ed. Early Native American Writing: New Critical Essays. Cambridge: U of Cambridge P, 1996.

———. "From the Time Immemorial: Native American Traditions in Contemporary Short Fiction." Since Flannery O'Connor: Essays on the Contemporary American Short Story. Ed. Loren Logsdon and Charles W. Mayer. Macomb: Western Illinois University, 1987. 54–71.

Johnston, Basil. Ojibway Heritage. New York: Columbia UP, 1976.

Jones, Malcolm. "Life, Art Are One for Prize Novelist." Conversations with Louise Erdrich and Michael Dorris. Ed. Allan Chavkin and Nancy Feyl Chavkin. Jackson: UP of Mississippi, 1994. 3–9.

Kehoe, Alice B. North American Indians: A Comprehensive Account. Englewood Cliffs, NJ: Prentice-Hall, Inc. 1981.

Kroeber, Karl. "Deconstructionist Criticism and American Indian Literature. Boundary 27.3 (1979): 73–89.

———. Introduction. SAIL 9.1 (1985): 1–4.

———. Retelling/Rereading: The Fate of Storytelling in Modern Times. New Brunswick, NJ: Rutgers UP, 1992.

———, comp. and ed. Traditional Literatures of the American Indian: Texts and Interpretations. Lincoln: U of Nebraska P, 1981.

Krupat, Arnold. Ethnocriticism: Ethnography History Literature. Berkeley: U of California P, 1992.

———. The Voice in the Margin: Native American Literature and the Canon. Berkeley: U of California P, 1989.

La Flesche, Francis. *The Middle Five: Indian Schoolboys of the Omaha Tribe*. 1900. Madison: U of Wisconsin P, 1963.

La Framboise, C.J. Telephone conversation. 27 November 1995.

Lacapa, Michael. *Antelope Woman: An Apache Folktale*. Flagstaff: Northland Publishing Co., 1992.

Landes, Ruth. *Ojibwa Religion and the Midéwinin*. Madison: U of Wisconsin P, 1968.

Larson, Charles R. *American Indian Fiction*. Albuquerque: U of New Mexico P, 1978.

Larson, Sidner. "The Fragmentation of a Tribal People in Louise Erdrich's Tracks." *American Indian Culture and Research Journal* 17.2 (1993): 1–13.

Le Guin, Ursula K. Rev. of *Love Medicine*, by Louise Erdrich. *SAIL* 9.1 (1985): 5-6.

Lévi-Strauss, Claude. *The Raw and the Cooked*. Trans. John and Doreen Wightman. New York: Harper and Row, 1969.

Lewis, Robert W. Rev. of *Love Medicine*, by Louise Erdrich. *American Indian Culture and Research Journal* 9.4 (1985): 113–16.

Lincoln, Kenneth. *Native American Renaissance*. Berkeley: U of California P, 1983.

Longfellow, Henry Wadsworth. *The Song of Hiawatha*. New York: Penguin, 1996.

Lord, Albert B. *The Singer of Tales*. Cambridge, MA.: Harvard UP, 1964.

Magalaner, Marvin. "Of Cars, Time, and the River." *American Women Writing Fiction: Memory, Identity, Family, and Space*. Ed. Mickey Perlman. Lexington: U of Kentucky P, 1989. 95–107.

Malinowski, Bronislaw. *Coral Gardens and their Magic II: The Language of Magic and Gardening*. Bloomington: U of Illinois P, 1965.

Malotki, Ekkehart, ed. *Hopi Animal Tales*. Lincoln: U of Nebraska P, 1998.

Mann, Susan Garland. *The Short Story Cycle: A Genre Companion and Reference Guide*. New York: Greenwood Press, 1989.

Maristuen-Rodakowski, Julie. "The Turtle Mountain Reservation in North Dakota: Its History as Depicted in Louise Erdrich's *Love Medicine* and *Beet Queen*." *American Indian Culture and Research Journal* 12.3 (1988): 33–38.

Masnick, George, and Mary Jo Bane. *The Nation's Families: 1960–1990*. Boston: Auburn House Publishing Company, 1990.

Maszewska, Jadwiga. "Functions of the Narrative Method in William Faulkner's *Absalom, Absalom!* and Louise Erdrich's *Tracks*." *Faulkner, His Contemporaries, and His Posterity*. Ed. Waldemar Zacharasiewicz. Tübingen: Franche, 1993. 317–21.

Matchie, Thomas. "Louise Erdrich's 'Scarlet Letter': Literary Continuity in *Tales of Burning Love*." *North Dakota Quarterly*. 63.4 (1996): 113–23.

Mathews, John Joseph. *Sundown*. 1934. Norman: U of Oklahoma P, 1988.

———. *Talking to the Moon*. 1945. Norman: U of Oklahoma P, 1981.

Matthiesen, Peter. *In the Spirit of Crazy Horse*. New York: Viking, 1983.

McKenzie, James. "Lipsha's Good Road Home: The Revival of Chippewa Culture in *Love Medicine*." *American Indian Culture and Research Journal* 10 (1986): 53–63.

McNickle, D'Arcy. *Runner in the Sun. A Story of Indian Maize*. 1954. Albuquerque: U of New Mexico P, 1987.

———. *The Surrounded*. 1936. Albuquerque: U of New Mexico P, 1978.

Meisenhelder, Susan. "Race and Gender in Louise Erdrich's '*The Beet Queen*.'" *ARIEL* 25.1 (1994): 45–57.

Melville, Herman. *Moby Dick*. Boston: Houghton Mifflin, 1956.

Messerschmidt, Jim. *The Trial of Leonard Peltier*. Boston: South End Press, 1983.

Momaday, N. Scott. *House Made of Dawn*. New York: Harper and Row, 1968.

———. "The Man Made of Words" *Literature of the American Indians: Views and Interpretations*. Ed. Abraham Chapman. New York: New American Library, 1975. 96–110.

———. *The Names: A Memoir*. 1976. Tucson: U of Arizona P, 1987.

———. "The Native Voice." *Columbia Literary History of the United States*. Ed. Emory Elliott. New York: Columbia UP, 1988. 5–15.

———. *The Way to Rainy Mountain*. Albuquerque: U of New Mexico P, 1969.

———. "A Word Has Power." *The Way: An Anthology of American Indian Literature*. Ed. Shirley Hill Will and Stan Steiner. New York: Alfred A. Knopf, 1972.

Morriseau, Norval. Selwyn Dewdney ed. *Legends of My People the Great Ojibway*. Toronto: The Ryerson Press, 1965.

Morrison, Toni. *Playing in the Dark: Whiteness and the Literary Imagination*. Cambridge, MA: Harvard UP, 1992.

Mourning Dove [Christine Quintas Ket]. *Cogewa, the Half Blood: A Depiction of the Great Montana Cattle Range*. 1927. Lincoln: U of Nebraska, 1981.

Moyers, Bill. "Louise Erdrich and Michael Dorris." *Conversations with Louise Erdrich & Michael Dorris*. Ed. Allan Chavkin and Nancy Feyl Chavkin. Jackson: UP of Mississippi, 1994. 138–50.

Murray, Stanley N. "The Turtle Mountain Chippewa, 1882–1905." *North Dakota History* 51.1 (1984): 14–37.

Native American Graves Protection and Repatriation Act. 1990.

Neihardt, John G. *Black Elk Speaks, Being the Life Story of a Holy Man of the Oglala Sioux, as told through John G. Neihardt*. 1932. New York: Washington Square Press, 1959.

Niatum, Duane, ed. *Carriers of the Dream Wheel: Contemporary Native American Poetry*. San Francisco: Harpers, 1975.

———. "On Stereotypes." *Recovering the Word: Essays on Native*

American Literature. Ed. Brian Swann and Arnold Krupat. Berkeley: U of California P, 1987. 552–62.

Ong, Walter J., S. J. "Literacy and Orality In Our Times." *ADE Bulletin* 58 (1978): 1–7.

———. *Orality and Literacy: The Technologizing of the Word.* London: Methuen, 1982.

———. *The Presence of the Word: Some Prolegomena for Cultural and Religious History.* New Haven, CT: Yale UP, 1967. Rpt. New York: Simon and Schulter, 1970, and Minneapolis: U of Minnesota P, 1981.

Orlick, Alex. *Principles for Oral Narrative Research.* Trans. Kristen Wolf and Jody Jensen. Bloomington: U of Indiana P, 1992.

Oskison, John Milton. *Black Jack Davy.* New York: Appleton, 1926.

———. *Brothers Three.* New York Macmillan, 1935.

———. *Wild Harvest: A Novel of Transition Days in Oklahoma.* New York: Appleton, 1925.

Overholt, Thomas W., and J Baird Callicott. *Clothed-in-Fur and Other Tales: An Introduction to an Ojibwa World View.* Washington D.C.: UP of America, 1982.

Owens, Louis. "Acts of Recovery: The American Indian Novel in the 80's."*Western American Literature* 22.1 (1987): 53–57.

———. *Other Destinies: Understanding the American Indian Novel.* Norman: U of Oklahoma P, 1992.

Parry, Milman. *The Making of Homeric Verse: The Collected Papers of Milman Parry,* ed. Adam Parry. Oxford: Clarendon P, 1971.

Pasquaretta, Paul. "Sacred Chance: Gambling and the Contemporary Native American Indian Novel." *MELUS* 21.2 (1996): 21–33.

Passaro, Vince. "Tales from a Literary Marriage." *Conversations with Louise Erdrich & Michael Dorris.* Ed. Allan Chavkin and Nancy Feyl Chavkin. Jackson: UP of Mississippi, 1994. 157–67.

Peirce, Charles Sanders. *Peirce on Signs: Writing on Semiotic by Charles Sanders Peirce.* Ed. James Hoopes. Chapel Hill: U of

North Carolina P, 1991.

Peterson, Nancy J. "History, Postmodernism, and Louise Erdrich's *Tracks*. *PMLA* 109.5 (1994): 982–94.

———. "Indi'n Humor and Trickster Justice in *The Bingo Palace*." In *The Chippewa Landscape of Louise Erdrich*. Ed. Allan Chavkin. Tuscaloosa: U of Alabama P, 1999. 161–181.

Pittman, Barbara L. "Cross-Cultural Reading and Generic Transformations: The Chronotope of the Road in Erdrich's *Love Medicine*." *American Literature* 67 (1995): 777–92.

Pokagon, Simon. *Queen of the Woods*. 1899. Berrien Springs: Hardscrabble, 1972.

Posey, Alexander Lawrence. *The Poems of Alexander Lawrence Posey*. Ed. Mrs. Minnie H. Posey. Memoir by William Elsey Connelly. Topeka: Crane, 1910.

Propp, Vladimir. *Morphology of the Folktale*. Trans. Laurence Scott. Ed. Louis A. Wagner. Austin: U of Texas P, 1968.

Public Law 280 (PL 280). 1953.

Purdy, John. "Against All Odds: Games of Chance in the Novels of Louise Erdrich." *The Chippewa Landscape of Louise Erdrich*. Ed. Allan Chavkin. Tuscaloosa: U of Alabama P, 1999. 8–35.

———. "Betting on the Future: Gambling Against Colonialism in the Novels of Louise Erdrich." *Native American Women in Literature and Culture*. Ed. Susan Castillo and Victor Da Rosa. Porto, Portugal: Fernando Pessoa UP, 1997. 37–56.

———. "(Karen) Louise Erdrich." *Dictionary of Native American Literature*. Ed. Andrew Wiget. New York: Garland Publishing, Inc., 1994.

Radin, Paul. "Ojibwa and Ottawa, Notes." N.p: American Philosophical Society, 1926.

———. *The Trickster: A Study in American Indian Mythology*. New York: Bell Publishing Company, Inc., 1956.

Rainwater, Catherine. "Ethnic Signs in Erdrich's *Tracks* and *The Bingo Palace*." *The Chippewa Landscape of Louise Erdrich*. Ed. Allan Chavkin. Tuscaloosa: U of Alabama P, 1999. 144–160.

———. "Reading Between Worlds: Narrativity in the Fiction of Louise Erdrich." *American Literature* 62.3 (1990): 405–22.

Ramsey, Jarold. *Reading the Fire: Essays in the Traditional Indian Literatures of the Far West.* Lincoln: U of Nebraska P, 1983.

———, ed. *Coyote Was Going There: Indian Literature of the Oregon Country.* Seattle: U of Washington P, 1977.

Ridge, John Rollin. *Life and Adventures of Joaquin Murieta, the Celebrated California Bandit.* 1854. Norman: U of Oklahoma P, 1977.

Riley, Patricia. "The Mixed Blood Writer as Interpreter and Mythmaker." *Understanding Others: Cultural and Cross-Cultural Studies and the Teaching of Literature.* Ed. Joseph Trimmer and Tily Warnock. Urbana, IL: NCTE, 1992. 230–40.

Robinson, E. B. *The History of North Dakota.* Lincoln: U of Nebraska P, 1966.

Rockwell, David. *Giving Voice to Bear: Native American Indian Myths, Rituals, and Images of the Bear.* Nivot, CA: Roberts Rinehart Publishers, 1991.

Roemer, Kenneth. "Context and Continuity." *Smoothing the Ground: Essays on Native American Oral Literatures.* Ed. Brian Swann. Berkeley: U of California P, 1983. 39–54.

Rollins, Peter C., and John E. O'Connor, eds. *Hollywood's Indian: The Portrayal of the Native American in Film.* Lexington: U of Kentucky P, 1998.

Ronnow, Gretchen. "Tayo, Death, and Desire: A Laconian Reading of Ceremony." *Narrative Chance: Postmodern Discourse on Native American Indian Literatures.* Ed. Gerald Vizenor. 1989. Norman: U of Oklahoma P, 1993. 69–90.

Rosenberg, Bruce. *Folklore and Literature: Rival Siblings.* Knoxville: U of Tennessee P, 1991.

Rothenberg, Jerome. *Shaking the Pumpkin: Traditional Poetry of the Indian North Americas.* Garden City: Doubleday, 1972.

Rowlandson, Mary. "The Sovereignty and Goodness of God." Ed. Neal Salisbury. Boston: Bedford, 1997.

Ruoff, A. LaVonne Brown. *American Indian Literatures*. New York: MLA, 1990.

———. "Old Traditions and New Forms." *Studies in American Indian Literature: Critical Essays and Course Designs*. Ed. Paula Gunn Allen. New York: MLA, 1983. 147–68.

———, and Jerry W. Ward, Jr., eds. *Redefining American Literary History*. New York: MLA, 1990.

———. "Three Nineteenth-Century American Indian Autobiographies." *Redefining American Literary History*. Ed. A. Lavonne Brown Ruoff and Jerry W. Ward. New York: MLA, 1990. 251–69.

Ruppert, James. "Mediation and Multiple Narrative in *Love Medicine*." *The North Dakota Quarterly* 59.4 (1991): 229–41.

———. "Patterns of Life." Rev. of *Love Medicine*, by Louise Erdrich. *Wicazo Sa Review* 2.1 (1986): 47–51.

Russell, David. *Writing in the Academic Disciplines, 1870–1990: A Curricular History*. Carbondale: Southern Illinois UP, 1991.

Ryan, Marya. *Gender and Community: Womanist and Feminist Perspectives in the Fiction of Toni Morrison, Amy Tan, Sandra Cisneros, and Louise Erdrich*. Diss. U of Illinois, 1995. Ann Arbor: UMI, 1996.

Sanders, Karla. *Healing Narratives: Negotiating Cultural Subjectivities in Louise Erdrich's Magic Realism*. Diss. Penn State U, 1996. Ann Arbor: UMI, 1996.

Sanders, Scott R. Rev. of *Love Medicine*, by Louise Erdrich. *SAIL* 9.1 (1985): 6–11.

Sands, Kathleen M. "American Indian Autobiography." *Studies in American Indian Literature: Critical Essays and Course Designs*. Ed. Paula Gunn Allen. New York: MLA, 1990. 55–65.

———. Rev. of *Love Medicine*, by Louise Erdrich. *SAIL* 9.1 (1985): 12–24.

Sarris, Greg. *Keeping Slug Woman Alive: A Holistic Approach to American Indian Texts*. Berkeley: U of California P, 1993.

Schimmoeller, Kathleen. *Humor in the House: Wendell Berry, Rachel*

Carson, Edward Abbey, and Louise Erdrich*. Diss. U of California, Davis, 1998. Ann Arbor: UMI, 1999.

Schneider, Lissa. "*Love Medicine*: A Metaphor for Forgiveness." *SAIL* 4.1 (1992): 1–13.

Schneider, Mary Jane. *North Dakota's Indian Heritage*. Grand Forks: U of North Dakota P, 1990.

Schweninger, Lee. "A Skin of Lakeweed: An Ecofeminist Approach to Erdrich and Silko." *Multicultural Literatures through Feminist/Poststructuralist Lenses*. Ed. Barbara Frey Waxman. Knoxville: U of Tennessee P, 1993. 37–56.

Schultz, Elizabeth A. "The Insistence Upon Community in the Contemporary Afro-American Novel." *College English* 41.1 (1979): 170–84.

Schultz, Lydia. "Fragments of Ojibwa Stories: Narrative Strategies in Louise Erdrich's *Love Medicine*." *College English* 18 (1991): 80–95.

———. *Perceptions from the Periphery: Fictional Form and Twentieth Century American Women Novelists*. Diss. U of Minnesota, 1990. Ann Arbor: UMI, 1991.

Schumacher, Michael. "Louise Erdrich and Michael Dorris: A Marriage of Minds." *Conversations with Louise Erdrich & Michael Dorris*. Ed. Allan Chavkin and Nancy Feyl Chavkin. Jackson: UP of Mississippi, 1994. 173–83.

Secco, Anna. "The Search for Origins through Storytelling in Native American Literature: Momaday, Silko, Erdrich." *Rivista di Studi Nord Americani* 3 (1992) 59–71.

Seeger, Charles. "The Folkness of Non-Folk vs. the Non-Folkness of Folk." *Folklore & Society: Essays in Honor of Benjamin A. Batkin*. Ed. Bruce Jackson. Hatboro, PA: Folklore Associates, 1966. 1–9.

Sergi, Jennifer Leigh. *Narrativity and Representation in Louise Erdrich's Fiction*. Diss. U of Rhode Island, 1993. Ann Arbor: UMI, 1994.

———. "Storytelling: Tradition and Preservation in Louise Erdrich's *Tracks*." *World Literature Today* 66.2 (1992): 279–82.

Shaddrock, Jennifer. "Mixed Blood Women: The Dynamic of Women's Relations in the Novels of Louise Erdrich and Leslie Silko." *Feminist Nightmares: Women at Odds: Feminism and the Problem of Sisterhood.* Ed. Susan Osttrouweisser. New York: New York UP, 1994. 106–21.

Silberman, Robert. "Opening the Text: *Love Medicine* and the Return of the Native American Woman." *Narrative Chance: Postmodern Discourse on Native American Literatures.* Ed. Gerald Vizenor. 1989. Norman: U of Oklahoma P, 1993. 101–20.

Silko, Leslie Marmon. *Ceremony.* New York: Penguin Books, 1977.

———. "Here's an Odd Artifact for the Fairy-Tale Shelf." Rev. of *The Beet Queen,* by Louise Erdrich. *Impact Magazine* 7 October 1986: 9–12.

———. "Landscape, History, and the Pueblo Imagination." *Antaeus* 57 (1986): 83–93.

———. "Language and Literature from a Pueblo Indian Perspective." *English Literature: Opening the Canon.* Ed. Leslie A. Fiedler and Houston A. Baker, Jr. Baltimore: Johns Hopkins UP, 1981. 54–72.

———. *Storyteller.* 1981. New York: Arcade Publishing, 1989.

Skinner, Alanson. "The Cultural Position of the Plains Ojibway." *American Anthropologist* 16 (1914): 314–19.

Slack, John. "The Comic Savior: The Dominance of the Trickster in Louise Erdrich's *Love Medicine.*" *North Dakota Quarterly* 61:3 (1993): 118–29.

Smith Jeanne Rosier. *Writing Tricksters: Mythic Gambols in American Ethnic Literature.* Berkeley: U of California P, 1997.

Standing Bear, Luther. *My People, the Sioux.* Transcribed by E. A. Brininstool. 1928. Lincoln: U of Nebraska P, 1988.

Stands in the Timber, John. *Cheyenne Memories.* Transcribed by Margot Liberty. 1967. Lincoln: U of Nebraska P, 1972.

Stansfield, Carol, and John Stansfield. "Guidelines for Using Traditional Stories from Native American Sources in the Four

Corners Region." *Personal Communication.* 10 March 1995.

Stansfield, John. "Reclaiming the Past: Storytelling and Education." *Storytelling* (1994): 16–18.

Stripes, James D. "The Problem(s) of (Anishinaabe) History in the Fiction of Louise Erdrich: Voices and Contexts." *Wicazo Sa Review* 7.2 (1991): 26–33.

Svensson, Frances. *The Ethics of American Politics: American Indians.* Minneapolis: Burgess Publishing Company, 1973.

Swann, Brian, ed. *On the Translation of Native American Literatures.* Washington: Smithsonian Institution Press, 1992.

———, ed. *Smoothing the Ground: Essays on Native American Oral Tradition.* Berkeley: U of California P, 1983.

Swann, Brian, and Arnold Krupat, comps. *I Tell You Now: Autobiographical Essays by Native American Writers.* Lincoln: U of Nebraska P, 1987.

———, eds. *Recovering the Word: Essays on Native American Literature.* Berkeley: U of California P, 1987.

Tedlock, Dennis, trans. *Finding the Center: Narrative Poetry of the Zuni Indians.* 1972. Rev. ed. Lincoln: U of Nebraska P, 1978.

Toelken, Barre. *The Dynamics of Folklore.* Boston: Houghton, 1979.

Trigger, Bruce, and Wilcomb Washburn, eds. *North America.* Vol. 1 of *The Cambridge History of the Native Peoples of the Americas,* part 2. 3 vols. Cambridge: U of Cambridge P, 1996.

Trueheart, Charles. "Marriage for Better or Words." *Conversations with Louise Erdrich & Michael Dorris.* Ed. Allan Chavkin and Nancy Feyl Chavkin. Jackson: UP of Mississippi, 1994. 115–21.

Twain, Mark. *Tom Sawyer.* New York: Viking, 1987.

Utley, Francis Lee. "Folk Literature: An Operational Definition." *The Study of Folklore.* Ed. Alan Dundes. Englewood Cliffs, NJ: Prentice-Hall, 1965.

Van Dyke, Annette. "Of Vision Quests and Spirit Guardians." *The Chippewa Landscape of Louise Erdrich.* Ed. Allan Chavkin.

Tuscaloosa: U of Alabama P, 1999. 130–43.

———. "Questions of the Spirit: Bloodlines in Louise Erdrich's Chippewa Landscape." *SAIL* 4.1 (1992): 15–27.

Vecsey, Christopher. *Traditional Ojibwa Religion and Its Historical Changes.* Philadelphia: The American Philosophical Society, 1983.

Velie, Alan R., ed. *American Indian Literature.* 1979. Rev. ed. Norman: U of Oklahoma P, 1991.

———. "The Trickster Novel." *Narrative Chance: Postmodern Discourse on Native American Literatures.* Ed. Gerald Vizenor. 1989. Norman: U of Oklahoma P, 1993. 121–40.

Vizenor, Gerald. *Crossbloods. Bone Courts, Bingo, and Other Reports.* 1976. Minneapolis: U of Minnesota, 1990.

———. *Darkness in Saint Louis Bearheart.* St. Paul: Truck, 1978.

———. *The Everlasting Sky: New Voices from the People Named the Chippewa.* New York: Crowell-Collier Press, 1972.

———. *Griever: An American Monkey in China.* Normal: Illinois State UP and Fiction Collective, 1987.

———. "Minnesota Chippewa: Woodland Treaties to Tribal Bingo." *American Indian Quarterly* 13.1 (1989): 31–57.

———. *The People Named the Chippewa: Narrative Histories.* Minneapolis: U of Minnesota P, 1984.

———. *The Trickster of Liberty: Tribal Heirs to a Wild Baronage at Petronia.* Emergent Literatures. Minneapolis: U of Minnesota P, 1988.

———. "Trickster Discourse." *American Indian Quarterly* 14.3 (1990): 277–87.

———, ed. *Narrative Chance: Postmodern Discourse on Native American Literatures.* 1989. Norman: U of Oklahoma P, 1993.

Walker, Victoria. "A Note on Narrative Perspective in *Tracks.*" *SAIL* 3.4 (1991): 37–40.

Wallace, Karen. *Myth, and Metaphor, Archetype and Individuation: A Study in the Work of Louise Erdrich.* Diss. U of California, Los

Angeles, 1998. Ann Arbor: UMI, 1999.

Warren, William W. *History of the Ojibway Nation*. Minneapolis: Ross & Haines, Inc., 1974.

Waters, Frank. *Book of the Hopi*. New York: Penguin, 1963.

———. *The Man Who Killed the Deer*. 1942. Athens, Ohio: Swallow P, 1970.

———. *Masked Gods: Navaho and Pueblo Ceremonialism*. Athens, Ohio: Swallow P, 1950.

———. *Pumpkin Seed Point: Being Within the Hopi*. Athens, Ohio: Swallow P, 1969.

———. *The Woman at Otowi Crossing*. 1966. Athens, Ohio: Swallow P, 1987.

Weatherford, Jack. *Indian Givers: How the Indians of the Americas Transformed the World*. New York: Fawcett Columbine, 1988.

———. *Native Roots: How the Indians Enrich America*. New York: Fawcett Columbine, 1991.

Welch, James. *The Death of Jim Loney*. 1979. New York: Penguin, 1987.

———. *Fools Crow*. New York: Penguin, 1986.

———. *Winter in the Blood*. 1974. New York: Penguin, 1986.

Whitman, Walt. *Leaves of Grass*. The Harper Single Volume American Literature. 3rd ed. New York: Longman, 1999. 1152–1254.

Whitson, Kathy J. *Louise Erdrich's* Love Medicine *and* Tracks: *A Culturalist Approach*. Diss. U of Missouri, 1993. Ann Arbor: UMI, 1994.

Wiget, Andrew. *Critical Essays on Native American Literature*. Boston: G.K. Hall & Co., 1985.

———. "His Life in His Tail: The Native American Trickster and the Literature of Possibility." *Redefining American Literary History*. Ed. A. LaVonne Brown Ruoff & Jerry W. Ward, Jr. New York: MLA, 1990. 83–96.

———. *Native American Literature*. Boston: Twayne, 1985.

———. "Singing the Indian Blues: Louise Erdrich and the Love That Hurts So Good." *Puerto Del Sol* 21.1 (1986): 166–75.

Willard, William. "Chippewa Puzzle." Rev. of *Love Medicine*, by Louise Erdrich. *Wicazo Sa Review* 2.1 (1986): 49–51.

Wilson, Michael. *Writing Home: The Oral Tradition as a Philosophical and Stylistic Basis for a Tradition of Written American Indian Literature*. Diss. Cornell U, 1995. Ann Arbor: UMI, 1994.

Winter, Kari. "Refusing the 'Sovereign Territory' of Language: The Trickster Nanapush vs. a Storm of Government Papers." *Northwest Review* 35.3 (1997): 541–55.

Witt, Shirley Hill, and Stan Steiner, eds. *The Way: An Anthology of American Indian Literature*. New York: Alfred A. Knopf, 1972.

Wong, Hertha Dawn. "An Interview with Louise Erdrich and Michael Dorris." *Conversations with Louise Erdrich & Michael Dorris*. Ed. Allan Chavkin and Nancy Feyl Chavkin. Jackson: UP of Mississippi, 1994. 30–53.

———. *Sending My Heart Back Across Years*. Oxford UP, 1992.

Woodward, Pauline Groetz. *New Tribal Forms: Community in Louise Erdrich's Fiction*. Diss. Tufts U, 1991. Ann Arbor: UMI, 1991.

Zitkala-Ša [Gertrude Bonnin]. *American Indian Stories*. 1921. Lincoln: U of Nebraska P, 1986.

INDEX

A

Adare, 85, 141, 210n. 14
  Adelaide, 109, 110, 121, 141
  Dot, 47, 49, 65, 68, 82–83, 85, 92, 99, 100–1, 110, 113, 114, 120, 121, 122, 129, 130, 132, 141–42, 145, 146, 166, 183, 205n. 19, 208n. 4
  Karl, 47, 68, 88, 89, 90, 92, 109–10 120, 121, 122, 130, 141, 145, 160, 166, 167, 208n. 18
  Mary, 47, 65, 68, 89, 90, 92, 99, 109–10, 120, 121, 122, 130, 141, 146, 166
Alexie, Sherman, xi
Allen, Paula Gunn, 6, 8, 10, 11, 14, 16–17, 19, 26, 44–45, 61, 64, 69, 70, 108, 116, 148, 149, 175, 177, 178, 180, 186, 189, 197n. 17, 195n. 11
  tribal gynocracies, 149
  Sacred Hoop, The, 15, 197n. 17, 200n. 21
  Spider Woman's Granddaughters, 189, 216n. 17
  Woman Who Owned the Shadows, The, 60
Almost Soup (The Antelope Wife), 50, 172, 173
American Indian Movement (AIM), 18, 93, 222
American Indian Religious Freedom Act (1978), 17
American literary canon, 4, 175–79
American myth, 185
American studies,
  shift from myth to rhetoric (see Philip Fisher), 4
Amiotte, Arthur, 20–21
Anglo literary perceptions of Native people, 2
animal transformations, 147–48, 169–72
Anishinaabe (Anishinaabeg), also see Chippewa, xiv, 51, 82, 86, 92, 103, 114, 115, 116, 147, 152, 160, 165, 172, 173, 174, 191n. 1, 204n. 14, 207n. 14, 211–12n. 4
Antelope people, 169–72
Antelope Wife (Sweetheart Calico), xiv, 67, 115, 143, 144, 146, 150, 171, 172, 173, 174, 187, 204n. 16
Apes, William, 2, 62, 181,

193n. 3
Argus, North Dakota, 83, 84, 90, 91, 109, 110, 112, 114, 118, 120, 136, 141, 158
autobiography,
   Erdrich's use of, 60–69
   Native American, 39–40, 61
   twentieth-century, 63–64

B

Baker, Jr., Houston, 10, 175–76
Banks, Russell, 83
Barnouw, Victor, 161, 164, 198n. 19, 211n. 1
Barton, Gay, 106
Bataille, Gretchen, 62, 64, 197n. 18, 200n. 21
Beidler, Peter, 106
Benjamin, Walter, 41, 187, 188
Bevis, William, 37
Black Elk Speaks, 63
blood quantum, 6–7, 194–95n. 10
Blue Prairie Woman (*The Antelope Wife*), 114, 115, 142, 143, 144, 171, 172
Boas, Franz, 30, 31, 198n. 19, 201–2n. 3
Boccaccio, Giovanni, *Decameron*, the 48, 182
Bonetti, Kay, 57, 70, 192n. 2, 209n. 6
Bonnin, Gertrude Simmons (Zitkala–Ša), 2, 193n. 4
Borland, Hal (*When Legends Die*) 5, 193n. 6

Boudinot, Elias, 2, 9, 193n. 4
Bright, William, 11
Brown, Dee, 45, 51
Bruchac, Joseph, 53, 54
Brumble, H. David, 62, 198n. 17, 207n. 11
Bureau of Indian Affairs (BIA), 54, 75, 88, 92, 102
Bynum, David, 37, 38

C

Camp, Gregory, 77, 81, 169
Campbell, Joseph, 149
Cane (Jean Toomer), 182
Canterbury Tales, The, 48, 182
Carter, Forrest (*The Education of Little Tree*), 5, 58, 193n. 6
Catt, Catherine, 155, 192n. 2
Chambers, Ross, 188, 189
Chippewa (Ojibwa, Anishinaabe), 191n. 1
   animal helpers and totems, 152, 211n. 4
   bear in the Ojibwa culture, 155–58
   clans, 74
   contemporary, 80, 81–82, 97
   family structure, 75
   formation of the band, 77–79
   formation of reservation, 80–82
   grandparents, 65–66, 75–77, 103, 109, 117
   historical, 70–71
   important historical dates,

219–22
love medicines, 74, 145, 210n. 17
manitous, 72, 73, 118, 123, 126, 153, 154, 156, 159, 160, 161, 162, 165, 168, 169, 173, 174
maps, xvii–xix
Midéwinin, 72, 74, 150, 153, 155–57, 160, 173, 213n. 12, 216n. 15
reservations, 207n. 14
storytelling, 22
treaties, 80–81
Turtle Mountain Band, 13, 51, 52, 53, 70, 71, 77–82, 195n. 10
types of narratives, 46
urban (see *The Antelope Wife*)
Woodland culture, 71–77
Chippewa-Sioux Sweet Corn Agreement, 77
Chona, Maria, 63
Clark, Joni, 151, 158, 160, 165, 191n. 2
Clifford, James, 17
Coleman, Sister Bernard, 22, 145, 148, 210n. 17, 211n. 1
Coltelli, Laura, 19, 26, 27, 57, 60, 70, 108, 206n. 7
Convocation of Indian Scholars (1970), 8
Cook, Marlis, 101, 113, 131, 132
Cook-Lynn, Elizabeth, 57–58, 194n. 7
Cooper, James Fenimore, 2, 192n. 2

Copeway, George (Kah–ge–ga–gah–bowh), 9, 62, 181, 193n. 4
Cox, Jay, 155, 199n. 21
Creighton, Joanne, 182, 183

D

Dartmouth College, 54, 55, 181
Dawes Act (1887), 81, 86, 93, 154, 220
Deloria, Vine, Jr., 51
Delorme, David, 77, 78, 79
Derrida, Jacques, 184
Dewdney, Selwyn, 155, 156, 157, 158, 161, 162, 211n. 1
Dorris, Michael, xiii, 5–6, 8–9, 45, 46, 54, 55–57, 60, 70, 89, 108, 122, 142, 195n. 11, 196n. 13
 collaboration with Erdrich, 55–56, 192n. 2
 Crown of Columbus, The, 56
 views on Native American literature, 5–6
 Yellow Raft in Blue Water, A, 9
Dubliners, The (Joyce), 183

E

Eastman, Charles (Ohiyesa), 63
Eliot, T.S., 26, 27
Erdrich, Louise, 1, 14, 19, 148,

176, 179, 181, 189, 195n. 11
  children's book, *Grand-
    mother's Pidgeon*, 56
  critical work on, xiii
    191–92n. 2
  life, 53–57, 206nn. 5, 7, 9
  multiple narrators in the
    novels, 42, 47–50
  mythic presence in the
    novels, 148–50, 187
  novels:
    Antelope Wife, The, xii,
      xiii, xiv, 1, 36, 42, 45,
      49–50, 56, 65, 67, 76,
      85, 101–3, 105, 114–17,
      133–34, 142, 145, 169,
      171–173, 209n. 5
    Beet Queen, The, xiii, 9,
      42, 47–48, 49, 53, 56,
      65, 67, 71, 82, 83, 84–85,
      88–92, 109–10, 112,
      120–22, 126, 129, 130,
      142, 166, 182
    Leslie Silko's review of,
      xiii, 40–41
    Bingo Palace, The, xiii, 42,
      48, 49, 56, 65, 73, 84,
      93, 95, 96, 97–99, 100,
      108, 111–12, 116, 123,
      124, 125–126, 130, 139,
      146, 155, 159, 160, 164,
      167, 212n. 5
    Birchbark House, The, 56,
      209n. 5
    Crown of Columbus, The
      (collaboration with
      Dorris), 56
    Love Medicine, xiii, 2, 8,
      9, 15, 38, 42, 46, 47, 49,
      50, 56, 84, 91, 92–97,
      100, 107, 108, 110–11,
      121, 122–25, 129, 130,
      142, 166, 182, 196n. 13,
      203n. 10, 205n. 19,
      206–07n. 10, 217n. 2
    North Dakota novels
      (T, BQ, LM, BP, TBL),
      1, 19, 36, 45, 48, 53, 56,
      71, 83, 84, 85, 101–2,
      106, 117, 126, 129, 133,
      134, 141, 149, 150, 166,
      168, 174, 182, 196n. 14,
      213n. 8
    Tales of Burning Love, xiii,
      42, 49, 53, 56, 65, 67,
      82, 85, 95, 99–101, 105,
      112–14, 129–33, 205n.
      19, 209n. 12
    touchstone stories, 117–34
      Antelope Wife, The,
        133–34
      Beet Queen, The,
        120–22
      Bingo Palace, The,
        125–29
      Love Medicine, 122–25
      Tales of Burning Love,
        129–33
      Tracks, 117–20
    Tracks, xiii, 9, 40, 42,
      46–47, 53, 56, 59, 60,
      73, 74, 84, 86–88, 108,
      109, 110, 112, 116,
      117–20, 122, 124, 135,
      151, 163, 166, 167–68,
      196n. 14, 205n. 2
  nonfiction:
    Bluejay's Dance, 56,

208n. 3,
Route 2, 56
novels of families, 105–6, 108, 134–45
novels as storytelling sessions, 45–50
place in the Native American literary renaissance, 12
poetry:
Baptism of Desire, 56
Jacklight, 56
popularity, 1, 206n. 9
tribal storyteller, xiii, 1, 41–45, 52, 58, 59, 69, 85, 103, 149, 184, 187, 189, 190, 206–7n. 10
use of the autobiographical voice in her work, 60–69
use of story cycles in her work, 69–70, 182–84
voice, 51–52
ethnometaphysics, 147

F

family stories (circular structure), 108–34
Faulkner, William, 2, 26, 27, 82, 183, 184, 217n. 3
Absalom, Absalom!, 184
As I Lay Dying, 184
Go Down Moses, 183
Sound and the Fury, The, 184
Unvanquished, The, 184
Fisher, Philip, 4–5, 185–86
Flavin, Louise, 46, 192n. 2, 204n. 17, 206n. 10
Foley, John Miles, 31, 34, 35–36
folklore,
and Native American narratives, 31–32
definition, 28–29
folklorist, 28–32
Bascom, William, 201n. 2
Bauman, Richard, 30
Ben-Amos, Dan, 30, 33, 202n. 4
Bronner, Simon, 201n. 2
Dorson, Richard, 30
Dundes, Alan, 28, 31, 203n. 8
Georges, Robert, 29, 30, 31, 202n. 7
Hymes, Dell, 30
Jansen, William, 30
Malinowski, Bronislaw, 201n. 2
Radcliffe-Brown, R., 201n. 2
Seeger, Charles, 29–30
Utley, Francis Lee, 29
Forbes, Jack, 180, 181
Foucault, Michel, 23, 24
functionalists, 30

G

Gates, Henry Louis, Jr., 176
Godzich, Wlad, 187–88
Goody, Jack, 40, 203n. 9, 204n. 11
Gourneau, Patrick, 53, 78, 79, 135, 207–08nn. 16, 17

H

Hallowell, A. I., 46, 147, 148, 149
Harjo, Joy, xi
Havelock, Eric, 40, 204n. 11
Hogan, Linda, xi, 8, 148, 195n. 11
Hopkins, Sarah Winnemucca, 2, 62–63, 193n. 4
Howard, James, 77, 79, 97, 135, 158, 160, 161, 163
Hymes, Dell, 11, 30, 199n. 20, 202n. 7

I

Indian, the term, 6–8
Indian Citizenship Act (1924), 17
Indian Civil Rights Act (1968), 17
Indian Claims Commission, 77
Indian Relocation Act, 137
Indian Reorganization Act (1934), 17
In Our Times (Hemingway), 182
Iser, Wolfgang, 25

J

Jahner, Elaine, 19, 39, 40, 59, 200n. 21
James, Celestine, 47, 65, 68, 85, 89–90, 91–92, 99, 110, 120, 121–22, 132, 141, 145, 166
James, Dutch, 84, 91
Jaskoski, Helen, 182
Johnson, Albertine, 47, 48, 67, 76, 95, 96, 97, 111, 112, 122, 128, 139, 140
Johnston, Basil, 72, 73, 76, 152, 153, 160, 211n. 1, 211–12n. 4
Joyce, James, 26–27, 39

K

Kashpaw, 38, 48, 75, 85, 86, 87, 92, 96, 102, 109, 119, 122, 138–39, 144, 163, 209–10n. 13
  Aurelia, 122
  Eli, 47, 65, 74, 87, 94, 95, 111, 119, 120, 138, 139, 145, 146, 167, 168, 208n. 19, 213–14n. 13
  Gordie, 47, 94, 95, 111, 122, 139, 207n. 12
  King, 94, 135–36, 139, 207n. 12
  Margaret, 86, 87, 110, 119, 136, 138, 146, 163
  Nector, 47, 65, 66–67, 75, 76, 84, 86, 88, 92, 93, 111, 122, 124, 125, 126, 136, 138, 139, 145, 146, 163, 166, 167
  Resounding Sky, 138
  Russell, 68, 85, 89, 91, 94, 120, 121, 139, 140, 166

Index

Zelda, 67, 76, 98, 111, 122, 123, 124, 127, 128, 139, 145, 146, 209n. 8
Kozka (*The Beet Queen* and *Tracks*), 85
Fritzie, 110, 118, 141, 146
Pete, 84, 141
Sita, 47, 68, 89–91, 92, 99, 110, 120, 121, 141, 182
Kroeber, Karl, 19, 22, 24, 25, 191n. 2, 197n. 18, 199n. 21
Krupat, Arnold, 19, 44, 61–62, 105, 107, 197n. 18
The Voice in the Margin, 3–4, 177–78, 204n. 14

L

La Farge, Oliver (*Laughing Boy*), 2, 5, 192n. 2, 193n. 6
La Flesche, Francis, 63
Lake Matchimanito, 112, 163, 213–14n. 13
Lamartine, 38, 48, 75, 87, 92, 95, 102, 122, 124, 125, 135, 137
Bev, 94, 137
Henry, Jr., 47, 95, 97, 123–24, 125, 127, 137
Henry, Sr., 94, 137
Lulu Nanapush Morrissey, 43, 46–47, 48, 59, 64–65, 76, 86, 88, 92, 93, 96, 97, 98–99, 109, 112, 122, 123, 124, 125, 128, 129, 137, 139, 140, 145, 146, 166, 208n. 19, 209nn. 8, 9, 213n. 7
Lyman, 48, 66, 75, 92–93, 95, 97–98, 100, 112, 123, 124, 126, 127, 128, 130, 137, 138–39, 140, 144, 207n. 12
Landes, Ruth, 74, 75, 145, 155, 156, 210n. 17
Larson, Charles, 9, 11
Lazarre, 87, 88, 92, 109, 119, 122, 135, 136
Boy, 87, 118, 158
Geezhig, 126
Lucille, 95, 122, 126, 127, 136
Marie, 47, 64, 65, 76, 84, 92, 93, 95, 96, 97, 98, 99, 111, 122, 123, 124, 125, 130, 136–37, 138, 139, 143, 145, 146, 166, 209n. 8, 215n. 13
Le Guin, Ursula, 59, 192n. 2
Leonard, 126, 127
Leopolda, Sister (also see Pauline Puyat), 47, 67, 84, 86, 91, 96, 99, 109, 118–19, 120, 122, 124, 130, 133, 136–37, 145, 158, 159, 164–65, 166, 167, 196n. 14, 213–16n. 13
Lévi–Strauss, Claude, 25, 184, 185, 199n. 20, 201n. 2
Lewis, Robert, 183–84
Lincoln, Kenneth, 5, 11, 19, 27, 28, 39, 43, 57, 59, 107
Little Shell, Chief, 79, 80, 220
Lord, Alfred, 34, 38–39, 40, 50, 202nn. 5, 6

M

Mann, Susan Garland, 182
Matchie, Thomas, 113
Matchikwewis, 115–16, 143
Mathews, John Joseph, 18, 64, 200n. 23
Mauser, Jack, 48, 49, 65, 68, 82–83, 99, 100, 101, 112–14, 126, 129, 130, 131, 132, 133, 137, 138, 145, 146
McCumber Agreement (1892), xix, 81, 83, 220–21
McNickle, D'Arcy, 18, 200n. 23
Métis, 66, 71, 78–79, 80, 87, 92, 119, 120, 135, 137, 207n. 16, 216n. 16, 219, 220
Michif, 71, 79
Miller, Jude Adare, 130
Milou North, 56–57
Missepeshu, 118, 123, 150, 154, 156, 161–66, 167, 168, 173, 196n. 14, 212n. 5, 213n. 11, 213–16n. 13
mixed–blood, 7–8
Momaday, N. Scott, xi, xii, 3, 6, 9, 14, 20, 21, 27, 28, 37, 40, 44, 45, 50, 60, 148, 175, 176, 177, 179, 187, 188, 189
House Made of Dawn, 3, 5, 8, 36, 41, 60, 107, 175, 188
Names, The, 39–40, 64
Way to Rainy Mountain, The, 13, 39, 40, 64
Morriseau, Norvel, 145, 151, 162, 165, 210n. 17, 211n. 1
Morrison, Toni, 176, 180–81
Morrissey, 38, 47, 87, 88, 92, 102, 109, 119, 122, 135, 136
  Bernadette, 87, 118, 135, 136, 213–14n. 13
  Clarence, 87, 135
  June, 38, 47, 48, 49, 76, 84, 92, 95, 99, 100–01, 110–11, 112, 113, 114, 122–23, 124, 126–27, 129, 132, 136, 146, 164, 208n. 4
  Lipsha, 47, 48, 66, 73–4, 76, 92, 95, 96, 97–98, 99–100, 110–11, 112, 122, 123, 124, 125–26, 127, 129, 134, 135, 139, 140–41, 145, 146, 155, 159, 164, 166, 167, 174, 182, 207n. 12, 209n. 8, 212n. 5, 213n. 7, 216n. 14
  Napoleon, 118, 124, 125
  Sophie, 87, 119, 135, 136, 145, 167, 213–14n. 13
Mourning Dove, 18, 200n. 23
multiculturalism, 175–79
Murray, Stanley, 77, 78–79, 80, 81, 216n. 16

N

Nanabozho, 72–73, 74, 115–16, 140, 143, 147–48, 154, 156, 160, 172, 207n. 15, 211n. 3
Nanapush, 16, 46–47, 53, 59, 65, 66, 73, 74, 86, 87, 88, 109, 110, 117–18, 119, 122, 127, 138, 140, 145, 146, 154, 158, 160, 163, 165,

166, 167, 169, 187, 208n. 15, 211n. 3, 215n. 13, 216n. 14
  Gerry, 16, 48, 92, 93–94, 95, 99, 100, 101, 111, 122, 125, 126, 129, 130, 132, 140–41, 145, 187, 204n. 16, 205n. 19, 208n. 19, 208n. 4, 211n. 3, 213n. 7, 214n. 7, 216n. 14
  Shawn, 129, 132, 142, 145, 205n. 19, 210n. 14
Nanapushes, 86, 87, 102, 119, 122, 138, 140, 155
narrative clusters, 37–38
Native American Graves Protection and Repatriation Act (1990), 17
Native American life, twentieth-century, 3
Native American Literary Renaissance, 2, 3–6, 12
Native American Literature
  and the American literary canon, 177–79
  characteristics, 12–17
  contemporary, 10
  critical work in, 10–12, 196–200nn. 16, 17, 18, 19, 20, 21
  definition, 6–10
  1970s, 8, 195–96n. 12
  pre-twentieth-century, 2
Native American novel, 9–10
Native Americans portrayed by Anglo authors, 2
Niatum, Duane, 8, 17

O

Occum, Samson, 2, 193n. 4
Ojibwa (see Chippewa)
Ong, Walter, 36–37, 38, 40, 203n. 9, 204n. 11
oral residue, 36–37
oral tradition, 11, 12–14,15, 19, 22–23, 28, 197n. 18
Oral-Formulaic Theory (see Milman Parry)
orality theory, 19, 32–38
Orlick, Alex, 33
Ortiz, Alfonso, 8
Ortiz, Simon, 12, 27, 196n. 12
Oshkikwe, 115–16, 143, 172, 216n. 17
Overholt, Thomas and J. Band Callicott, 147, 148, 173, 211nn. 12
Owens, Louis, 6–7, 9, 19, 23–24, 59, 89, 91, 94, 192n. 2, 196n. 16, 204n. 18, 208n. 18, 209n. 7, 211n. 3

P

Pantamounty, Candice, 68, 101, 113, 131, 132
Parry, Milman, 33–34, 38, 202nn. 5, 6, 202–3n. 7
Peltier, Leonard, 94, 208n. 20
Pembina Band, 169, 216n. 16
Peterson, Nancy, 46, 158, 191–92n. 2, 204n. 17, 205n. 3, 206n. 10

Pfef, Wallace, 65, 68, 85, 89, 90, 110, 120, 121, 122, 141, 145, 146
Pillager, 48, 72, 74, 75, 86, 87, 88, 92, 118, 119, 122, 123, 125, 126, 127, 128, 138, 140, 141, 142, 145, 150, 163, 210n. 14, 216n. 14
    Fleur, xiv, 46, 75, 76, 84, 86, 87, 96, 98, 109, 112, 118, 119, 120, 122, 123, 125, 126, 127–28, 138, 140, 145, 149–69, 173, 174, 187, 204n. 16, 210n. 14, 213nn. 7, 8, 11, 12, 214–15n. 13, 216nn. 14, 15
    bear power, 151–52, 155, 158–60
    historical, 153–54
    Moses, 86, 96, 140, 145, 146, 154, 155, 203n. 10, 209n. 9, 213n. 7, 215n. 13
Pokagon, Simon, 2, 193n. 3
Propp, Vladimir, 25–26, 199n. 20, 201n. 2
Pukwan, 94, 128, 138, 154
Puyat, 87, 92, 109, 122, 135, 136, 141
    Pauline (see Sister Leopolda)
    Regina (Kashpaw James), 118

R

Radin, Paul, 16, 73, 199n. 21
Ramsey, Jarold, 16, 189, 199n. 21

Red River Valley, xix, 54, 80, 216n. 16, 219
regionalism, 4
Ridge, John Rollin, 181, 193n. 4
Riley, Patricia 148–49
Rockwell, David, 151, 152, 157
Roemer, Kenneth, 40, 204n. 14
Rose, Wendy, 195n. 11
Rothenberg, Jerome, 11
Roy (*The Antelope Wife*), 102, 114, 115, 133, 142, 143, 144–45, 171
    Augustus, 114, 133, 143, 144
    Mary, 65, 66, 76, 102, 115, 133, 142, 143, 204n. 16
    Matilda, 171, 172
    Rozin (see Whiteheart Beads)
    Scranton, 114, 116
    Zosie, 65, 66, 76, 102, 114, 115, 133, 142, 143, 204n. 16
Ruoff, A. LaVonne Brown, 8, 11, 19, 61, 62, 193n. 4, 196n. 16, 198n. 19
Ruppert, James, 50, 69, 192n. 2, 206n. 10

S

Sands, Kathleen, 39, 46, 50, 61, 62, 64, 191n. 2, 197n. 18, 206n. 10
Sarris, Greg, vii, xi, 8, 148, 177, 195n. 11
Schlick (*Tales of Burning Love*)

Anna, 101, 131, 145, 146
Eleanor, 49, 68, 99, 101, 113, 114, 130–31, 132, 133, 145
Lawrence, 99, 101, 146
Schneider, Mary Jane, 77, 81
Schultz, Elizabeth, 188
secondary heroes (Joseph Campbell), 148–51
Sequoyah, 13
Shawno (*The Antelope Wife*), 102, 114, 115, 133, 134, 142, 143, 144, 171
Cecille, 102, 103, 143, 146
Frank, 102, 103, 133, 134, 143, 145, 146
Klaus, 50, 67, 102, 143–44, 171–72
Silko, Leslie Marmon, xi, xii, iii, 8, 9, 14, 21, 27, 40–41, 50, 148, 175, 176, 179, 187, 204n. 12
Ceremony, 13, 36, 40, 41, 44, 45, 60, 107, 188, 204n. 12
Storyteller, 19, 41–44, 45, 46, 204n. 13
Skinner, Alanson, 72, 77
Standing Bear, Luther, 63
Stansfield, John, 58
story cycles, 44–45, 69–70, 104, 182–84
storyteller, 12, 13, 21–22, 23, 38
communal, 23–24, 41–45
Native American, 3, 21 (also see oral tradition)
structuralists, 25, 29–30, 199n. 20, 201n. 2
Stryses, James, 85, 192n. 2

T

Tapahonso, Luci, xi
Tatro, Jewel Parker, 127, 161
Tedlock, Dennis, 202n. 7
"ten-cent agreement," xix, 81, 221
Toelken, Barre, 202n. 7
Toose (*The Bingo Palace*)
Redford, 98, 128, 139–40, 146
Shawnee Ray, 48, 73, 97, 98, 99, 112, 126, 127, 128, 139, 140, 145, 146, 167, 174
Xavier, 97, 128, 140, 145, 146, 174
traditional Native American narratives (see oral tradition)
transitional texts (also see Native American autobiography), 38–45
trickster, 11, 15–16, 20, 36–37, 65, 76, 92, 117–18, 129, 140, 147–48, 154, 155, 168, 172, 204n. 16, 207n. 15, 211n. 3
Turtle Mountain Band of Chippewa Indians (see Chippewa, Turtle Mountain)

V

Van Dyke, Annette, 163, 164, 165, 170, 192n. 2, 205n. 3
Vecsey, Christopher, 72, 74, 75,

153, 154, 157, 162, 163, 164, 213n. 10
Velie, Alan, 14, 199n. 21, 211n. 3
Vizenor, Gerald, xi, xii, 7, 8, 10, 14, 16, 26, 27, 36, 75, 94, 103, 108, 148, 176, 189, 191n. 1, 195n. 11, 199n. 20, 199–200n. 21, 207n. 14
  Darkness in Saint Louis Bearheart, 8, 16, 36, 200n. 21
  Griever: An American Monkey King in China, 9, 16, 200n. 21
  People Named the Chippewa, The, 191n. 1
  Trickster of Liberty, The, 16, 200n. 21

W

Warren, William, 74, 93–94, 153, 163, 181, 213n. 6
Waters, Frank, 5, 193n. 6
Welch, James, xi, xii, 9, 14, 27, 45, 176, 187
  Death of Jim Loney, The, 36, 60
  Fools Crow, 9, 85
  Indian Lawyer, 85
  Winter in the Blood, 8, 13, 36, 41, 60, 107, 188
Wetherford, Jack, 217n. 4
Wheeler-Howard Indian Reorganization Act (1934), 81
Whiteheart Beads (*The Antelope Wife*), 102, 114, 115, 133, 171
  Cally, 50, 65, 102, 103, 114–16, 133, 134, 142–43, 144, 146, 172, 174
  Deanna, 133, 134, 142, 143
  Richard, 102, 133, 134, 143, 144
  Rozin, 50, 65, 66, 76, 102, 103, 133–34, 142, 143, 145, 146
Wiget, Andrew, 11, 19, 193n. 4, 196–97n. 16, 201n. 1
Winesburg, Ohio (Anderson), 182, 183, 184
winter counts, 52, 85, 103
Wong, Hertha, 85, 142, 194n. 7, 197n. 18
words, power of, 6, 13–14, 27–28, 37, 194n. 9, 203n. 10, 217n. 3

Z

Zepeda, Ophelia, 175

American Indian Studies

Elizabeth Hoffman Nelson and Malcolm A. Nelson, General Editors

The American Indian Studies series represents a growing group of important books on the literatures and cultures of America's indigenous peoples. The series is inclusive and open to a wide variety of approaches. We welcome scholarly literary studies and interdisciplinary studies of languages and cultures by American Indians, First Nations writers, and non-American Indians.

Original primary texts by American Indian and First Nations authors, thinkers, and religious and political leaders are especially encouraged.

For the submission of manuscripts, contact:

Heidi Burns, Senior Editor
Peter Lang Publishing, Inc.
516 N. Charles St., 2nd Fl.
Baltimore, MD 21201
(410) 385-5362
e-mail: hburnsplp@aol.com

To order other books in this series, please contact our Customer Service Department:

(800) 770-LANG (within the U.S.)
(212) 647-7706 (outside the U.S.)
(212) 647-7707 FAX

Or browse online by series:

www.peterlang.com

www.ingramcontent.com/pod-product-compliance
Lightning Source LLC
Chambersburg PA
CBHW050627300426
44112CB00012B/1685